I COME FROM THE STONE AGE

I Come from
the Stone Age

HEINRICH HARRER

translated from the German by
EDWARD FITZGERALD

NEW YORK
E. P. DUTTON & CO., INC.
1965

Contents

Maps in Text

Illustrations

5

AUTHOR'S PREFACE

THE wheel has turned full circle: I had left civilisation behind, and from the year of our Lord nineteen hundred and sixty-two I had gone back to something like three thousand, or even five thousand, years before Christ. And now I have returned to my own time.

My journey back to the Stone Age began in Munich, where Lufthansa arranged a press conference before my departure. The plan I explained to the assembled journalists seemed to interest them. I had left my own solidly built house with its electric light, its hot and cold water, its glass windows, its comfort and its security behind well-fitting doors. My aim was to journey to an unexplored part of an island where about a hundred thousand people live, people who go to sleep when night falls, drink water from streams in their cupped hands, have never seen through a pane of glass, don't know what a wheel is, and who continue in this day and age to regard a knife made of bamboo and an axe made of stone as the last word in man's technical equipment. They have no pots to cook in, no metal to forge, no cloth with which to make themselves clothes, and no written language to record their small store of words. They are good-natured and playful like children, they are as helpful as Samaritans, their behaviour is as incalculable as that of young puppies—and their cruelties set us aghast. These people are the Danis of West New Guinea.

The astonishingly rich experiences of my expedition to them filled me with delight, though it was a harsher and more laborious expedition, and one that involved greater privations than any other, and though I came near to death on several occasions, and though I left the island with a badly mauled body and broken bones.

The first stage of my journey into the Stone Age took me into the stony waste of New York, the extreme opposite civilisation to that I was about to visit. The stone here was quarried and dressed, framed in steel, bound in chromium, nickel and bronze, and relieved at frequent intervals by vast panes of glass. The future had already begun here. In Central New Guinea the past had not yet ceased. The stone there was not quarried, and where the Danis had succeeded in splitting it, sheer chance had more to do with its form than deliberate intention. The difference between the hanging gardens of Babylon and the snowcapped peaks of the Himalayas is no greater contrast than that between New York and New Guinea.

I have often been asked why I chose objectives for my expeditions such as the north face of the Eiger, the peaks of the Himalayas, Tibet, or the Stone Age island of New Guinea. And I could only say that all my life I have been fascinated by contrasts, and by the differences between our civilised world and the world of strange, out of the ordinary people, and strange, out of the ordinary things, since they give us new standards by which to judge life. On the Eiger I was attempting to prove myself, in the Himalayas I learnt the meaning of loneliness, in Tibet I met extraordinary people. On the island of New Guinea I found everything at once: dangerous and torrential streams and rivers; the as yet unconquered north face of a sixteen-thousand-foot mountain, a tropical giant marvellously covered with glaciers and eternal snow; the loneliness of an untrodden peak, the nights alone in my tent with the rain pelting down on the canvas; and, finally, the Danis themselves, men who are almost incomprehensible to us, and who still live the lives of our own remote forefathers in grey primeval times.

I thought I had a fair idea of what to expect, and I also thought I was well prepared to cope with it. But how much did I really know?

In the summer of 1937—I was making my preparations for climbing the north face of the Eiger—I heard for the first time about a Dutch expedition which had just penetrated into the interior of New Guinea and reported finding a chain of "ice mountains" there. Its highest peak (16,600 feet) they had named after the man who was the first European to see the snow over the jungles of New Guinea three hundred years ago: Jan Carstensz, a seafarer in the service of the Dutch government.

I already knew that in Africa and South America there were snow-

8

and glacier-covered mountains in the neighbourhood of the equator; Chimborazo, 20,560 feet, in the Ecuadorian Andes, and Ruwenzori, 16,794 feet, in Central Africa. But I found it difficult to believe that there was anything of the sort on an island in the Pacific, towering above palm trees, orchids and warm and humid jungles.

The Portuguese discovered New Guinea in 1526, but they sailed along the north coast of the island, and high ranges nearer the coast unsighted them for the snow-capped miracle in the interior. Almost a hundred years later, in 1623, other Europeans, led by the Dutchman Jan Carstensz, sailed along the south coast of New Guinea in the two vessels *Pera* and *Arnheim*. There are no high ranges near the coast here, and Carstensz and his men must have encountered one of those crystal-clear days over land and sea that are nowhere more rare than in New Guinea. In consequence Jan Carstensz went into history as the first man from the West to see a snowcapped peak glistening on the far horizon in that part of the world. It is possible that at first he thought it was a white cloud, but its immovability must soon have convinced him that it was a snow-covered mountain. When he returned to Europe he told them what he had seen, only to find himself laughed at. But although he was not believed at the time his story was not forgotten, and almost three hundred years later a British expedition penetrated into the interior, and returned with confirmation of what Jan Carstensz had said: a mountain of unimaginable beauty towers over the jungles of New Guinea in fantastic contrast to the hot and humid country that surrounds it.

And now I was on my way there. But before I started on the last stage of my journey into the Stone Age I allowed myself a luxury that only our highly civilized modern age can offer: I took a plane in New York and flew to the Hawaiian Islands, where, as a dedicated skier, I fulfilled a long-felt desire to ski on the ocean waves.

This pleasurable interlude did not last long, because time was running short, and I wanted to be in New Guinea by the first half of January at the latest. On the other hand I had also determined to get to know as much about the Pacific area as I could. In any case I had to leave my Hawaiian paradise, though, for the time being, only to visit another—Tahiti.

In Tahiti I began my immediate preparations for my expedition

9

into the interior of New Guinea. For one thing I collected a store of cowrie shells—which gives you some idea of the totally different world into which I proposed to penetrate. Normally, of course, before going to a strange land you first visit your bank to get a supply of the appropriate currency. But the sort of currency the Danis of New Guinea use is not quoted at any Bureau de Change; and, as I say, I first had to collect a store of it—cowrie shells. By the time I left Tahiti in the direction of Japan I was, as far as the Danis are concerned, a well-to-do man, since I had collected cowrie shells most industriously.

The next stage of my journey began with a disappointment. I wanted to see the sacred mountain Fujiyama, or, as the Japanese call it, Fuji san. Unfortunately it was concealed by thick cloud, and I had to make up my mind that I shouldn't be able to see it after all. In fact I was to be generously compensated for the preliminary disappointment, because on the way from Tokyo to Hongkong my plane flew over Fujiyama, and its peak jutted up crystal clear and glistening from the sea of cloud below.

I took advantage of my stay in Hongkong to search for *objets d'art* from Tibet. This probably sounds a bit absurd, because Lhasa, the capital of Tibet, is something like fifteen hundred miles away from there. However, for some time there had been a persistent rumour that after their occupation of Tibet the Red Chinese had seized all the works of profane and religious art they could lay their hands on, and, in the absence of a market of their own for such things, had disposed of them in Hongkong. I don't know what gave rise to this rumour, and all I can say is that I found practically nothing there to substantiate it.

From Hongkong I went on to Bangkok, where I made inquiries about the possibility of a further expedition at a later date to North Thailand, and then I flew on to Australia, where I gave a number of lectures to the Bushwalkers, and met a young medico named Russel Kippax. He was a splendid type, and when he heard what I intended he was enthusiastic about it all—and my expedition had found its doctor.

The next and final stage before New Guinea was New Zealand, where I delivered a lecture to the Alpine Club of Christchurch on mountaineering in the Alps and the Himalayas. In this connection I mentioned my plan to climb the Carstensz Peak in New Guinea. I found a volunteer at once in young Phil Temple, who had taken part in an expedition into the interior of the island the previous year, and in him I had the third man for my own expedition. It was arranged that he should join me in New Guinea in January.

I took a plane back to Sydney, and from there I flew to Lae in the Australian part of New Guinea. At the beginning of January Kippax arrived, and a little later Temple. Our expedition into the Stone Age could now begin, and the approach to the Carstensz Peak was close ahead, exactly 339 years after its discovery by Jan Carstensz. We now started our journey into the interior of the second largest island in the world, where human beings are more primitive, the jungle thicker, and the rivers more dangerous than anywhere else in the world. At the same time we were entering the biggest natural history museum left anywhere on earth. We were entering an area in which every false step, every ill-considered movement, could mean death.

Huddled up in a tent, crouched on a rock, or leaning against a great jungle tree, rested or tired out, hungry or satisfied, fit or with a smashed kneecap, by day or by night, I jotted down the story of our adventurous expedition on the spot. This is how this "diary of the Stone Age" came to be written.

December 1962.

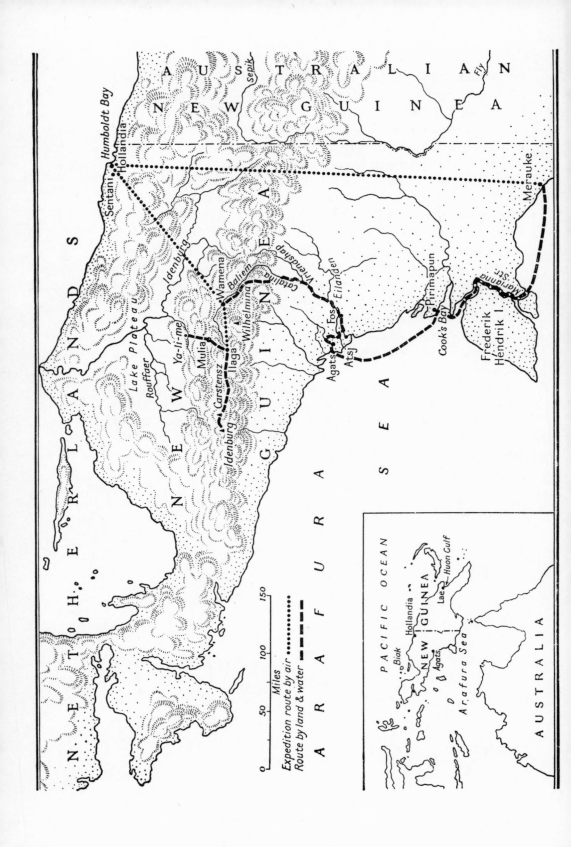

PART ONE

The Equatorial Ice

Asti, asti bandar ko makaro!
Softly, softly catchee monkey!
(Old Indian Proverb)

Final Preparations in Lae   *January 4*

BEFORE us the Huon Gulf shimmers softly in the last light of the
day. Behind us the first lights of the night are going on in Lae.
Only a little farther back, just behind the town, begins the jungle of
the Huon Peninsula, lying there dark and threatening.

Russel Kippax has arrived. This thirty-year-old Australian
doctor is one of the three white men who are going with me to the
Carstensz mountains. This is our last evening in Lae. We are sitting
on the raised terrace of one of the usual pile houses here and listening
to the familiar noises of the jungle. They are familiar, but I have to
get used to them again, a strange and fascinating symphony of animal
sounds, cracking branches and rushing water.

Tomorrow we shall leave that part of New Guinea which is under
Australian administration and go by plane to Hollandia in the Dutch
part of the island to complete our final preparations for our approach
to the Carstensz range. I wonder how long that will take? I just don't
know. And Kippax shrugged his shoulders, and the corners of his
mouth turned down. We have the generous support of the Dutch
Government and its administration here, but all the same, we mustn't
judge by European standards. When you get near the equator you
find that no one is in much of a hurry about anything, so we'll just
have to be patient.

On board the Kroonduif. Flight from Lae to Hollandia   *January 5*

Bathed in sweat we climbed into the plane, and then sat there, almost
at the point of exhaustion, waiting for the Kroonduif to start. We took

off and after a while we came to cooler regions. All the same there are beads of perspiration on the powdered face of our stewardess, a plump blonde Dutch girl, as she attends to us—all ten passengers. Everyone else on board thinks Russel Kippax and I are mad because we're leaving the plane at Hollandia and not flying on to Biak to change to international airways.

I've got to get used again to the enormous distances involved. Most of us Europeans know the Pacific area only on "world atlas" scales; something like 1:3,000,000 or even 1:50,000,000—with the result that many people at home are inclined to regard New Guinea as quite a smallish island. But the air line from Lae to Hollandia is about 560 miles, and from west to east the island is something like 1,250 miles long—that's farther than from the Baltic across Austria down to the toe of Italy; and the total area of New Guinea is two and a half times as great as that of Britain.

We are flying over a thickly carpeted jungle area with winding rivers and medium mountain chains. Here and there are clearings in the jungle, like small islands in a vast sea. You can hardly make out the huts of the natives. There are also deep gorges with great waterfalls, and the white spray looks like steam rising out of the dark jungle background.

Early afternoon: We are circling over Hollandia with its picturesque islands and bays. In Humboldt Bay I can see huts as though on the water, built on piles. They are the first fishing villages. The otherwise quiet scene is enlivened by moving outriggers, the local native fishing boats. Here and there I can see the evidence of a not so quiet past: the wreckage of Japanese and American vessels, a sad legacy of the Second World War.

We are turning inwards now, flying over the great Sentani lake. The pilot is making for the airfield at Hollandia. The nose of the Kroonduif is turning down now and we are coming in to land. The earth and its humid heat rise to meet us.

Hollandia   *January 5*

Rafael den Haan, the Dutch Commissioner for the New Guinea mountain area, is at the airfield to welcome us. He looks quite splendid with his magnificent moustache and his dark glasses. He speaks five languages fluently.

Thanks to his presence the customs examination was a mere formality, and soon after our landing we were all seated in his black Fiat. Ahead of us the road curves interminably. Nothing but curve after curve—about thirty miles of them. That's the distance from the airfield to the town of Hollandia.

Our first discussion took place in the office of the District Commissioner, and when I said that it was only fair, and, indeed, the usual custom amongst mountaineers, that when they made a first attempt a national of the country concerned should go with them, Den Haan introduced me to one of his Patrol Officers, a young Dutchman (twenty-five years old) named Bert Huizenga, a blond giant of a man, and proposed that Huizenga should accompany us, to which I immediately agreed. I was also asked if I would allow a Dutch geologist to join the expedition, and when I agreed to this too, the Director of the local Mining Board, Dr Willem Valk, decided to come along himself.

Tomorrow the last member of the expedition, the New Zealander Phil Temple, is due to join us here. He has had a certain amount of experience, having, as I have already said, been a member of an expedition into the mountains in 1961.

People keep asking me doubtfully whether it isn't risky to carry on with my expedition in view of the imminent threat of an Indonesian invasion. I always give them the same answer: if you were to let your plans depend on threatening crises, and on political happenings in general, you'd never get anywhere or do anything. Not that this means I'm just sticking my head in the sand and ignoring disagreeable possibilities. I have already given careful thought to the dangers our party might encounter if there were large-scale Indonesian landings. In fact I have even taken practical precautions, and amongst the expedition kit is sailing tackle, sail needles, stout thread, rope and so on. And for improvised sails there are ten ponchos. We are also well provided with maps and charts of the southern coastal area as far as Australian New Guinea, and if it became necessary we could sail from there to Australia, so I'm not worrying. We shall be prepared for all eventualities.

17

Phil Temple and Bert Huizenga have already flown off to Bokondini, and from there they will go on to Ilaga, from where we shall
make our approach to the Carstensz Peak. Perhaps Phil has already
left for the site on which we propose to pitch our main camp, where
his job is to build huts for us. He knows the place from last year's
expedition.

Dr Valk, Russel Kippax and I are still in Hollandia. Dr Valk and
I have bought food, and, in addition, a hundred axes and as many
matchets. In addition we have about a hundredweight of cowrie
shells, and something like half as much again of various trinkets,
watches and whetstones—the wages for our porters, who have to be
recruited in Ilaga. The whole day goes in packing. It's hot and humid
and my very first movements make the sweat break out on my forehead. When I bend down it runs together into larger drops and falls
from my forehead onto packages and sacks.

Kippax, our expedition doctor, is as happy as a sandboy with the
great assortment of medicaments I brought with me from Europe.
He has sorted them into three medical kits with great love and care.

Tomorrow we shall be leaving Hollandia. The Kroonduif plane is
scheduled to take off at nine o'clock in the morning. The first stage
of our flight is to Wamena, and from there, presumably the day after
tomorrow, we are to fly on to Ilaga and join our advance guard.

Sukarno's threat to "liberate" New Guinea is hotting up, and for
this reason no fewer than sixty journalists have arrived in Hollandia
during the past few days. They're falling over each other in the two
small hotels the Dutch Government runs here. Talk of war is in the
air, but we aren't letting it bother us. At eight o'clock tomorrow
morning we shall start loading our tons of baggage, and an hour
later we shall start off.

Wamena   *January 12*

The organisational side of it is working well; when we arrived here
we found everything ready. Johanson, the pilot of the M.A.F., Missionary Aviation Fellowship, flew to Ilaga with the first supplies soon after

we landed. I reckon he'll have to make three or four such journeys, and we'll follow on tomorrow. This evening we propose to visit a number of Dutchmen here to thank them for the generous support their Government has given us.

Ilaga January 13

When our two small planes were circling before touching down on the airstrip at Ilaga we noticed that a great crowd of people had gathered to welcome us. When we landed and clambered down from our planes we were immediately surrounded by hundreds of Danis, the natives of the mountainous region of New Guinea, all shouting their characteristic "Wa-wa-wa!" Phil and Bert had some difficulty in making their way to us. The landing on the sloping airstrip turned out to be easier than I had expected. Somewhat relieved we stood together and watched the two planes taxi-ing faster and faster down the slope and finally taking off as easily as birds to fly through the deep valley. A few minutes later they disappeared behind the jungle-clad range to the east. An impressive sight.

Our camp lies about three hundred feet lower than the airstrip. A cooking hut had been set up and a trench dug round the whole camping place, which is itself surrounded by fields of sweet potatoes, the mainstay of local native nourishment. As we expected, it is raining.

January 15

We made ourselves comfortable in the tents, and despite the rain our spirits were high. My thoughts are completely taken up with planning the expedition. When everything is ready I hope to have some time over for ethnographic research.

Just as everywhere else in the world, it is difficult to find porters here too. Bert Huizenga spends all day doing his best to engage them. So far we've got only a hundred—about half the number we need. And, of course, there have already been a few incidents with the native Danis. They live spread out over the whole highlands. Their numbers are estimated at about two hundred thousand, of whom about six thousand live in Ilaga valley. They are divided into tribes, and the tribes are subdivided into clans. They speak a variety of dialects, which I have to get to know for the various stages of the expedition. They have no written language, and, of course, this necessarily leads to misunderstandings. So far the various incidents have been more amusing than serious.

The male Dani is a big, powerful fellow with a dark skin and a proud carriage. But though their appearance inspires respect, it takes some time before you can look at them without smiling to yourself. They smear their faces with pork fat and soot, and the only article of clothing they wear is the outer rind of an elongated pumpkin-like fruit which they slip over the penis. Whether they are alarmed or merely elated, they always shout their "Wa-wa-wa" excitedly, and accompany it by tapping frenetically with their fingernails on the hard outside of their pumpkin penis sheaths.

The Dani female is smaller than the male, but hardly less strong. She wears a loincloth which she weaves very expertly and attractively from fibres taken from the bark of trees or from yellow orchids.

The sort of reserve which has become natural to us is unknown to the Danis, either men or women. Whether I'm walking around, standing still, sitting or lying down, they swarm around me, touching my hat, or my pipe, laughing, gesticulating, and, of course, shouting: "Wa-wa-wa!" It sounds like a pack of excited dogs barking.

There was a bit of excitement yesterday when a snake came wriggling between our tents. The Danis all fled for their lives shrieking "Wa-wa-wa!", and only after Bert Huizenga had severed the reptile's head with a matchet did they slowly and cautiously return.

This morning Phil Temple went off with ten porters to set up our main camp and to finish off the shelters at intervals along the way. Our intention is to establish a potato store between here and the main camp, and in this way we hope to negotiate the second stage of the journey more easily. But this plan depends on our finding enough porters. As a precautionary measure we also considered the possibility of using planes to drop foodstuffs where necessary. Just three days more now, and then, I hope, we shall be able to start. *Asti, asti bandar ko makaro*—Softly, softly catchee monkey. I am constantly reminded of this old Indian proverb and its English version here.

Each of us—Dr Valk, Phil, Bert, Russ and I—has a sort of personal servant. I called "my man" Oskar, but it turned out that the Danis have some difficulty with the letter "s" so we've compromised on "Okar."

This morning the wireless news reported that Indonesian troops had tried to land at Etna Bay. The attempt was repulsed by the Dutch, but further attacks are expected. Understandably this news has aroused misgivings amongst my partners. However, I think I have succeeded in communicating some of my own enthusiasm for the expedition to them. I had a chat about matters with Temple and Huizenga. They are both willing to carry on with our plans. Whatever happens we will do our best to get to Carstensz. Unfortunately Dr Valk has had to abandon the idea of accompanying us. He's developed tummy trouble.

At home my pipe is just a pleasure. I sit perhaps in a comfortable armchair thinking quietly, and its puffs of blue smoke carry my thoughts along happily and contentedly. Here my old friend is a pleasure too, of course, but it's also something more—it serves a very useful purpose. Our morning reveille is the loud grunting and slobbering of the pigs the natives keep. Unfortunately they are always surrounded by swarms of small and quite disgusting flies which are a real nuisance. The only thing they don't seem to like is tobacco smoke, so as soon as the grunting wakes me in the morning I light up and get my tent full of smoke before I open the flap. In this way I manage to get a little peace from those horrible flies.

A little later the Danis themselves arrive and crowd round our tent openings, shoving, pushing, chattering and making a tremendous din. This morning Bert lost patience with them, drew his pistol and fired a bullet into the ground. They fled in terror, shrieking "Wa-wa-wa!" at the tops of their voices, but when from a distance they saw that nothing else was happening they just laughed and were back again as noisy as ever. Bert gave up and hid himself in his tent.

Women often join in the audience. They are usually carrying nets full of sweet potatoes, and they squat around our tents and just stare. Some of them occupy their time by weaving nets on a round frame-work, using orchid fibres. The dexterous way in which they work coloured patterns into the nets constantly arouses my admiration.

But the chief occupation of the Danis, both men and women, is just staring. Not a single item of our kit and equipment has escaped their close examination. As soon as they come across something they haven't seen before they all start to shout "Wa-wa-wa!" approvingly, and the men drum happily on their penis sheaths with their finger-nails.

Spirits are high in and around our camp, which has by this time grown to quite a respectable size. The small yellow-white dogs the Danis keep seem affected by the general atmosphere. From morning to night they sniff around us and our things, wagging their tails wildly. Like the dogs of the Pygmies in Africa, they seem to be Pharaonic, or Bazengi dogs. At all events they don't bark, and so they are particularly suited for hunting.

January 18

Russel Kippax and I are alone now. Dr Valk has taken his tummy trouble back to Hollandia. Phil Temple is preparing our main camp at the foot of the mountain range, and Bert Huizenga is in Wamena buying provisions. For extra porters we need at least another twelve cwt. or so of rice, which is to be dropped over our base camp.

This means that I must postpone the start of our expedition again. In order to spend the time of waiting usefully Russel and I started off early this morning on a three-day tour. No one has ever climbed the 12,800-foot Kelabo peak, so we're going to have a shot at it. On the way I want to have a look at Vonk Lake, about which I don't know a thing and in which I am therefore particularly interested.

As a result I have now got to know the trackless, slippery, moss-carpeted forest and its tricks, and, of course, I had to pay for my knowledge. First of all we descended about six hundred feet or so from our camp, which is about seven thousand feet above sea level, into the valley as far as the tumultuous Ilaga River, which empties

22

itself into the Rouffaer torrent. The only bridge we found was a large tree-trunk half under water. Our porters negotiated it elegantly, loads and all. They go barefooted, and tripping along a tree-trunk represents no difficulty at all for them, but the studs in my boots gave me no proper hold on the slippery trunk. Carefully I advanced along it step by step, balancing as well as I could. To left and right the rushing water foamed and swirled. To have straddled my way across would have been impossible, because the current was so powerful that to have subjected my legs to its pressure would have been enough to tear me off the trunk. I got the better part of the way across safely, and I had only about another half-dozen steps to make to the safety of the other side when my left boot slipped a little; not much, but enough. My only thought now was to do the rest of the way in a rush, but then my right boot slipped too, and at the next step I lost my balance completely. A last effort, a desperate jump, rock under my feet, wet, slanting rock, and for the fraction of a second I knew that I was going to hit it with my face as I fell. Instinctively I hurled myself sideways into the water against the current. It swept me against the tree-trunk at once and with all my strength I tried to cling to it, but my mountaineering instinct had played me false here in the water. The current sweeping powerfully beneath the trunk dragged me with it and I was sucked under at once. It was a desperate situation: the way to the surface was impossible because of the water pressure, the way back was impossible for the same reason, and in front of me was a network of branches through which the water was forcing its way. Don't panic, was my only thought, and in any case there was no time for any other. I had to act quickly. But there wasn't much room: just as much as I could feel with my hands as the water forced me against the branches. But at last I found a space between them. I grabbed hold of the branches and pulled my body through, and the force of the water did the rest. Suddenly I was through the opening and able to move freely again. The water now swept me to the surface like a cork. The force of the stream grew less and I was able to swim ashore without much difficulty, where "my man" Okar, grinning all over his face, dragged me ashore.

Once I had firm ground under my feet again it didn't take me long to realise where I'd gone wrong—I should have thrown myself into the water with the current, not against it. First of all, without that opening in the branches I should have been hopelessly lost; and secondly, the opening itself was an added danger, because as the water had to pass through a relatively restricted space it did so with still greater force than it needed on the downstream side of the tree where there was more room.

Okar felt me expertly all over, watched with interest by the other Danis, and when the result was obviously satisfactory they all shouted "Wa-wa-wa!" happily. There were no bones broken, and the only casualty was my old hat now being swept away out of sight downstream.

We now made our way up a steep slope on the other side of the river and went on into the jungle. Our progress was made difficult by gnarled roots and fallen tree-trunks, each lying in a different direction, and sometimes one on top of the other. We went forward like monkeys, gripping first one branch and then the other, dragging ourselves along, pulling ourselves up, and balancing our way along the tree-trunks. Finally we reached a narrow gully-like path through thick jungle. Here and there it went up steeply over liana-covered patches of chalk.

We had been going for five hours now, and by this time Russel Kippax was as wet from sweat as I was from water; and by the time we finally reached a pass neither of us had a dry stitch on our bodies. It was high time to have a rest, and our bones were aching.

Not so with our Danis. Laughing and shouting they were still moving with the ease and elegance of wild cats over the maze of gnarled roots, branches and trunks. It was difficult to get them to stop.

Russel tried to light a fire, but his matches were as damp as mine, and to make matters worse it had started to rain, so there we crouched and the advantages of civilisation were no good to us; our magic little sticks could conjure up fire only when they were dry!

For a while Okar watched us silently as we tried to get our matches to light, then he snapped off a branch, split it down the middle and put tinder in it, using the inner fibre of a plant for the purpose. Then he made a little heap with twigs and leaves and put his tinder-packed branch on top of it. Taking a rattan roll he always carried with him

24

on his upper arm he threaded it through the split branch and began to pull it up and down through the tinder, standing with one foot on each end of the branch to keep the rattan taut. His movements grew more and more rapid, and the rattan thread moved up and down faster and faster through the tinder until suddenly it broke. The friction set up by the rubbing had burnt it through. But in the meantime the friction set light to the tinder. We had witnessed the age-old "fire-saw" at work.

Russ and I made ourselves some Ovaltine, and the Danis put stones in the fire on which they then baked their sweet potatoes. In less than an hour we moved on again. Our halt was something like 11,000 feet up, and now our way went downwards.

After descending for about 640 feet we again came to a river. This one was rather more than thirty feet wide, quiet-flowing and easy enough to cross, but very dirty to make up for it. Everything was brown and muddy, the river bed, the water, the Danis, and as we waded across the river, Russel and I became so too.

But at least we'd done it safely. After crossing the river we went through a number of clearings, and the symphony in brown gave way to white chalk and red rhododendrons. Just when it was starting to rain again we came to some derelict huts. Whenever Danis halt, even if it's only for a temporary rest, they build themselves such huts of branches, bamboos, leaves and ferns to protect themselves from the rain. When they move on they either leave the huts standing or burn them down to the accompaniment of gleeful shouts. At their next halt they build more huts. There's no shortage of building material and it doesn't take them very long.

For Russel and me this first day with its long upward climb and its great differences in altitude was a bit too much. We're both dead tired, and our legs are scratched and bruised. I also notice that I've a bigger bruise on my thigh from my misadventure than I thought at the time. However, we're very comfortable in these low huts, and our porters have put more fern on the roof so that the rain now makes only a very subdued sound. A fire is burning—we lit it with matches this time—and sweet potatoes, frogs and vegetables are roasting over hot stones. We are waiting patiently until our Stone Age meal is ready.

25

There are ten porters with us. Actually we thought half that number would do, but you need porters for yourself, and then porters for your porters and their potatoes, so in the end you need more porters than you first thought.

January 19

We spent the night seven thousand feet up. This morning we first climbed down a little way until we again came to a rushing stream. Russ tapped me on the shoulder and pointed to the only "bridge"— a tree-trunk as before. But the water was tossing and boiling even more violently as it rushed on. A false step here would mean certain death. Our Danis went over the trunk in their bare feet as easily as before. Once bitten, twice shy, so I went only part of the way upright, and where the bark covering ceased and the trunk was smooth and slippery, I straddled it and made the rest of the way across like that. Russ followed my example. But the water rushed past our legs with such violence that now and again we had great difficulty in maintaining our hold. However, we managed to get to the other side safely.

Our way through the jungle after this can be disposed of very simply: either we were wading through an indescribable morass, or we were crossing a black and impenetrable confusion of branches and plants, balancing our way along higgledy-piggledy fallen tree-trunks. The result was that we were constantly in doubt as to which way to go—through the revolting morass, which was at least not dangerous, or over the clean but treacherous maze of tree-trunks. The rushing, roaring river was always close at hand, and we frequently had to cross tributaries that ran into it from the jungle. As it probably came from Vonk Lake we decided to call it Vonk River.

The landscape through which we were laboriously fighting our way was of simply fabulous beauty. The most magnificent orchids were growing everywhere, together with red and white begonias and other tropical flowers. The moss-covered tree-trunks with their grotesque protuberances looked like a stage setting for the witches' wood. The light that filtered through the rich foliage seemed equally unreal, and one could easily imagine long-extinct beasts prowling around in it.

It took us five hours to reach our present camp. Actually Russ and I had intended merely to make a short halt here, 1,200 feet up, but by this time it was clear that we had taken on a bit too much for the first days. We therefore decided to spend the night here. Russ is already asleep in fact. When we were pitching the tent he complained that he felt as though he had just climbed the summit of Mount Everest.

Our Danis obviously aren't feeling in the least exhausted—and each of them has been carrying a thirty-three-pound load! But you simply can't make them rest. They're shouting and howling around in the forest, and now and then not a single one of them is in the camp. Then suddenly they all appear again and crowd round our tent inquisitively and push their way in. This is typical of them. They don't regard themselves as in any way different from us, and they use our basins and spoons, even when we happen to be eating. And they are quite nonplussed when Russ or I push them out of the tent. Just now Okar discovered that I had gold stoppings in my teeth. He's dashing around outside now telling everybody else what's the matter with my teeth, and tapping excitedly with his fingernails on his penis sheath.

They return from their wanderings in the forest bringing all sorts of things back with them to eat: fruit, frogs, and sometimes mice and rats. They then throw the bodies onto the fire until the hair is burnt away, then they slit them up and remove part of the gut. The rest they eat.

January 20

We'll have to give up the idea of getting as far as Vonk Lake and climbing Mount Kelabo. We want to be back in Ilaga at the latest by tomorrow so we turned back early this morning, and we have already reached the river. Our great attraction is the Carstensz.

The way back through the wet forest was a pleasure compared with the way there. We are now making a short halt in yesterday's bivouac. Our porters are singeing the hair off an opossum at the moment. I found the dead brute in my Leica case just now. That's where they had put it unknown to me. You can't help laughing at their antics and making the best of their tricks, which are innocent enough. They just regard everything as their property. However, they have a marked sense of ownership for certain things. On the way we more than once came across vegetable patches by small huts, but no Dani would think of touching the growing vegetables—the patch belongs to someone else.

In the meantime we have pressed on and reached our last night's camp. Our route passes over the mountain chain between the Ila and Kelabo rivers. The last five hundred feet of our descent we had to cut ourselves a way with our matchets until we came to the enormous clearing. In the middle of it there is a large vegetable patch surrounded by a fence made of palings. It reminded me of similar palings at home in the Alps. Sweet potatoes, maize, beans, peas, pumpkins and cucumbers were all growing there. In return for a few cowrie shells we bought some "spinach" from the natives—in other words, the leaves of the sweet potato, or batata. And for each man two cucumbers, maize and beans. A Dani banquet is about to be prepared.

Gradually I have realised why it is the natives hardly ever drink anything—their food contains so much liquid that they rarely experience a real feeling of thirst. As they don't possess even the most primitive earthenware pot of any kind, both meat and vegetables have to be cooked on and between hot stones. The Stone Age knows nothing of the luxuries of our civilisation, and it produces only what is absolutely necessary for survival. And that isn't very much. Even the pleasure of taking a bathe, which we had promised ourselves this evening to crown the feast, was not all we had hoped —we had to use the muddy brown water of the River Ila.

January 21

Sunday: Five hours' march behind us and now we are surrounded by crowds of children who have invaded our main camp. Although we didn't get as far as Vonk Lake and didn't climb Mount Kelabo

28

our excursion was pleasurable—and useful: we have a fairly accurate cartographic record of Kelabo Valley; we know the rate of progress you can make through this sort of jungle; and we've had a chance of trying out our porters. They're certainly no worse than those I've had to hire in other parts of the world. They're willing, good-natured, good-tempered, strong and tough. But they're certainly not any better, since they have no sense of responsibility either, and they're inclined to be lazy. And finally, of course, the excursion gave both Russ and me a bit of excellent training. So all in all we had every reason to be satisfied with ourselves.

Bert Huizenga isn't back from Wamena yet, and we are happy to enjoy a rainless day for once, and without having any preparations to make. But although it's dry enough here, there are dark, heavy clouds hanging around our objective: the Carstensz mountains.

Russ and I are enjoying the peace of the evening, and each of us is obviously busy with his own thoughts. Mine are on the Hahnen-kamm races which are taking place today in Kitzbühel. It's still broad daylight there, and they're lining the track anxiously wondering whether "their man" is going to win the downhill race or not. If I were in Austria now I should be there too. Here in Ilaga a Dani is watching me, first with interest and then with horror as it takes me several matches to get my pipe going properly. All things in life are relative.

They're astonishing people these Danis, and they live in an astonishing world. Every bit of coloured paper you discard they carefully pick up and stick in their matted hair, or behind one ear, or through their bamboo armlet. They take the steel bands that held our cases together, hammer them flat with stones and wear them as belts. One day when Russ flung away a ball-pen because the ink was exhausted a Dani rescued it at once and stuck it through the hole bored in his nose. I expect it's still there now. This kind of nasal decoration is confined to the men. When a Dani is quite a child his family bores through his septum with a thin piece of wood. Gradually thicker and thicker pieces are inserted until the hole is big enough to take the decoration worn on festal days, a flat ground boar's tusk. On ordinary days the male Dani wears only a chicken bone or a piece of wood through the hole in his nose, though I take it that the Dani who was lucky enough to pick up Russel's ball-pen will wear it all the time. He probably thinks it's the most beautiful piece of decoration in any tribal nose. Their ear lobes are also pierced. Usually they wear pieces of bamboo stuck through them, but here too the achievements of our more technical age were soon seized on, and one Dani put a discarded long-cell torch battery through one ear. It almost came down to his shoulder. And his wife was delighted to use an empty sticking-plaster roll as an ear-lobe decoration. But the funniest piece of improvisation was the use of the envelope of a letter from my wife by one of their chiefs as a sort of fig-leaf.

The only musical instrument known to the Danis is a bamboo jaw's harp. Apart from this they don't even possess drums. But they have a very definite musical sense all the same, as it was not difficult to realise when you listened to the rhythmic and rather melancholy songs they sang on the march. And when there was Western music on our wireless they would crowd around and listen with evident enjoyment.

January 22

Bert Huizenga has just returned from Wamena with the news that the day after tomorrow the final batch of our food supplies will be dropped by plane—provided the weather is suitable, that is. The day after tomorrow is Wednesday, which means that if all goes well we can make a start on Thursday. However, even if the weather should prove bad and delay the drop Russ and I propose to go on with some of the porters. In that case Bert will have to stay behind to wait for favourable weather and the food drop.

Our main camp looks rather like an army camp at the moment. Piles of sacks and cases and a huge mound of several thousand tins of food are keeping us busy weighing and sorting the loads. The sacks which are to be flown to our base camp in the mountains have to be very carefully packed indeed. The contents are first wrapped in a waterproof plastic cover and then put into two jute sacks. We are anxious to make quite sure of our precious salt and the other valuable foodstuffs such as sugar—even if a sack should burst on hitting the ground. The tinned stuff is just put in one jute sack. Pork we need too. We have one pig Bert shot with his revolver, and the pork is already packed up ready for dropping.

We're happy that everything seems to be on the move satisfactorily now. We have had a variety of experiences, and occasionally my patience has been put to the test during the waiting, but one of the most important items of equipment in any expedition happens to be patience. And if anyone thinks he can hurry up governments, civil servants, or even native porters, he'd do better to stay at home— remember the old Indian proverb! In the tropics, in the Himalaya highlands, and above all here in this stifling jungle country a philosophy of "take it easy" is absolutely essential. It's the only way to adapt yourself to a new and strange rhythm of life, and it is you that have to do the adapting. After all, I want something from the natives; they don't want anything from me. We need the Danis; they don't need us. This was made very clear even on our minor excursion into the valleys of the Ila and Kelabo rivers. They naturally led the way; not Russ or I. They knew the tracks, or found them; they did the hunting; they carried the loads, and they decided where we were to camp.

It hasn't rained very much today again, and now, towards evening, the fantastic peaks of the Messerschneid range are jutting through the vapour of the low-lying clouds—a magnificent sight. There's another unexplored area on this fascinating island; further secrets, further adventures, a further slice of the unknown Stone Age. Everything an explorer ever dreamed of could be satisfied here.

But there's no time to dream. Ahead of us now there's our immediate objective, the highest peak in New Guinea, the peak of the Carstensz mountains.

Bert Huizenga reports that the Dutch authorities are having trouble again in the Baliem district. Fighting has broken out amongst the natives. Blood feuds are disturbing the area, and there have been a number of murders. A Dutch police patrol has been attacked by natives armed with spears. Whilst Bert was telling us all this we were sitting outside our tent in the moonlight and drinking Dutch gin. Huizenga was a District Officer for a number of years amongst the mountain Papuans, and so he has an interesting tale or two to tell about his experiences.

This morning some of Phil Temple's porters returned from the temporary base camp and brought a letter from him in which he particularly praised three of them. A little later Bert paid out their wages, and I realised what a bit of luck it was to have a man like him around. He knows how to manage Danis, and he organised a kind of parade and decoration ceremony. Each of the three porters who had particularly distinguished themselves was presented with a steel axe. What a thing like that meant to a Dani you can imagine when you remember that for him a stone axe is the very last word in human technical possibilities. So when Bert went on to promise them a matchet each in addition, and some of the best cowrie shells from Tahiti, they declared themselves willing, against their original intention, to go with us to the new base camp once more.

Russ and I still find it difficult to make the Danis understand us— or to understand them. Their language is extremely primitive, and many of the words they use sound very similar to us. They have only two pronounceable numbers: one and two. Anything beyond that has to be shown on their fingers. That may sound easy, but it isn't, and Bert has explained to me how it comes about that I keep getting things wrong when there's any counting to be done with the Danis. When a Dani raises his right hand, keeping the little finger and the ring finger bent, he doesn't mean "three" as you might imagine because the index and the middle finger are raised together with his thumb. No, he means "two"! It's the bent fingers that "count," not the straight ones, and when a Dani raises his clenched fist he actually means "five." No wonder Russ and I could never get it right at first!

As an example of how short of words the Dani language is: the Dani word for "mother" also means everything directly connected with the idea of "mother," including pregnancy, birth and suckling. But there is one simple sentence I soon mastered—right from the very first day. And there's hardly a day on which I don't hear it: "*Maajo uragin*"—"It's going to rain." And it always does.

With the first words you learn you also begin to establish relationships. You get to know each other better; come closer to each other.

32

1. Make-up: pork fat, soot and ochre

I privately gave all my porters names from their own language, and this helped me to learn it. One of them I call Tavo, because he's always smoking. This helps me to remember that *tavo* means approximately "tobacco"—and, of course, "smoking" too. A little girl who was always laughing we called Niniki, which is the native word for "heart," and also joy. But don't think it's as easy as all that; the same word also means sorrow and weeping, and every other kind of emotion. The toughest of all the porters I call Vam-eik, because he wears the most impressive boar's tusk through his nose. His wife I call Yavi in my private Dani language, because she wears a particularly beautiful bast loincloth made of orchid fibres and *yavi* is the native word for the bird of paradise.

In this way I am gradually getting closer to these strange people and their peculiarities, and at the same time I am learning something of their language, their feelings and their character. A strange habit the men have is constantly grinding their teeth. That takes a bit of getting used to.

Russ is in a particularly favourable position for getting more closely acquainted with the Danis, because every day he holds a "surgery," at which he treats injuries, boils and so on; and there is nothing more calculated to win over primitive people than relieving them of pain and curing their sicknesses, which they think are caused by demons and evil spirits generally.

There are one or two things I want to add to this diary because I had too little time in the beginning. In particular there is the visit of the paramount chief of the Uhunduni tribe. As far as science and the art of living are concerned he is just as primitive as his subjects, but nevertheless there is a certain dignity about him. He carries his head higher than the others, and all his movements are more deliberate. I showed him a few peasant tricks from my own country; the way the lads try out their strength: finger hooking and hand pressing against hand with the elbows fixed, and his childlike naïveté immediately became apparent. Usually he lost, but when I told him I'd like to have him for my son he was very pleased, and forgot all his mortification at being beaten. Russ watched us at these games and he discovered a particularly developed muscle all the Danis had, probably as the result of a good deal of running. It is a muscle in the

33

2. *The whole village was there to welcome us*

3. *Clothes are a joke if you've never worn them before*

hollow at the back of the knee. We have it too, of course, but with us it is not to be seen outwardly, whereas with the Danis it sticks out like a biceps. Now I know why it is that after about five hours of tramping through their jungles I feel dead beat and have to rest, whereas our porters can still do gymnastics amidst the tree-trunks like monkeys.

Whilst I am sitting entering up these matters in my diary the three "heroes" decorated by Bert for their good services as porters to Phil are in my tent sharpening their new axes. They are simply bursting with pride and it is quite clear that they want to be admired. Three happy savages. Savage? They're not savage at all. It's just that their society has different standards from ours, and it is quite certain that they would be as unhappy with our laws as we are with their dirt. It is also quite certain that it would be utterly wrong to try to impose our way of life on these people within a short space of time.

January 24

The last day in Ilaga. Tomorrow we set off for our base camp, towards the ice and snow only just a few degrees south of the equator. We've had to abandon our wireless transmitter. Early this morning Bert tried to get into touch with Bokondini, but the apparatus seems defective. A technical breakdown. However, it has its good side: there'll be less to carry. If we have to get into touch with the coast we shall have to send a runner to the Mission, which is in daily contact with Wamena and Hollandia; though it would take a runner several days to get from our base camp to the Mission. The American missionary Gordon Larson has amiably consented to pass on any messages.

I reckon that we shall need six days to get to our base camp, which means that we should be there on January 30. I'm a bit worried by the fact that some of the Dani porters want to take their wives with them. I'm afraid that will make the party too big. I must talk to Bert about it.

Inwardly I have already said good-bye to Ilaga. I went once more to the landing-strip. It has hardly rained at all today and I therefore had the most wonderful view over to Table Mountain and to the

34

steep peaks of the Messerschneid range. But my thoughts are all centred on tomorrow now, and that means: the start of our journey to the Carstensz mountain.

In Dani language the neighbourhood of the Carstensz is called "Dugundugu," or in English "Reed Flower." The Danis have in mind the white hanging seed flower of the reed plants that grow so luxuriantly in the marshland there—a poetic comparison with the snow and ice of the mountains.

January 25

Yesterday over a ton and a half of foodstuffs were dropped by plane at our base camp, and now we've been on our way for a couple of hours. When we got up at six o'clock it was still dull. When we started at seven the clouds parted and it became clear. What I was afraid of has happened: some of the Dani porters have brought their wives with them, and now a long caravan is passing through the last villages on our way—at least two hundred men and women, shouting, shrieking and laughing.

Bert, it appears, didn't want to upset the porters so he allowed the women to come part of the way. At the moment we are making a short halt and he is now engaged in settling "the woman question." It isn't merely that if they stay with us we shan't have enough food; here in the thick jungle there's a very serious danger that men of other clans might rape the women, and that would mean big trouble and the outbreak of violence: blood vengeance and perhaps all-out war. In the end the Danis allowed themselves to be convinced and so the women are going back to Ilaga.

Midday. We are resting near a hut Phil Temple set up on the way to our base camp. It took about an hour before our whole caravan arrived here. Even without the women there are a hundred and twenty of us. As usual, the Danis are tireless; no sooner have they put their loads to the ground than they begin to prance around, doing handstands and collecting wood. Before long the first fires were going and a scene of tremendous activity developed. They were finished by seven o'clock in the evening, by which time it was quite dark. But in our bivouac in the rhododendron jungle we now have

35

seven huts, and their roofs keep out the rain even better than those in Ilaga.

The Danis build their own huts either round or square from trunks and branches, and for the roof they like to use the bark of a juniper tree, but if there are pandanus palm trees in the neighbourhood they use their hard leaves instead. These leaves have the advantage that they can be fitted into each other like roof tiles.

During our morning march the peace between us and the Danis was threatened for a while. One of the chiefs suddenly got the idea that he would like to take his men off along another path. This caused a clash with Bert, and Bert got angry. Gesticulating with his matchet he accidentally sliced off the top of the chief's penis sheath. Such a thing represents an insult for any Dani, and as for a chief— well, it's deadly, because it damages his prestige amongst his tribal brothers. For a few minutes it looked as though the best that could happen was that our porters would desert us, and the worst that they would attack us. Bert Huizenga had to summon up the whole weight of his experience and exercise his art of persuasion to the full to put the matter to right.

However, peace reigns once more and the unfortunate incident has happily been forgotten. Danis are vindictive only where blood feuds are concerned; otherwise they very quickly forget everything, including their own misdeeds. Bert told me that it was very difficult to haul a Dani before the courts and punish him for anything at all, because as there is usually quite a long interval between the offence and the trial and if in this period the spirits don't punish him for his offence then the Dani just can't imagine that anyone else should want to do so after such a length of time. To cope with a situation like this, a Dutch District Officer who felt that he just had to punish a Dani, did to him what they do to each other. The man had committed a theft, so the D.O. just set fire to his hut. This is the sort of thing Danis understand, and when it happens to them, they just rebuild their huts, and feel quite certain that they have been punished by the spirits. However, this particular native had heard something about the white man's ways, and so he appealed. The appeal went on and on through all the appropriate stages and finally landed up before the United Nations. In the meantime, of course, the Dani had long ago forgotten all about it, but the whites, the U.N. officials, were still earnestly discussing the matter at great length. Were such measures at all right and proper and in accordance with the White Man's Burden? It is not surprising to learn that the primitive grass hut had grown into a "house" during the deliberations.

Fires are burning all around and, their dancing flames are sending the shadows of trees racing to and fro across the clearing like dark spectres. Thick smoke is rising above the huts. It is black, red and yellow in the glow. Quite a romantic picture. The Danis haven't settled down for the night yet. There are trees to be felled, because the fires must be kept going throughout the night. We are something like 8,000 feet above sea level here, and without the fires the naked Danis would be very cold. Some of them are crouched around the cooking holes they have dug, attending to the roasting batatas. Others are scouring the surrounding forest for animals suitable for provender. Just now one of them brought in a bat. It didn't strike me as particularly attractive as food, but the Dani was of a different opinion, and his flat nose was made even broader by a wide grin of satisfaction, and his mouth obviously watering at the thought of the delicacy awaiting him. Not only customs, but tastes differ from country to country too.

January 26

Our camp was alive at six o'clock this morning. The first thing I heard on waking was Okar and a couple of his friends under the canvas awning of my tent, and the first words I heard were: "*Maajo uragin.*" It's going to rain. "Of course it is," I thought. Nothing new in that, and I opened the flap of my tent. The three of them were huddled up in jute sacks like embryos. During the night each man had put another sack over his head, and slept that way.

We started off at about seven o'clock. Our route went through deep gorges with streams coming from Table Mountain. The ground was mossy and slippery. Now and again on raised ground we came to open spaces which would have provided us with a view, but "*Maajo urame*"—it is raining, so there was no view. In the grey mist and rain bare trees stand around like many-armed spectres. Then followed a further balancing session over fallen tree-trunks with water gurgling threateningly so far down below that we couldn't even see it.

Having made our way up to between nine and ten thousand feet we stopped for a rest. Once again it took about an hour before our trailing caravan of 115 porters was fully assembled. Bert found a note that Phil had left for us, but he thought it was just a piece of paper Phil had thrown away, so he threw it away again—unread—which only shows you that it's every man to his job: even a good colonial officer needn't realise how important it is for any expedition that it should get any messages left behind by its advance party.

From this spot we have our last sight of the Ilaga Valley and our first glimpse of the rise up to the plateau. By tomorrow we shall have reached its foot and the end of the wet forest.

Camp II lies in deep jungle, and there wasn't much room, so after a short rest we pressed on. At midday we found another note from Phil. He told us that his porters had caught two dogs and eaten them that same evening.

I am lying in my tent. It is strangely quiet today, apart from the steady pelting of the rain on the canvas. Just now and again you can hear a bird. I went outside to see if I could spot them, but the trees in which they were singing were too tall and the foliage was too thick. There are hardly any animals to be seen on the ground, just an occasional lizard scuttling over the tree roots.

January 27

We have arrived at Camp III. According to our altimeter we are now 10,272 feet above sea level. The climb was laborious, and during our short rest I had no opportunity to write.

Bert, Russ and I had a brief discussion and decided that when we get to our base camp we will introduce fixed rations for our Danis. We have plenty of food but those fellows are like young dogs. No matter how much you give them they will eat it—even if they have to make themselves vomit in order to be able to eat more. Ideas such as "rationing," or keeping something by for another time, just don't exist for them, and there's no way of expressing them in their language—if there's anything to eat you just eat it.

The weather has been a bit better, and once we even saw the sun. Its presence conjured up an improbable magnificence of colour in the neighbourhood of our camp, which is situated on a mountainous ridge amidst marvellous violet-red and orange-yellow stem orchids. Amongst them are small trees something like our firs with needles and white flowers that look like Christmas stars. In the midst of tropical luxuriance I am reminded of home—fir trees and snow! At this height the other trees and bushes—like cedars, junipers and rhododendrons—are already smaller. But the mosquitoes and sand-flies are unfortunately just as big up here as they were down in the valley, and they're just as much of a nuisance. Incidentally, the size of our party has remained unchanged. Despite the occasional differences of opinion which are unavoidable when so many people are together, not one single porter has deserted us. I hope it stays that way.

January 28

Sunday in the jungle. Quite early this morning there was tremendous excitement. One of the Danis found a rain cape made of pandanus leaves, and there were blood stains on it. No one could imagine where the blood came from, and this was very mysterious and disagreeable for the Danis. For them it was a bad omen, and it meant that beyond all doubt we should be attacked today. Bert did his best to argue them out of it, but it was no good. The incident delayed our start, and when we finally got away at about eight o'clock, most of our porters had provided themselves with juniper staves which they turned into spears by sharpening the points and hardening them in the still glowing camp fires.

Owing to this delayed start we did not reach our next camp until the afternoon, and on the way the Danis showed us who were the lords of this particular jungle—they and not us. With one accord they refused to follow the route Phil had reconnoitred, and we had to go the way they wanted to go. However, we had no cause to regret it.

This last part of the way went through a real fairy-tale wood. The going was easy and we advanced rapidly. Singing rhythmically and waving their spears the Danis marched on, and now and again—

probably when they remembered the blood-stained cape—they burst into their war cry. Suddenly the wet forest came to an end. We had reached the wide high plateau. Another hour's march brought us to Yenengena-Hokayogu Lake by the side of which we are now camping. We were here by midday. Our camping ground is marshy. Only a few tall ferns break the monotony.

Russ is in high spirits. Before our tents were up he was off duck shooting. I am lying half in and half out of my tent sketching the neighbourhood. To the left of our route—that is to say, to the south —rise the chalk peaks of the Willem chain. They are so white you might mistake them for snow-covered mountains. Between us and the mountains lies the lake, calm and smooth. We can't yet see anything of the real snow mountains, in "Dugundugu." As usual, they are hidden in thick cloud.

January 29

I stand here lost in enthusiasm at the majestic beauty of the scene: two enormous rock faces, broken by glaciers, with a few clouds overhead. Sometimes a ray of sunlight moves across the blue shimmering ice. I can hardly find words to describe how moved I am. Indeed, where am I? In the Alps? In the Himalayas? No, I am not far from the equator, in Melanesia. Only yesterday I came out of the hot, humid jungle, and now I am standing before a tremendous mound of rock and ice.

A little more than an hour ago we left our camp by the lake. It had been raining; the whole of nature was solemnly still; only a few wild duck skidded across the surface of the lake. Ahead of us there was a gently rising slope, easy to negotiate, and then we came to the ridge above. Before us lies the Carstensz range, and almost all its peaks are still untrodden.

The mountaineering history of the Carstensz range began just fifty years ago when the Englishman A. F. R. Wollaston came here from the south. If he had brought back a single photograph of this magnificent scene I am sure that the ice-covered peaks would not still be unconquered today. Such a photograph would have drawn mountaineers from all over the world. But we must go on. Russ is also beside himself with delight, and anxious to press on. Bert Huizenga is trying to persuade the Danis to move. It is raining so hard now that they would sooner build themselves huts and stay in them out of the rain. But we are going on—now that our objective is right before our eyes.

Our porters kept up the march for three hours, and I really believe they have been affected by our enthusiasm. We crossed ridge after ridge, and wet and cold penetrated our clothing. But then the leading porters found a shelter, and by the time we came up it was hopeless to expect them to go on: cold and steaming they crowded together in the hut, and we couldn't persuade them to move. Gradually the others came up. They were moving in a long file and with their pointed rain hats made of leaves they looked like brownies making their way to their glass castle with the work of the day done. We had no alternative but to agree to another rest. With difficulty the Danis lit fires, still very careful to keep their head coverings on to protect their matted hair from the rain. "Papua" is, by the way, the Malay word for "woolly hair." It is a male privilege to wear the hair long and done up in a net, whilst the women have to keep theirs short. At last a few fires were got going, and our brownies crouched around them. I was beginning to feel the cold myself now and I pushed my way to one of the fires to warm myself. Then suddenly—I could hardly believe it had happened—one of the porters seized me from behind and hurled me away from the fire. He was one of the toughest of the Danis, and I realised at once that this was mutiny, and that unless I was to lose all control over them I should have to act vigorously. Instantly I snatched off his hair net and seizing the curved boar's tusk which was pushed through his nose I slowly drew his face up to mine. For a moment or two his eyes glittered balefully and it was doubtful how the incident would end. I was only too well aware of the situation Bert, Russ and I were in—three white men against a fortyfold superiority of natives. They could overwhelm us at once if they felt like it.

After all, we were interlopers in their world. And not only did they live like men of the Stone Age, but no doubt they also has its outlook. And what was that outlook exactly? We didn't really know. We knew practically nothing about them, and I had never realised this so clearly as I did at that moment. I could feel the eyes of the others on us. Quite naturally they must feel themselves on his side and against me. And then I saw the eyes in the face so close to mine change their expression. The look became gentler, almost pleading. I threatened him that he would hear more about it and then I released him. He cleared off at once, and his fellows turned their eyes away and continued to stare expressionlessly into the fires. I hoped they had learned a lesson from the incident.

But now I no longer had any desire to stand with them at the fire, even though I was very cold and hadn't a dry stitch on my body. I felt miserable, and even the lovely dark red rhododendron, a darker red than in the valley, did nothing to raise my spirits. Suddenly I got the idea of going ahead on my own, and off I went, but I hadn't gone more than a few hundred yards when I heard the familiar shout "*Novok!*" It was the signal for a start. Bert had once again managed to persuade the Danis to move off.

For three and a half days I had done my best to jump over the deepest puddles, and to find shallow fords to cross the streams. At least in this way I kept the upper part of my body dry. But sooner or later there came a stream—usually just before the end of the day's march—which seemed to gurgle mockingly: "You've had it, chum. You've got to get over and there aren't any shallow fords." Today it was different: I was already so wet that I could afford to treat the streams with contempt, and I waded through them almost with pleasure, not bothering about shallow fords. At least I had the satisfaction of reaching the other side cleaner than when I started—and I couldn't get any wetter.

I was so far ahead of the rest by this time that they didn't catch up with me. Suddenly I saw smoke rising from a narrow valley, and I immediately realised that Phil, who was expecting us tomorrow, had come a day's march to meet us. And then I saw him making his way towards me through high grass. We greeted each other warmly, and he asked me whether it was Monday or Tuesday. I told him it was Monday, and there we stood, twenty-four hours earlier than planned, not far from his base camp. The Danis had guided us well.

It is the evening of January 29, and here I am lying in my tent out of the rain with dry clothes on. Good God, I had almost forgotten how agreeable dry clothes can be. Nothing more wonderful when you've been wet for so long.

Phil was happy too, for he had spent a very lonely time completely on his own—his last porter had deserted him days ago. At least I could give him satsifactory news that our lot were still all with us. And when our Danis finally reached our objective, tired and cold as they were, they quickly recovered their good spirits. With loud shouts of "Wa-wa-wa." they finished building the incompleted huts. We "Tuans" levelled a place for our tents, and when everything was ready the four of us stood under the canvas awning and toasted each other with the whisky I had kept for Phil, but which he now insisted we should all share. So far we could only guess just where the peaks were hidden above us in the clouds, and for the moment we were more interested in our marshy camp site than in the proud mountain we had come to climb. But shortly before dusk the weather cleared up—the final gift of nature on a hard, eventful but satisfactory day—and there, rising almost vertically above us, were tremendous towering rock faces with hanging glaciers between them. Swathes of mist moved across them in the last rays of the sun. The view remained only for a few seconds, and then everything was covered with a veil of mist again. But we had seen our mountain almost near enough to touch, and I was filled with an indescribable feeling of happiness and thankfulness for such a day. Tired out, now all I wanted was to sleep.

January 30

Work is seldom such a pleasure as it has been today. The job of finishing off our base camp went with a swing, and Phil took the porters and fetched the drop from the valley. The loads are all undamaged except one—a sack of rice burst whilst still in the air. Phil told us that the rice streamed down like the tail of a white comet.

In the afternoon Bert gathered all the porters and asked which of them would like to stay on with us as we should need a few men to help us prepare the advanced camp. Almost half the Danis volunteered, and Bert was able to choose fifteen powerful fellows who looked reliable. The others were rewarded for their efforts with steel axes, matchets and cowrie shells. But before they were allowed to go Bert set up a court to deal with the fellow who had pushed me away from the fire. The Danis all sat around in the rain with their pointed pandanus leaf hats over their heads—an extraordinary picture in the grey mist. Bert now hauled the offender before his court, but before he had time to charge him one of the older tribal chiefs stood up and declared that as he had witnessed the offence he would see to it that the man was punished. Bert declared himself satisfied with this and contented himself with seizing the cowering offender and hurling him into the mud. Everybody was obviously very happy that the incident had gone off with so little trouble. The Danis now all got to their feet; we heard the shout "*Novok*" from a hundred voices, and off they went on their way back to Ilaga. Gradually the sound of their singing died away in the bare forest, and things were now very quiet in our base camp. This evening it is reminiscent of a small, contented town. Russ has tuned in our transistor receiver and is listening to the news. One of the items was a report that our expedition had set out from Ilaga. It was strange to hear that the outside world was interested in our progress through the Stone Age, particularly now when at any moment the Dutch were expecting more landings by Indonesian troops. It appeared that the first Indonesian parachutists had landed right in the middle of the cannibal area.

From now on our expedition is composed as follows: Leader: Heinrich Harrer. Doctor: Russel Kippax. Chief Scout: Phil Temple. In charge of porters: Bert Huizenga. With Bert were two Papuan soldiers from the coast. In addition we have five personal servants and ten porters. Our total strength is therefore twenty-one.

January 31

Tomorrow we shall start off again. Russ and Bert would really like to start today, but a day's rest will do us all good.

The day began with fine rain, but now and again the clouds parted and we saw the glacified north wall of our mountain rising almost vertically above our camp. It reminded me a little of the Dolomites, which, like the Carstensz mountain, consist in part of ice-covered limestone. But how much more tremendous this mountain is, and how much more magnificent!

Generally speaking I can now say that not only our Danis, but also the other Papuans with whom we have come into contact, make a peaceable impression. They are not very intelligent, but they cannot be denied a certain cunning. They are prepared to help without payment, but once you start negotiating with them about wages they are quite capable of bargaining for more. And if they once realise that whoever wants something from them is well supplied with cowrie shells they take advantage of it. On the other hand, when we have had to cross dangerous rivers they have, without being asked, relieved us of the last awkward piece of baggage to make the crossing easier for us. Yes, they are certainly helpful.

Feuds and enmities exist between the individual clans, and they are fought out with great cruelty. They will pursue blood vengeance for years with extraordinary persistence. Their relentlessness will go so far that one tribe which has been attacked and defeated by another will voluntarily submit to a third tribe, mingle with it, live with it and till its land with no other object in view but to be strong enough when the day for vengeance comes. Bert Huizenga and other Dutch officials have told us that sometimes five, eight and even more years will pass before the counter-blow is delivered, but then the hostile village is razed to the ground.

Each tribe usually has a valley to itself, and when they are living in peace they trade with each other. Such trading relationships continue even when the territory of a third tribe with which one or the other is on bad terms lies between. How the friendly tribes communicate with each other through enemy territory is quite mysterious.

Bert explained something to me which at first astonished me. I noticed that some of the Danis, even quite young ones, had fingers missing. The explanation is strange and horrifying: if a Dani suffers great emotion, for example sadness at the death of a near relative, or perhaps if he is upset because a war has been lost, he will just cut off one of his fingers with a stone axe. In order to reduce the pain of the operation he will knock his elbow violently against a door post or a rock, so that the arm becomes numbed. Another but more

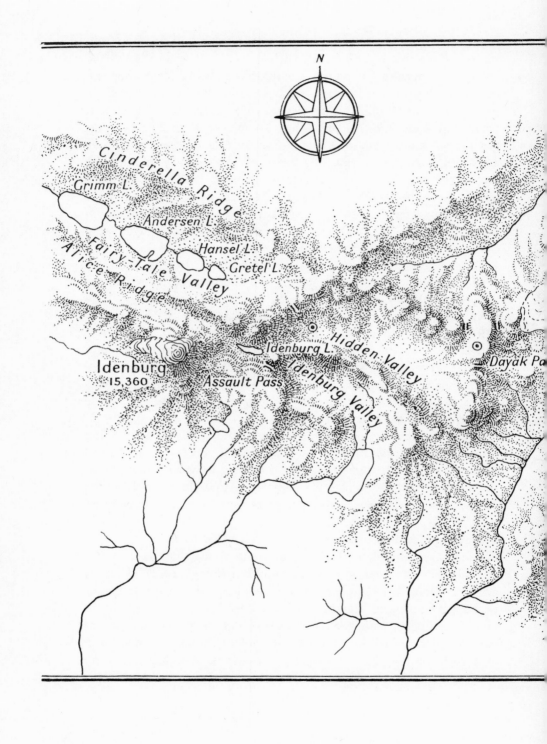

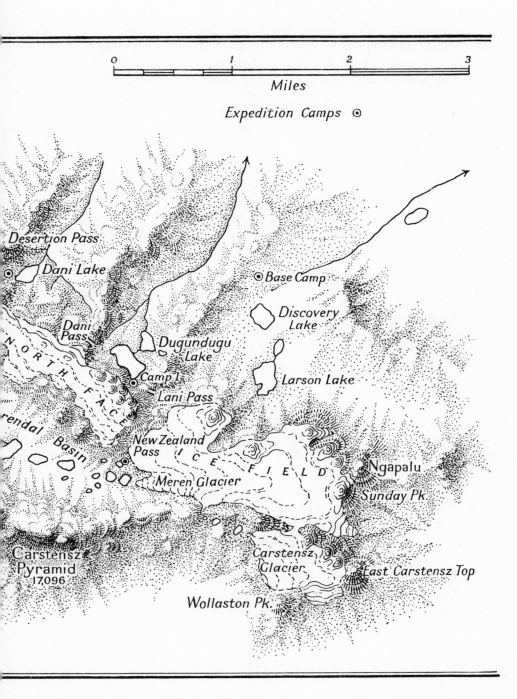

Expedition Camps ⊙

Miles

Desertion Pass

Dani Lake

Dani Pass

NORTH FACE

rendal Basin

Dugundugu Lake

Camp 1

Lani Pass

New Zealand Pass

Meren Glacier

Carstensz Pyramid
17096

Wollaston Pk.

⊙ Base Camp

Discovery Lake

Larson Lake

ICE FIELD

Ngapalu

Sunday Pk.

Carstensz Glacier

East Carstensz Top

protracted way of achieving the same thing is to tie the finger up so tightly with bast thread that in the end it dies off. A friend with a stone axe can then give it the *coup de grâce*. But this way means going around for weeks with the pain of the constricted finger. The first finger to go is the little finger of the left hand. The next is the ring finger, and so on. And if necessary the process can go on to the right hand. The thumbs are never amputated in this way. For the same reasons the upper part of the ear will sometimes be sacrificed. The wound is then smeared with clay. Bert told me that this sort of thing is so widespread that I should be bound to come across examples of it. I did, in fact, see Danis who still had their thumbs, but no fingers. Not a very pleasant thought before going to sleep, but I'm tired, and we've got a hard day ahead of us.

February 1

We shall be leaving our base camp in about an hour, and our approach to the Carstensz pyramid will have begun. At last! A very agreeable feeling.

We have been up and about since six o'clock, and there has been a great deal to do. For one thing we have had to dress our Danis. This meant a good deal of work, but it was well worth it and gave us a good deal of fun. In my mind I called it our Christian Dior session. Now and again it was richly comic. These men had never worn a pair of trousers before in their lives, or had boots on their feet, or proper headgear. They thought the buttons were there just for ornament, and as for the buttonholes—they were just holes in the cloth. Bert had to explain the practical relationship between buttons and buttonholes to them. It was almost as difficult to get them to understand the practical difference between trouser legs and jacket or shirt sleeves. Left to themselves some of them would attempt to put the trousers over their heads, or their legs into sleeves. When all these misunderstandings had finally been cleared up the biggest problem of all arose: each Dani had to be persuaded individually to abandon his penis sheath. There was just no room for it in an ordinary pair of trousers, because some of these hard pumpkin-like gourds came up to their chests. I remember a remark Russ made when we

48

4. On the North Face of the Carstensz Pyramid
5. The daily rain rolls up (OVERLEAF)

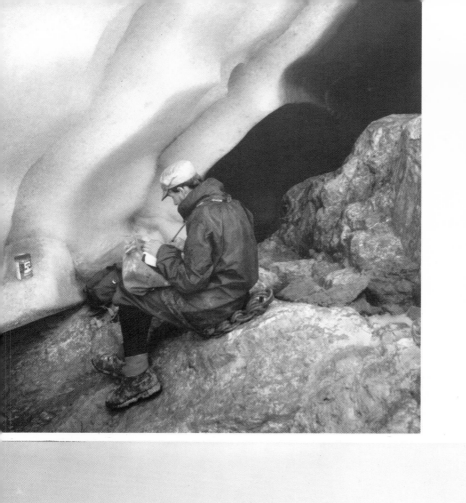

came across a row of these elongated fruit growing. He looked at them for a while in silence and then commented: "Gentlemen's outfitting."

After about an hour everything was in place. The Danis all had trousers on, and the discarded penis sheaths were scattered around all over the camp. The Danis joined us in our hearty laughter at the sight.

Our mountaineering headgear was the most popular item of clothing. They knew at once what it was for, and they put on their caps immediately, and insisted on wearing them around the camp all the time, though it was quite warm. There they stood and admired each other, and although Bert did his best to persuade them to take their caps off and put them into their pockets until it was necessary to use them, this time even his powers of persuasion proved unequal to the task—a cap seemed to strike a Dani as being every bit as important as his hair net.

Since I wrote the above we have been six hours on the way. We left our base camp at about ten o'clock, and before long we had reached Lake Discovery, which is very beautifully situated. Our way went on through tropical moss-carpeted forest with bright flowers growing all around. Occasionally we had to cut our way through liana, and to balance once more over fallen tree-trunks. Finally we reached the edge of the forest and the tree line. A little farther up we came to a pass, and there before us rose the broad north face of the Carstensz.

It was here, at 12,800 feet above sea level, that we established Camp I. By the site was an enormous rock, and with his mountain boots on Russ started to climb it. The rest of us watched him, and when he was almost at the top I jokingly said to our porters that if they really wanted to go with us they would have to be able to do that sort of thing too. The effect of my words flabbergasted me: they all took off their mountaineering boots and socks, and ran towards the rock in their bare feet. They jumped up on to the rock and ran up it as though there were suction pads on their feet. All of them quickly overhauled Russ and went on ahead, leaving him staring after them in amazement.

A little later Phil and Bert returned with the porters to our base camp.

49

6. *The new glacier cairn*
7. *The Pyramid still hidden in mist*

Russ and I are lying in our tent and enjoying the silence. Neither of us is a great talker. Both of us prefer to think over the aims of our expedition to ourselves and consider the mountains that we are going to climb and name. Above us now is peak after peak right over to Ngapalu in the east, around which veils of mist are wreathing. A very beautiful day is drawing to its close. We feel that we have got over the worst and that there should be no insuperable difficulties ahead of us now. In fact what lies ahead should be nothing but sheer joy for explorers and mountaineers.

February 2

That was a hard day! Hard certainly, but beautiful all the same. The weather was excellent when we left Camp I—clear and cold, quite extraordinarily cold for the tropics in fact. We climbed steeply upwards over jagged rocks with stretches of grass in between, and finally we reached the Carstensz ice at an altitude of 13,000 feet. Then our way went downwards a little through snow. Traversing in order to get a better view I suddenly saw the pass I was looking for. It was far away below us, and quite unattainable from where we were. There was no solid ice covering such as I had been led to expect by the twenty-five-year-old expedition report, but it would seem that big changes can take place very rapidly in the tropics. Instead there were steep, ice-free hangs ahead. There was no question of roping our porters—we should have to find another route. The only way open to us was the broad belt that runs across the whole north face. Following it we went down to about 13,000 feet. It was disagreeable but necessary. Moving eastward we passed through completely new terrain that twenty-five years before had been covered by glacier ice. In honour of the previous year's expedition we named it "New Zealand Pass." New Zealand mountaineers, led by Colin Putt, had already tried to find this crossing, but a combination of supply difficulties and lack of time had forced them to give up. Our Phil had been with this expedition, and his knowledge of the terrain now came in very useful for our own approach.

We ended up practically in the Merendal Basin below with a view over seven small turquoise-coloured lakes. Above them towered the tremendous face of the Carstensz Pyramid. It had been a laborious detour, but at least we had found the way through the north face into the horseshoe shaped arena of the Carstensz chain, and we had been the first to do so. With this we had opened up a route that can be used by porters who are not mountaineers.

We have photos of this landscape taken twenty-five years ago. The change brought about by the retreat of the glaciers is almost unbelievable. The place is hardly recognisable. Several miles of glacier must have melted away in the meantime, and in consequence enormous vertical rock faces have been laid bare. Lakes that did not previously exist have been formed. An altogether new area of the earth's surface has been opened up. It is in such circumstances that you begin to get some idea of the power of natural forces, and feel a breath of that original blast of creation. Towering above it all is the 2,500-foot north face of the Carstensz Pyramid—still waiting to be conquered. I can understand now how it was the Dutch failed twenty-five years ago. They were good mountaineers, but they were not familiar with the piton and roping technique that this giant probably requires.

Russ and I searched for a route over this virgin territory, and we found it. In order to make it easily negotiable in the mist we set up about fifty stone cairns.

It was late afternoon by the time we got back, tired but happy. It was raining again, but this meant more time for me to bring my diary up to date. Russ is also writing, but I can see that he is just as tired as I am. I feel quite fit though, and the altitude isn't troubling me. But my nose has a thick crust of scurf from sunburn, because at this altitude the sun is very strong, and the mist droplets act like lenses.

February 3

Russ and I have reconnoitred an ice-free approach in the direction of the Idenburg Top. I was anxious to find this way in order to spare our Danis the way across the glacier. They are experts at negotiating rocks and tree-trunks, but they would have difficulty here, and to make matters worse they would have to wear dark glasses.

But along the route we found today they will be in their element.

On the way we sat down for a while on broad bands of rock reminiscent of the Kugys Götterbänder in the Julian Alps in the Upper Engandine, and we took snaps of the fiery red rhododendrons growing there. We had seen something similar at lower altitudes as bushes. We found sprays of these flowers under chalky overhangs. They were quite white, calcified and brittle—as though preserved for all eternity.

On our return to camp Phil received us with the very disagreeable information that three of our porters had gone down with dysentery. Russ has already left for our base camp to attend to them. Phil and six of the porters are remaining here. Tomorrow we are going into Merendal (lake valley), and there we shall wait for Bert and Russ, who can get there direct from the base camp.

February 4

Despite pouring rain Phil and I enjoyed a proper Sunday in Merendal. We are sitting in our rainproof tent at the foot of the massive north face, and the ice of the glacier which sweeps down from Ngapalu is quite close to us.

Our six Danis went with us up the steep grassy slopes to the northern section of New Zealand Pass. We didn't make very rapid progress because they were quite considerably troubled by the intense cold and the rarefied air. But when we once got to the pass they quickly forgot all their exertions because for the first time in their lives they made the acquaintance of ice and snow. Their immediate and impulsive reaction was to embrace Phil and me in gratitude for having brought them into their "Dugundugu." Then they rushed at the ice, which they certainly took to be salt, because when they hacked big lumps off and ate them they marvelled that they had no taste. In their joy and delight they were so beside themselves that they now did a sort of mad snow twist. Their reaction once they had time to think was amusing and very typical: each man made himself a heap of the crystal treasure as his own personal property, after which they compared notes with great glee. It wasn't easy for us to persuade them to go on at all, and before they would consent to move we had to promise them that on the way back they could take some of the "Dugundugu" with them down into the valley.

Unfortunately, soon after that it began to rain, and the Carstensz Pyramid was once again hidden from us. Because of the rain our porters were feeling miserable and we had to rope them forward part of the way. Their usual agility had completely deserted them and they were like unhappy children. It was midday before we stopped, and then we pitched our tent in a stony waste of rubble at the edge of a green moraine lake. The change brought about by the retreat of the glaciers became more and more evident. The thickness of the ice must have been enormously reduced since the days of the Dutch expedition, and the actual volume which has melted is more important than the distance the ice has receded. Tomorrow morning we are going to look for the stone cairns the Dutch left behind twenty-five years ago. Only when we have found them will we have a real idea of the changes that have taken place in the meantime.

The area was thoroughly explored by a small expedition at the end of 1936, and once we had found a route over New Zealand Pass into it, the notes made by the Dutch expedition headed by Dr A. H. Colijn, accompanied by Flying Officer F. Wissel and the geologist Dr J. J. Dozy, proved very useful.

February 5

It is evening now. The day was depressingly dull, and very little happened to raise our spirits. At the time the Dutch had set up their cairns about two hundred feet from the tongue of the glacier, but our search for them now began to look pretty hopeless. A notebook was also said to have been left behind. All we had been able to see so far was a great waste without a single sign of life—there wasn't even moss or grass, only a couple of glacier lakes. We were already beginning to fear that the cairns had disappeared into these lakes when Phil suddenly shouted: "I can see one!" He was right. Far out on a moraine ridge running laterally across the valley we could now see the first of the stone cairns we were looking for. It jutted up out of the mist, and when we got there we found that it was overgrown with moss. Inside it was a tin, very rusty, but otherwise intact. We took it back to our tent to open it. The rust had affected the folded document inside, and the neat handwriting of Dr Dozy was decipherable only at the edges. In any case, it contained no information we did not already possess from the report of the Dutch expedition. We now very carefully wrapped the precious document in a plastic cover, and whilst we were thus engaged a bird began to sing sweetly outside the tent as though to say: "You see! There's life even here."

Now we must look for the two upper cairns, but they ought to be much easier to find now that we know approximately how far the ice has retreated. The only thing I really can't understand is that on two occasions geologists have been here since without searching for the cairns. Not that I mind, of course: their omission left it to me to find the tin, which had been lying there untouched for twenty-five years.

February 6

It was bitterly cold this morning, but at least the sun was shining. We spread our clothes out on the ground in the hope that they would dry a little. In the meantime we have built a stone wall round our tent to protect it against the wind and the rain during the night. We spent the rest of the day exploring the horseshoe-shaped basin. During our exploration we came across the other two Dutch cairns, and we found a zinc box in one of them containing the notebook the Dutch had left behind. Its pages were damp and stuck together, but to strike gold could hardly have been more exciting. I will send the notebook to the Dutch authorities to be forwarded to Dr Dozy, and I hope he will be as pleased about the discovery as we are. Once again we were granted a marvellous view of the smooth face of the Pyramid, and we could see the small ice cap of the Idenburg Top in the west. Clouds were gathering in the south, and the jagged, serrated outline was even more graphic by contrast.

Russ was in camp when we got back. He had come up from our base camp with seven porters, and he told us that Bert was already in Camp I, and that the sick porters were getting better. Unless the weather upsets our plans we shall be able to bivouac at the foot of the north face tomorrow.

The ice is just as great a sensation for our seven new porters as it

54

was for their fellows. They have carefully put some of it in tins to take back to the valley to demonstrate the miracle of the Dugundugu to their friends. Impossible to persuade them that all they will have in their tins when they get back is water. They just have no idea what freezing and thawing means. There is no room in their heads for such incredible things, and naturally their tongue has no words to express them.

February 7

Phil, Russ and I have made a tour of exploration into the lower-lying "Carstensz Heath," where the Dutch expedition had its base camp. For hours we struggled through sharp, breast-high grass and over marshy ground. When we got back to our tent we found Bert there. He already had the water boiling for our tea, and rarely have I enjoyed a cup of tea so much as I did then. Despite our tiredness it turned out a very pleasant evening. The sky was clear for a change and there was a lambent crescent of moon against a sparkling background of stars. It was really like something out of a picture book.

Tomorrow the four of us are going to do our yesterday's tour all over again just for the sake of the training it will give us. We also propose to go on to a pass which will give us a view of the Wollaston Glacier. And if the weather holds we're going to try the as yet unclimbed East Carstensz Top.

February 8

The day began with dark, heavy clouds as usual, but we didn't let that put us off. It was just as well that we didn't because the clouds rolled away and we crossed the Carstensz Glacier and reached the pass in sunshine. But there was nothing to be seen. The Wollaston Glacier had just melted away. At every turn this landscape offers magnificent views and surprises. We climbed a rock face and named it Wollaston Peak. The view from the top was really unique: we could see the Arafura Sea fifty miles away. Standing in a world of ice we were looking down into the tropical jungle along the coast 16,000 feet below! We could clearly see the estuaries of at least ten rivers

55

along the coast. This was the area in which Indonesian landings were expected. And it was there that some of Jan Carstensz's sailors had been eaten by cannibals. It was also there that Jan Carstensz had been the first European to see ice and snow in the South Seas.

The weather held, and we pressed on over the broad Carstensz Glacier. Moving over a narrow arête of ice and snow we climbed the East Carstensz Top for the first time. The Dutch had tried it twenty-five years previously without success. By the time we were standing shivering in the wet mist and the sudden flurries of snow on the peak, five hours had passed since we had left camp. "It's damned cold here," said Bert abruptly. He was right too, and it was time to get back.

Our descent was hampered by mist, and, in addition, the snow was so rotten that we kept sinking up to our waists in it. We roped ourselves over the glacier, and then I went on ahead of the others to have hot tea ready for them when they arrived. On the way I was several times in trouble in "glacier morass," which is a sticky, muddy mixture of earth and water. Once in camp I washed all the muck away in clean glacier water. Then, still wet to the skin, but happy, I got the stove going.

Before long the others arrived and we celebrated our first peak victory with half a bottle of Dutch gin. We were keeping the other half for the Pyramid itself. We are now within reach of our objective, and it was a particularly fine performance on Bert's part, because he is not, after all, a mountaineer, and he waited for us two hours on the "fore" peak in the bitter cold whilst we also climbed the "aft" peak.

We are now hoping that the sun will shine tomorrow—we just must get our soaking things dry again somehow. Then in the afternoon we hope to get a closer look at the north face of the Pyramid itself.

The weather is one of the main themes of our conversation, of course. It reminds me of Bernard Shaw's remark about history—all it teaches you is that you can't learn anything from history. It's just like that with the weather. That's why we always set off no matter what the weather. If it gets too bad you can always turn back, after all, but if you hang about waiting for "good weather" you'd never get anything done.

In retrospect I feel that today was one of the most beautiful mountaineering days in my life. I shall never forget that breath-taking view from a height of 16,000 feet right over to the Arafura Sea beyond the dark jungle along the coast. We also saw the other peaks along the north side of the chain. Frankly, they weren't particularly impressive, but the point about them all is that each peak is as yet unconquered—which means, of course, that they are all our natural objectives, since I had determined to bag all the peaks of the Carstensz mountains.

Whilst we were sitting in our tent smoking our pipes, and I was writing up this diary, one of the favourite songs of my youth came into my head very appropriately:

"Was kann es schöneres geben, als nach Höhen streben,
die noch keines Menschen Fuss betrat. . . ."[1]

February 9

Rest day. I have given my feet the once over, because yesterday on the East Carstensz Top I had a disagreeable feeling that I was in for my fifth case of frostbite—they were beginning to feel very numb. However, the numbness wore off during the descent and they seem all right now, thank goodness.

February 10

We occupied the morning with glacier measurements. The result is astonishing. During the past twenty-five years the Carstensz Glacier has retreated 1,446 feet. And the Meren Glacier has retreated even farther—2,384 feet. We wrote down the new measurements, added the information that we are going to build another stone cairn higher up, then put the message in a water-tight tin and left it where the Dutch had left their tin.

By midday we were back in camp. Two porters and the Papuan policeman Navas arrived there just as we did. They brought a letter from the American missionary Larson. What it had to say first

[1] "What can be better than striving for heights, on which no man's foot has yet trod. . . ."

astonished us and then made us laugh. It appeared that to explain their premature return the porters who had deserted us had put it around in Ilaga that our party had first been decimated by hunger and sickness and then buried by a landslide.[1] Well, fortunately the truth is very different. Here we are, fit and well, and very much alive. All our thoughts are now concentrated on our forthcoming assault on the Carstensz Pyramid. What we are hoping for now in the way of weather is a few heavy snowfalls followed by a few days of good weather. That would be ideal. Tomorrow we propose to climb Ngapalu for training.

February 11

We set off early this morning through the steep broken rocks behind our camp and soon reached a vast rock terrace. At first there was very little snow on the old ice, but soon it became thicker at every step. Finally we were sinking in so deep that making a track became very difficult. After about three hours we found ourselves in thick mist. Almost without visibility we took turns in making a track through deep wet snow. In the hope of spotting unevennesses and crevasses in the diffuse, shadeless light we threw an empty tin ahead of us every few steps in order to fix a point ahead we could see. Towards the end Bert was in the lead, but he is a heavy fellow and he sank into the snow up to his waist, so after a while he started crawling along on his knees as otherwise he would have sunk right into the snow. But it was laborious progress. However, shortly after midday we were standing on the broad peak, freezing and exhausted, but we had made it. It had begun to snow, so now we started the

[1] The canard even got into the world press, and I subsequently read the following account in the *Salzburger Nachrichten*: "The Harrer expedition is reported missing. Reports from Hollandia say that nothing has been heard of Harrer and his companions for three weeks. The expedition set out to climb the 17,500-foot high Carstensz Top in Dutch New Guinea, and left Ilaga Valley in the mountainous area of Central New Guinea on January 29 last. The last news of the expedition comes from porters who returned to the expedition's base camp on February 1. Although the expedition is equipped with a wireless transmitter no contact has been established." Similar reports also appeared in other European news papers.

58

descent at once, and within an hour and a half we were back in camp. The second ascent of Ngapalu had been carried out without incident.

We all felt fit and well, and we decided that if the weather cleared up in the night we would tackle our main objective, the highest peak of the Carstensz chain, the Pyramid, the following morning.

February 12

The pattering of rain on the tent woke me. It meant that our assault on the Pyramid would have to be postponed. During the course of the morning the weather did improve, but just as it is on the Eiger after a storm, so it was here: there was wet, sloppy snow everywhere on the north face. It was sticking even to steep places where normally it would have slid away. An ascent in such circumstances would be very difficult. We've no choice therefore; we shall have to postpone our hopes till tomorrow. Fortunately we aren't pressed for time, since there's no summer here to pass, and no monsoon or rainy period to bother about. "Softly, softly . . ." Gently does it, and we'll take the trick in the end. So now we're lying on our bellies and writing letters, and I'm writing up this diary, and we're all hoping that porters will arrive from the base camp today to take the letters back with them.

February 13

When I went to sleep yesterday it was raining, and I woke up again about every two hours thereafter. In the end I got up and went outside. I still hadn't given up hope, and at about three o'clock the rain actually stopped. Once again I crawled out of my warm sleeping-bag and had another look outside. Yes, the rain had stopped, but the Pyramid was hidden in mist. Phil was awake too now, and when he noticed that the rain had stopped he started to make our porridge. At four o'clock we ate it, and at five o'clock, armed with pocket torches, we set off. It was still dark when we passed the two upper stone cairns on the glacier, but by the time we got to the former camp of the Dutch expedition the first light of day was creeping over the mountain ridges. There was still an old stone oven in the abandoned camp and in it we put our torches for safe keeping.

It was daylight now and the air was calm, but we still couldn't see much of the mountain. The whole of its upper part was still shrouded in mist. However, there was no point in waiting any longer for good weather, so we pressed on.

We went up over the steep rubble-strewn slope making for the point from which we had long planned to start climbing the face. Phil took our heavyweight Bert on the rope and had to negotiate an overhang almost immediately. All went well. The next rope-length brought us to another awkward spot, but Russ mastered it almost with elegance. After that we went up almost vertically in a crack. The limestone was so rough and with so many small flutings that with our rubber soles we could find a good footing even on almost vertical places. And with every foot we ascended the weather improved. The mist lifted and we could see blue sky shimmering above us. By the time we were half-way up almost all the North Face peaks on the other side were in brilliant sunshine. There was no need for hesitation now. Above us was the west ridge leading up to the peak, and below us, bathed in sunshine, was the horseshoe basin. We could also clearly see the approach route we had already reconnoitred from the Idenburg Top in the west. In high spirits we climbed on, went round a steep gully and by nine o'clock we had reached the serrated west ridge.

It consists of innumerable sharp, almost black limestone needles that look like a relief map of some ghostly landscape. The fine points cracked and broke underfoot. You could have got hold of them only with those thick leather gloves iron puddlers use.

For the most part upright, we balanced our way over the miniature "peaks" of this strange rock formation until we suddenly came to a vertical drop. It was no more than sixteen feet deep, and the crevasse was only seven feet across, but we had to drive a piton into the rock face and let ourselves down on the rope. Russ was the second to dare the jump over the fissure. We held our breath, but he managed it. The first part of the ridge was a real treat and from the standpoint of climbing technique the best part of the ascent.

Then quite suddenly the mist descended again and immediately

60

afterwards it began to snow. But we had no time to bother about the weather now. We were determined to get to the topmost peak of the highest mountain between the Himalayas and the Andes.

Once again a vertical fall yawned before us, a few hundred yards farther towards the north it was lost in milky-white nothingness. On the other side of the fall a great "mist tower" rose over the ridge.

We found a small rock-head on which we could rope ourselves down. Then we traversed along the south face, going up through soft snow over breaks and heaps of debris until we came to overhangs beneath which we sought shelter for a while against the wild snow flurries. We had been climbing for over five hours now, and we were chilled and wet to the skin. A rest seemed inevitable. But then the snow flurries parted and allowed us a short glance above. The rest of the way didn't look too difficult, and in fact the climbing now became easier. We crossed alternately snow with rock and ribs with steps, and reached the ridge again, and in this way we traversed from the south face into the north face. It was dangerous now, like a winter climb in the Alps. Once again we had to go through a gully. Carefully secured we ascended laboriously, making our way round a pillar of rock and balancing along a snow peak. And suddenly it was all over. All around us the only way was downwards. We were on the peak itself. The highest point on the island of New Guinea, 17,096 feet above sea level. I looked at my watch. It was two o'clock in the afternoon.

The peak is a small snow cone on which there was enough room for all four of us. We shook hands enthusiastically. Then we produced the four flags and a pennant we had brought with us. Bert Huizenga had a big Dutch flag which we spread out and weighted with stones. Next came the Papuan flag, and a hand-embroidered Australian pennant from Russel Kippax. Phil Temple contributed a small New Zealand flag which he left behind together with a note in a yellow cigarette tin; and finally I spread out a small red, white, red Austrian flag, which had been made by compatriots in Australia specially for the purpose.

There we stood—like a small harmonious and peaceful United Nations—the first men on the highest peak of the Carstensz mountains. With numbed fingers I wound up the release mechanism of my camera so that we could have a photograph of all of us together on the peak, and then we started the descent at once.

It had taken us eight hours to get to the top, and now we had to do the return journey to the foot in half that time if we were to have at least the face behind us before dark.

We just managed it in the last light of the day. Before dusk the clouds parted once more to give us a wonderfully beautiful view of the deep, dark jungle beneath us. We could even see a clearing with a village on a steep slope. Overjoyed but very tired we reached the old Dutch camp and recovered our pocket torches, and after another hour—more staggering than walking—we got back to our camp, fourteen hours after we had left it.

The climb was a good one, but it had not been made too easy for us. The degree of difficulty was somewhere about IV I should say, and all in all our undertaking had the typical characteristics of the classic first-timer—the sort of thing of which there's very little left in the world nowadays.

The rain is pelting down and we are crouching in our tent celebrating our success with hot tea and the second half of our bottle of Dutch gin. To add to the celebration there is also a fresh cucumber —well, when I say "fresh," it's been in my rucksack for the past three weeks, but it was fresh then. In any case, none of us is hungry. Whether that's due to our elation or our tiredness I don't know.

I think we owe our success to the fact that we make such a very good team: Bert Huizenga, who patiently and tirelessly interpreted and mediated; Russ, our excellent medico, and himself a first-class climber with some of the old Australian pioneering spirit; and finally the young New Zealander Philip Temple, who proved himself quite capable of mastering the most difficult snow faces the mountain had to offer. You could safely go sheep-stealing with men like that. And if it so happens that you climb a previously unclimbed mountain with them instead, you won't find yourself, or them, at a loss when it gets up to its worst tricks. They just happen to be the sort you can rely on in any circumstances. It's a real pleasure to be sitting with them after our victory over the mountain.

Today is a well-earned rest day. Russ wants to go back with Bert to Bokondini, leaving Phil and me to do some more climbing. In particular the two of us intend to tackle the second highest peak on the island, the Idenburg Top, which has also never been climbed.

Russ and Bert stayed on for another day, and in consequence Russ was privileged to take part in a memorable tour.

Phil, Russ and I were determined to climb the other peaks between Ngapalu and New Zealand Pass today in order, so to speak, to finish off the series. Rested and refreshed, we started off early, and within a few hours we reached the first of them. There was thick mist and it was impossible to get our bearings properly. However, we went on and climbed a second peak, which we guessed to be the so-called North Face Peak. But through the mist and snowfall, which was quite light, we caught a glimpse of a still higher peak. This one should have been Ngapalu, but it looked quite different. In any case, we beat a track on towards it. When we got there after an hour and a half we decided that it must be the North Face Peak after all, though we thought we had left that behind us long ago. I was still very doubtful, but because of the mist it was impossible to be sure. We went on through deep snow up to our waists and arrived at a fourth peak. We just stopped guessing now, but inwardly I was quite determined to solve the riddle in the end. And somehow or other we had to find Ngalapu Peak, since otherwise the series would not be complete after all. But it wasn't the fifth peak either—that was too flat and altogether too insignificant. So it must be the sixth: a splendid snow peak dropping away steeply on all sides.

Now it became clear to us that it was the fifth after all, the flat one, which was the North Face Peak, and that we were now on Ngapalu proper. But this meant that the snow peak we had climbed the previous Sunday in the belief that we were making the second ascent of Ngapalu was actually a nameless snow peak to the east, so we now named it "Sunday Peak." The peak on which we were now standing

63

was magnificent, and well worthy of being one of the three highest points of the Carstensz mountains. I can imagine the delight of the Dutch when they first climbed it twenty-five years ago.

We were quite excited about our discovery, and in particular I was very glad that we had not given up after the third peak, but had pressed on through the mist, the snow and the light flurries until we had solved the mystery.

Phil had obviously taken on too much and he was feeling a bit under the weather, and so for the most part I now tracked on alone. I think it was the excitement that kept me on the go—six peaks in one day! It was only in the afternoon when we had reached our tent again that I began to feel tired.

The Idenburg Top and the remaining peaks of the North Wall are now ahead of us, but I am going to do these with Phil alone.

This is our last evening in the heart of the Carstensz mountains. Tomorrow the porters are coming to take back everything which is still in Merendal to Camp I. Russ and Bert will go back to Ilaga, and Phil and I will go to the Idenburg Top.

It was a wonderful camp up here, both from the angle of landscape and mountaineering; it was a happy camp too. All the peaks we had set out to climb were climbed in heartening comradeship, including the most fascinating peak of all, the one that any climber who once saw its photograph would desperately want to conquer: the Carstensz Pyramid.

Tonight all the porters are in Camp I. Although I miss my amiable and helpful Okar I'm not sorry to spend this last night here just with Russ, Bert and Phil.

Apart from a pair of birds there is no other life in this new world which has been formed by the melting of the glacier. There are no trees and no flowers—though a little moss has started to grow over the barren surface. Oh yes! and there is just one tuft of poor grass whose seed was probably originally carried here by the wind. You couldn't imagine anything more desolate and inaccessible. This is probably what it looked like in Europe at the end of the last Ice Age.

64

8. The Carstensz Pyramid

The last stage of our Carstensz expedition has now begun. It was raining when we left our camp site, and that helped to make the parting easier. Our halt in the New Zealand Pass was amusing. This was where our Danis had stored their lumps of ice to take back with them into the valley to show their friends and relatives the marvel of the Dugundugu: amazing cold salt without taste! In the camp above they had already provided themselves with tins and other containers for the precious stuff. Now they started to pack it for the journey. By the time they get back into the valley all the ice will have disappeared of course, and they will marvel at the whole thing as magic, and no doubt they'll have the most extraordinary stories to tell. Some of them are embedding the ice in clay and then wrapping the whole in newspaper to go in their empty tins. With such careful packing it can't possibly get lost—at least, that's their idea.

It was pouring with rain, and it thundered and rolled in the north face. From all sides water is gushing down and making the otherwise quiet landscape lively and noisy. Behind us snow clouds are descending into the north valley. It is almost as though the world is preparing to end.

The general uproar is affecting our porters, and they are becoming restless and anxious. They are shouting and gesticulating as they go forward, and there is fear and menace in the air. The final steep descent into Camp I upset them completely, and one of the porters from Ilaga—completely naked—threw away his load and made as though to leap over the dangerous rock-face. He shrieked like a stuck pig and rolled his eyes wildly as he dashed off. Fortunately another Dani, a little more level-headed, seized him and did his best to pacify the hysterical fellow. Several other Danis now ran up and helped to drag him down. One of them now danced around hitting the ground with a stick and shouting at the top of his voice. He was obviously trying to exorcise the evil magic that had seized on the victim. When this had no effect he seized an ice-axe and hacked out a circle round the group in order to keep off the evil spirits. But the panic-stricken man continued to rave. In the end Russ and I tried our hands, spoke to him soothingly, and then led him between us

65

9. Fairy-Tale Valley

down the last four or five hundred feet of the descent to the camp. Behind us the other porters set up a tremendous shouting and shrieking. It sounded quite horrifying, but, in fact, they meant well—they were doing their best to drive away the evil spirits. The terrified man reached the camp and then he collapsed. One of his companions now gave him water to drink from his cupped hands. We were interested at this evidence that the Danis know the best treatment for shock— plenty of liquid, our "hot, sweet tea." When the man had drunk, the Samaratin seized him by his big shock of hair and began to pull it and hit him. This finally did the trick and the poor wretch came round, whereupon his "rescuer" basked in the admiration of his companions.

In this way the "Dugundugu," the ice, provided us with a dramatic denouement. But at least we didn't lose a porter. He hadn't even come to any harm or injured himself in any way.

February 18

I didn't get a chance of writing up my diary yesterday. Getting Russ and Bert off took up the greater part of the day. I shall certainly miss Russ in particular, his matter of fact comradeship and his stoical calm whatever the circumstances. Not that I shan't miss Bert's confident and effective way of dealing with the porters! The two of them are probably well on their way back to Ilaga by this time.

Phil and I are alone, and our two-man tent suddenly seems very big. It is unusually quiet.

February 19

We could get only five porters for the Idenburg Top, so Phil and I have to carry our heavy rucksacks. Although we have taken only what is absolutely necessary, our five Danis are all carrying overweight. In consequence, of course, we have to rest more often, and it took us five hours before we got beyond the two shallow Dani passes along the north face. In addition it was raining, and our porters didn't like that at all. They loathe marching through rain. But on the way Phil found a spiny ant-eater, and this improved their spirits. With shrieks of delight they danced round the heavily snorting beast,

66

which did not even raise its short white spines despite the obviously threatening danger. I take it that this is a sign of degeneration: the ant-eater has no enemies here, and in consequence it has probably lost the power to raise its spines any more. The Danis pranced round it merrily for a while and then one of them took an ice-axe and killed it. The whole thing was just a game for them. They have the thoughtless cruelty of children, but apart from that they are also very definitely good-natured.

After this incident we started on our way again. The porters ahead of me kept disappearing in the mist, and just as suddenly they were there again—it was a fantastic picture, like ghostly shadows that dissolved, formed again, turned grey, and disappeared once more. Now and again a pale ray of sun would penetrate the mist. The figures of the Danis ahead of me then stood out like steaming shadows against the light. It was like an illustration from a book of fairy tales.

In this way we finally reached the yellow marshes of Dani lake, and there we pitched our camp.

February 20

Once again we trod on new land, on ground that no human beings had ever trodden before. The mountains were hidden in mist, but our spirits remained high. We didn't even let it upset us when one of our porters fell ill and a couple of others deserted us. Perhaps they too will go back and spread the news that we have been buried by an avalanche. With only two able-bodied porters left we can't make very rapid progress of course, and so we transported our loads up to the next ridge in stages. When I thought we must be about two-thirds of the way up to the pass Phil surprised me with the agreeable news that we were there already. It was certainly high time, because the heavy load had just about brought me to the end of my tether, and Phil was in no better case. When our two remaining porters caught up with us at midday we pitched camp. Whilst we were setting up our tent we caught occasional glimpses through the mist of the confused limestone masses that lay between us and our objective, the Idenburg Top.

67

Because of the loss of three porters we changed our plans: we are sending the two porters we have left back to the lake camp, and Phil and I will go on alone. Phil's pack and mine consist of a sleeping-bag, a down stuffed jacket, an extra shirt and a pair of socks each, a Leica and food for four days. This means three main meals and the rest in the form of highly concentrated nourishment. We shall bivouac and hope to find overhangs for protection. Unfortunately this Carstensz landscape is not well provided with caves.

February 21

We have a heavy day behind us and we are now spending a pretty wretched evening. I have a head injury, an inner tendon of my left knee is damaged, and my hands are so cut about that I can hardly write. In addition we are both wet to the skin.

It was raining when we started off this morning. Phil and I are now alone. On our way we came across very many small lakes and streams, and when we looked down from above into the valleys we thought we could see the ancient frontiers of human civilisations. But it wasn't long before we realised that we had made a mistake. We laboriously made our way through breast-high grass, over heaps of rubble and between rocks which looked quite lovely because they were overgrown with moss in a great variety of colours. But behind this beauty there were treacherous dangers: the moss made the rocks very slippery, and there were funnel-like depressions everywhere, so that the whole route was one long balancing feat—hampered by heavy packs. However, I gradually felt more confident—too confident as it turned out. One piece of carelessness, and I slipped on a moss-covered rock, lost my balance and tried to grab hold of something, but the weight of my rucksack dragged me on against my will. My left foot slid into a steep funnel-like hole, and at last, with outspread arms, I managed to hold myself on its sharp edge. I tried to ram my ice-axe in above me, but in swinging it I hit my forehead just above the eye. Phil helped me out of this disagreeable situation, but it was some time before I could get going again.

As we fought our way upwards between rocks, through high tough grass, and over mud and rubble, the rain, which had originally been

68

quite light, changed into a downpour. Wet to the skin we made a halt to wait for it to end. But it didn't end, and so we went on again. We now came to the last and steepest part of the way up to the pass. I was no longer able to take the lead, so Phil went ahead. His hands were numbed with the cold, but at least they were not torn and battered like mine. At 14,000 feet we reached the pass and set up a stone cairn.

Exhausted now we looked around for some sort of shelter, and after about an hour we found an overhang which offered us at least a little dry ground in this harsh, bare and rocky landscape. Even then we had to work hard for about two hours in order to make the site suitable for our bivouac. Drops fell down on us from above, and our feet were in a narrow rocky crevice, but at least our heads were under the overhang. Phil squeezed out some moss to get water with which to make tea. It was brown before it came into contact with the tea-leaves. We're quite high up, but I can't really say we're on top of the world.

February 22

The morning did a good deal to recompense us. When we crawled numb and frozen out of our crevice the sun was there to greet us. We could see right over as far as the Arafura Sea. There was plenty of water there, of course, but we couldn't find even the tiniest trickle here, so now I started to press out some moss. It was daylight now so I could see very plainly how brown and dirty was the liquid I was managing to squeeze out. I suggested straining it through my handkerchief, but Phil said that on the whole he thought he would sooner have it strained through one of his socks. It only shows you that the tastes of civilised men can differ widely—even when they're in the wilderness together. In any case, we both drank the tea. The good spirits awakened by the sight of the sun began to disappear. Ahead of us was another day of streaming rain on our way to the Idenburg Top—and another day without porters at that.

We made our way through a valley which was so narrow and had such steep sides as to be practically invisible until you were on top of it, and so we named it "Hidden Valley."

It was here that we stopped for the night. We hope to be able to

69

tackle Idenburg Top tomorrow. A little sun would do us good. But we're not too depressed, because even in this dreary rain we have been exploring new country.

This was one of our best days, though we made a mistake which cost us at least twenty-four hours, which means that we certainly shan't be able to do the Idenburg Top today.

It began with a disagreeable night, cold, wet, and practically sleepless. The morning dawned with mist that wreathed through the narrow valley in thick swathes. Shivering we made our way westward through "Hidden Valley." We hadn't been going for long before we realised that we were crossing a watershed, and this meant that we were in a new valley. In order to get a better view of our position we clambered up one of the steep sides. Whilst we were fighting our way up through grass and rocks the mist lifted and an unexpected sight lay ahead of us: a valley of breath-taking beauty. Between the white limestone rock faces were three large and one small lake before the valley debouched westward into a plain. It was a small gem, and I can't remember any other landscape throughout our whole expedition that was so beautiful.

Nevertheless, at first Phil was a bit depressed because we had lost a day through our mistake. But in the end he agreed with me that this discovery was beautiful enough to be worth a day—even the Idenburg Top itself. It was obvious that our discoveries had to be named so we discussed the question and decided that as the whole place was so fairylike, so mysterious and so enchantingly beautiful we would name the four lakes Hansel, Gretel, Andersen and Grimm. The valley itself we called Fairy-Tale Valley, and the two rocky ridges Cinderella and Alice Ridges. The wide plain into which our fairy-tale valley debouched we called Peter Pan Plain; and the two ugly fissured peaks in the Alice Ridge we named Tweedledum and Tweedledee after Tenniel's two handsome lads in *Alice in Wonderland*.

We felt as though we were in a fairy-tale world. Well, isn't it a kind of fairy tale that on this old globe of ours circled by jet planes and space rockets we should still be able to find a valley with four

70

lovely lakes high above the villages of the Stone Age men of New Guinea, a valley which no other human beings had ever seen, not even from an aeroplane? It isn't marked on any map, and still farther to the west lies even more unexplored territory. But we have no time to explore that; our objective is still the Idenburg Top, and on March 1 the porters will arrive in our base camp to carry our expedition baggage back to Ilaga. This means that we shall have to do the Idenburg Top tomorrow and now go back to our bivouac in Hidden Valley.

Whilst we were entering the names on our map a robin appeared quite close to us and appeared to be scolding us. It may have been because we had taken the only place out of the rain for miles around.

February 24

Our last night without a tent is awaiting us now. It doesn't bother us any more, because we've done it—we've climbed the Idenburg Top. The 15,360-foot-high second highest peak in the mountains of New Guinea is now no longer untrodden.

The whole previous night I woke up about every hour. Each time it was raining. It rained in the evening; it was raining at midnight; and it was raining in the morning. It was still raining when we started off, with determination, but little hope of success, to tackle the Idenburg Top. The valley was grey and half-hidden in mist, and the rocky walls cast deep shadows over the lakes. There was nothing at all left of the entrancing picture that had so heartened us yesterday.

We tramped off, and every step squelched in the wet ground, but we made fair progress. It was now twenty to eight. Then suddenly the weather changed for the better. The rain became less and finally stopped altogether, and as we came into a mossy valley the Carstensz Pyramid rose slim elegant, and majestic in the east in full sunlight before us. Morning mist was wreathing around rock and ice. Without hesitation I should count this marvellous mountain as amongst the most beautiful in the world. Now that we could see it from the west I could understand why they called it the Pyramid. It is, in fact, a pyramid of matchless beauty. I am quite certain that if a photograph of the Carstensz Pyramid had been published in 1936 showing it as we could see it now an expedition to climb it would have set off the very following year. A bit of luck for us that no such photograph was published.

We succumbed again and again to the temptation to stop and admire the beauty around us. I doubt if I shall ever again in my life see anything so beautiful—at least, not for the first time, since the spaces still blank on our maps are rapidly diminishing. All the ice-peaks of the North Face were once again before our eyes. There was perpetual snow from Ngapalu to our own "Sunday Peak," and glaciers on the equator. An easy climb brought us into Idenburg Valley. Making our way between huge rock slabs we came to a high pass which we promptly named "Assault Pass." On its other side lay an enormous basin with a very beautiful lake in the middle. As far as we could see its mysteriously shining green depths were without any outlet. Incidentally, it is already marked on the map so it must have been seen from the air. It lies in the hollow formed by the steeply falling rocky slopes of Alice Ridge and Idenburg Top.

With this we were within reach of our objective, and we made our way up a steep rock face, alternately traversing across rubble and rock. After two successive rock levels came deep snow. The peak was rather less than a hundred feet above us now, and before long we were standing on its mist-wreathed ice cupola, 15,360 feet above sea level.

I looked at my watch. It seemed to have stopped. "What's the time, Phil?" I demanded. After a quick glance Phil shook his head. "Odd! Mine seems to have stopped too. It says only twenty-past eleven." It so happened that my Swiss chronometer said exactly the same, and a little further investigation showed that neither watch had stopped—we had just been unable to believe that we had finished the climb in less than four hours. And neither of us felt done up, or even tired. We were both in first-class form—if we hadn't been we could never have done the climb in that time.

We now built a stone cairn and left an air-mail letter in it for whoever should come after us:

"Idenburg Top. First ascent. February 21 1962. Heinrich Harrer and Philip Temple. P.T.O. Reached summit 11.20 a.m. three and three-quarter hours after leaving our bivouac in Hidden Valley. The two other summits are yours!" Together with the letter we left a small Austrian flag and then we began the descent.

After an hour we had the wall behind us and rested out of the rain for a bit under an overhang. We were laughing happily because of our success and the record time we had done it in. Neither snow nor rain mattered to us now—not even if the heavens had just opened and dropped it on us all at once. It wouldn't make any difference to our success: we had had our best mountaineering day of the expedition. Although we had not had to cope with any particular technical difficulties, we had made the approach without porters; this and our patience in waiting, and the speed with which we had finally made the climb turned it into a classic of its kind.

All the same, we have a few difficult days ahead of us. We must be in the main camp by March 1, and I want to end up by climbing the North Face peak lying to the west of New Zealand Pass.

February 25

As is right and proper on a Sunday we all had a longer lie in this morning. In any case it was raining again right from early on, so there was really no hurry. We drank tea, wrote a memo about the climbing route to the peak of the Idenburg Top, and left it together with a pennant in a tin that had once contained porridge oats. Finally I stowed away the faggots that had dried in the night. That was my good deed for the day. At some time or other someone would come to this cave on the way to explore the rest of the countryside and he would be glad of this wood for his fire.

And then we lost our way hopelessly in the mist. It is true that on this account we found another pass, which we promptly named "Welcome Pass," but unfortunately it didn't live up to its name: down below was a flat morass which ended abruptly in a sea of mist. We had a feeling that things weren't going to turn out too well, so we scrambled and slid down over the rubble, crossed the morass and then found ourselves facing a yawning precipice. A powerful waterfall hurled itself into the depths over a vertical face at least 650 feet deep. It was so deep that you couldn't see where the water finally hit the ground below. There was nothing jutting out of the sheer face,

73

no rock head which would have allowed us to rope our way down—just nothing. And very likely the other side rose just as steeply. At first there seemed nothing for it but to go back the whole way and search for our old bivouac site. But then Phil gave a shout. He had spotted a possibility: grass-overgrown stretches which would allow us to overcome the obstacle by fairly easy clambering. At least it meant that we still had some hope of reaching our tent before nightfall.

It took us many laborious hours all the same, and the exertions of the previous day coupled with a shortage of proper food began to make themselves felt. However, a cube of concentrated nourishment helped us to get through the final stage.

By half-past four we had reached our tent at last, and there we took off our wet clothes, flung them down on the ground and crawled thankfully into our sleeping-bags, though they were damp and cold too. I'm now lying on my belly, freezing but doing my best to scribble. At least we're both in good spirits. Phil has made the tea, and that's putting a bit of warmth into us. We've had seven solid hours of clambering up and down, sliding and scrambling and falling over slippery, moss-grown rocks, and hours of struggling through breast-high grass over slimy ground in snow and rain. Total altitude variation: 3,200 feet. Tiredness is overcoming us, but now at least we no longer have to listen to the rain pelting down on the rocks. We are in our tent, there is a canvas roof over our heads, and we are dry at last.

February 26

The loneliness of the mountains and the jungle has something magnificent about it; the peace and quiet induce a mood of solemnity. Phil and I preferred to enjoy it without words. It was only after we had succeeded in climbing the Idenburg Top that we broke the tremendous silence with singing and yodelling. That was just the elation of our victory, but generally speaking the only noises we heard were the sound of the rain, the rushing of the waterfalls, and just now and again, though not often, the twittering of a bird.

Since early morning, however, all that has changed. At seven o'clock we heard the first shouts of "Wa-wa-wa!" from the advance party of our Danis. They met us at "Desertion Pass," the place where a few days before two of our porters had just cleared off without a word. At last we were able to share our loads once more, but Phil and I still had to carry our rucksacks.

Our Idenburg tour is now over. Our porters are in good spirits because we are now back in Camp I, and at last there are cheerful fires again to warm us up. Phil and I are satisfied too: we are dry and we are lying in a snug tent with mounds of wet clothing piled up in front of it. For the last time I can see Dugundugu Lake. A pair of wild ducks, their tails stuck up comically in the air, are searching for food beneath the surface. Now that I'm warm and dry the very thought makes me shiver: if there's one thing I shouldn't like to be it's a wild duck.

February 28

After a rest day Phil and I set off at about half-past seven this morning up the steep gully above Camp I to the ice line again. It gave us a bit of trouble, but by eleven o'clock we were on the 1936 peak which we now named Dozy Peak in honour of the previous Dutch explorers.

When we had built our usual stone cairn we went on over a steep snow crest and an hour later we had reached the centre mound of the three that form Colijn Peak, and there we built another stone cairn. The third and smallest, Wissel Peak, we decided not to bother about as Phil wasn't feeling too good and complained of stomach pains. We made our descent in the direction of the New Zealand Pass and reached our tent again by the early afternoon.

We have now climbed sixteen peaks, and with one exception they were all first-timers. That's a very satisfactory performance. However, weather permitting, I'd still like to take in a few of the western North Face peaks. I haven't got much time left for it, though, because from tomorrow on the porters from Ilaga will be waiting for us at our main camp.

Phil stayed in the tent today, but I started off at about seven o'clock and first made my way to the gorge that descends to the west of Camp I from the North Face. The clouds were riding very high. It wasn't long before I found my ascent blocked by enormous rocks. I managed to negotiate a couple of overhangs, and then for about three-quarters of an hour I tried to get the better of a great rock and a waterfall, but in the end I had to give it up. I dare say I could have managed to get upwards, but I had no rope with me, and I had to think of the return journey, which would have been impossible without a rope, so I clambered back to the great belt, and taking this way I easily reached the ice by a detour. From here, acting on a sudden decision, I made my way eastwards to find an approach to the 1936 peaks. The first was easy and ice-free, but then I had to make a track through deep snow to get to the second. These two pinnacles were not very high, but now very temptingly above me was the western "Dugundugu." I didn't hesitate for long, and started to climb. It took me exactly an hour and a half to reach it, and another quarter of an hour to get to the top of the eastern peak.

I was just considering in which direction I should go down when through the thick mist and the light snow flurries I thought I heard the characteristic howling of our Danis. Apparently the porters had arrived, so I decided to give up the remaining peaks and go straight back to our tent. But when I got there there was no one to be seen. I now remembered that I had experienced something of the sort on the way to the Idenburg Top. Phil and I both thought we heard the sound of voices where there were no voices. Later we learned from our Danis that there are wild dogs in the neighbourhood and that their barking and melancholy howling can often easily be mistaken for human sounds.

Phil was asleep in the tent. I woke him up and he said that he felt better.

Phil is completely able-bodied again, and early this morning we set off in different directions in order to reconnoitre as many peaks as possible. The weather and the visibility were both unusually good when we started.

The first thing I discovered was that I had made a mistake yesterday. Because of the thick mist and the snow flurries I didn't know when I had reached the snow and ice line. Today I realised that yesterday I had reached the ice too far to the west. This explained why it had taken me so long to get from the second peak to Dugundugu. I had to go round the whole gorge, which I couldn't recognise in the mist. So yesterday's result was properly: two Lani peaks, and two large and one small "Dugundugu." With this all the eastern peaks of the North Face have now been climbed, something I would hardly have thought possible.

Today therefore I was able to devote myself completely to the west; first of all the third Lani peak, which was difficult to climb. On the other hand, the fourth and fifth peaks were quite easy—they are sheer rock and lie about 150 feet from the ice of the great, solid snow cover of the North Face.

I continued to clamber westwards and in doing so I had a great surprise. I went over several rock peaks of the Lani group, and after the fourth I found myself once again facing a deep gorge. But here the glaciers obviously didn't extend right to the North Face. But where did it end? There must be a "gap" somewhere, because at the big Lani peak—at least that was my impression—it appears again as a small glacier, an independent island of ice separated from the main mass. What I wanted to find now was, so to speak, "the land connection" between them. In fact, after the last gorge the glacier broadened out southwards, and I thought I had found its end. But when I was standing on the big Lani peak I saw that I was surrounded on three sides by glaciers. To the south I couldn't see the end of the ice however, because I was unsighted by a somewhat lower peak. The "gap" must therefore be beyond it. But I wanted to be quite certain so I also climbed the smaller advanced spur to the south, and there I saw at last that the glacier has no "gap," no "island," no "land connection." The permanent snow of the North Face forms a solid covering of ice from New Zealand Pass right to the end against Dayak Pass. And wherever we saw ice over this great distance it belonged to the main mass of this enormous glacier. That much was now certain.

Delighted that I now had exact information I turned back. I had climbed nine peaks on my own and set up stone cairns on them all.

When Phil returned I was already in the tent sketching the newly-recognised form of the eternal snow cover of the North Face into my map. Phil had climbed the third of the three Dutch peaks, the Wissel Peak. With this there is nothing left for us to do in the horseshoe shaped Carstensz arena. Every peak, thirty-one in all, has now been climbed, and all but one were first-timers. For days on end we have explored ground on which no human foot had ever trodden before. We discovered our Fairy-Tale Valley and many previously unknown lakes. We have lived together with men who are three thousand years behind us in cultural and civilised development. And together and separately we have experienced the endless loneliness of the world of the mountains. It was always the tremendous silence that impressed me most when I stood on those peaks. It is the silent moments which leave the deepest and most lasting impression. These are the moments in which you learn to know yourself.

March 3

The porters arrived at last at nine o'clock this morning. We packed our things and went back to our base camp.

Phil went off on his own, and I have been here in this dry tent for some time, but he has not turned up yet. He wanted to make the detour by Larson Lake "to have a look round the corner" as he said; that is, to get a view of the steep face of the Carstensz Top from the east.

The greater part of the afternoon was gone and it was still raining when quite unexpectedly a Papuan policeman appeared and handed me some scraps of metal which obviously came from a plane. In short, disconnected sentences he told me that he had also found a human bone, and he thought a plane had crashed, probably a missionary plane. I had hardly managed to understand it all when Dugundugu, Phil's porter, appeared with a note from Phil in which he told me that he proposed to go on searching for the crashed plane. The next to appear was my own personal porter, Okar, with another message to say that Phil had found parts of the wreckage, and that therefore he would not get back to the base camp until later in the day.

I was quite bewildered because the last news I had had from Russ had been four days ago, and he had said nothing about a plane crash, though as he had written from Ilaga he would have known. The only conclusion was that a plane must have crashed within the last two, three or four days, probably searching for us.

At dusk Phil finally got back. He was carrying a wet parcel and when he opened it there were teeth, fragments of jawbone and two small wallets wrapped in a piece of parachute silk. At least the mystery was now solved. From the papers in the wallets we discovered that the crashed plane was an American machine that had met with disaster as long ago as 1945. A small piece of paper revealed the whole tragedy of the disaster: it was a receipt for toys the pilot had bought for his small son in the United States. It was a macabre end to our Carstensz tour. At least it was some consolation to know that it was not, as I had at first feared, a plane which had crashed searching for us. We will hand the papers to the Dutch authorities for them to get in touch with the relatives of the dead pilot.

March 4

The affair of the crashed American plane hardly let me sleep. Phil was also tossing and turning throughout the night. The result was that we started the day, Sunday, unrested and depressed. In the meantime we have descended to the Twin Lakes and pitched our tent. The weather and the way were both as usual: water above and water below. But now at least we're in a dry tent again, and the Danis have built their huts around us.

We are back again in human society, primitive though it still is. The most certain sign—late that afternoon we heard the kind of giggling we had almost forgotten. I looked inquiringly at Okar, and he answered with one word "*kuliga*"—girl. As I obviously looked

79

a bit doubtful he explained to me circumstantially that the real wife of a Dani has to stay behind in the settlement. Other countries, other customs. When I had a look at the porter girls they didn't seem the ugliest girls I had ever seen. Or was my taste changing?

Our main porters have suddenly become positive dandies. This has probably got something to do with the five stocky girls. They don't want to carry the ordinary loads any more. They fancy themselves, striding around with axes over their shoulders. They are also wearing the army rejects we clothed them in, and playing around importantly with the leather gloves we provided them with. And they talk to their fellows who weren't with us in the upper camp as though they were subordinates. They obviously want to make it quite clear that they are now superior persons. Perhaps they are also thinking of the ice from "Dugundugu" they have brought back with them in their tins. They will probably unpack it at the most impressive moment—and then find there's nothing left for all their trouble.

March 5

Two days' journey lie ahead of us and then we shall be in Ilaga again, the starting point of our first expedition and of the second expedition we plan. New porters arrived today, but unfortunately without any letters. All they brought with them was a note from Russ. He did not climb Kelabo, but on the wireless he heard the first report of our Carstensz climbs.

The world around is getting livelier. Today we saw a great many beautifully coloured birds, and a small but resplendently white rhododendron flower with red points. This makes fourteen different kinds we have now found.

March 6

At half-past eight we started on the descent into the narrow river valley. On the map the river is marked as the Zenggilorong, but our Danis don't know it by this name; they call it the Paerap.

We have reached Ilaga. We started off at eight o'clock and at about midday we came to the first huts and were warmly greeted by the natives. Early in the morning we saw Kelabo rising over the jungle mists, and on the edge of the forest I discovered another species of rhododendron previously unknown to me. This time it wasn't so much its marvellous appearance that fascinated me as its overwhelming scent. It is the first scented flower I have come across here. It smells something like jasmine—at least I think so—but even more agreeable. I have pressed two of its flowers between the pages of my diary, and stuck another one in my hat, so that for the rest of the way its wonderful scent was in my nostrils.

Our reception in Ilaga was very friendly. The women presented us with the biggest sweet potatoes they could find but I don't think this was on account of our successful conquest of the Carstensz peaks. I have rather the impression that it was because they were happy to see their men safely back again, and this I can understand: they weren't altogether happy about the magic of the "Dugundugu." I told our men that now that they had been there they no longer need to wear amulets to protect themselves and their families. But then they unpacked their precious ice, and, of course, found nothing left—despite the clay and newspaper they had wrapped it in, and the tins in which they had packed it away so carefully. The result was that the magic of the "Dugundugu" was as powerful again as it had been on the first day. For us the whole thing was a simple natural process: with the higher temperatures the ice melted and the water disappeared in the clay. But for the aboriginals of New Guinea, for our Stone Age men, it was just a miracle. And what you can't explain is magic.

Our Carstensz expedition is described as follows in a report given by one or two of the West Danis to a monthly bulletin: "As far as the Tuans are concerned I'll tell you of Tuan Huizenga and Tuan Harrer, who is their older brother and leader. They went in order to climb the snow peak of the Carstensz. They went with the Danis from the west; that is, with the men from the Wakketokka tribe, the Mytip Watnipho tribe, and the Woda Tapvny tribe. All of them, except the last named, went to the top of the Carstensz. After they had gone to the Carstensz and had marvelled at the Tuans, one of the Tuans flung down one thing after another onto the plain from the Wooloo ship, the aeroplane. After he had thrown these things down, the Danis from the west went the whole way up to the rock peak of the Carstensz, and whilst they were climbing up, the Tuans sent many of the men who had gone with them back again. When they had climbed to the top of the rock peak they all slept there. They climbed the snow peak. Whilst they were climbing to the snow peak a moon came and went, which means it lasted a month. Then, after a moon had come and gone, Tuan Huizenga and another Tuan and some of the Danis from the west went back. They all came back and gave axes and pearls and cowrie shells to everybody. Now as to the Tuans who are on the mountain, they climbed from the rock peak of the Carstensz to the Kelabo mountain, and all the other rock peaks round about, which means here in Ilaga. After they had climbed it they climbed all the others except the last."

PART TWO

The Source of the
Stone Axes

IT was just about eight weeks ago that I first arrived here in Ilaga. That was on January 13, and it was on that day, for the first time too, that I held in my hand one of those marvellous stone axes every native here possesses.

I had already heard about them in Wamena from Europeans, and the question that always puzzled me was: where do the mountain Papuans get the stones with which to make them. And the only answer I got was: "We don't know."

Now that I was amongst the Danis and the Uhundinis, the men who make the axes, I asked the same question. But—at first at least—I couldn't obtain a satisfactory answer either. The origin of the stone was obviously a carefully-guarded secret. The source was taboo for all strangers. And I was a stranger. I was answered pleasantly enough, but in words that told me nothing. Even cowrie shells couldn't buy a real answer: the answers certainly got more friendly, but not more informative. In the end my personal servant Okar informed me as though he were betraying a secret: "Stones come from quarry." I could have worked that much out for myself, of course, but it was all I could get out of him. After all, I was a stranger.

But this changed. Friendships can readily form in the space of eight weeks. Thanks to us the Danis saw the ice of the Dugundugu. They touched it. They even broke it off and ate it. In consequence they became more friendly, not only in their relationship to us—they were friendly from the first—but also in their attitude to what was a tribal secret and what wasn't. And in reply to my repeated questions they now told me at least the name of the quarry from which the stone came—"Ya-Li-Me" or source of the stone axes. *Ya* means stone axe, *li* means place and *me* means source. The American missionaries Larson and Ellenberger were indispensable interpreters.

All the same, I can't see anything very clearly yet. There seems to be some cult connected with the production of these stone axes. What I want now is to visit the source itself, and I think that with Phil and a few porters I shall be able to manage it. I have reckoned three weeks for the job, including a week in reserve. I'm certainly not going to be in too much of a hurry. I've already learnt enough to know that you need time for everything here.

March 9

Today the Uhundinis, who live on the south side of the valley, have arranged a feast. Phil and I were there as guests. The food consisted of the red fruit of the pandanus palm. Ellenberger brought some down to the plains from his last journey. The fruit contains a good deal of fatty oil, and the Papuans like it very much because to them it tastes very much like pork fat, of which they are very fond. To them it is a delicacy. Phil and I still have a disagreeable taste of the stuff in our mouths, but we had to go through with the whole thing from the preparation, on to the distribution, and then to the final and most disagreeable part of it all, the eating. Generally speaking it is my principle to eat mainly what the natives eat, but for the moment my taste was too pampered.

The Uhundinis first dug the cooking-hole, which they lined with large leaves. The hole was then half-filled with glowing hot stones, and between the stones they bedded the thick red peels of the fruit together with various kinds of vegetables. After this the edges of the large leaves, which jutted out above, were turned down over the small oven and so carefully weighted with other stones that they could not unfold. The following hour was taken up with talk, during which I repeatedly brought the conversation round to the question of "the source of the stone axes," though without any success. Finally the food was ready. The kiln-oven was opened up, and the fruit rinds and the vegetables were cooked, braised in their own juice. The red fruit rinds found their way into the hands of the men, and the women then went for the vegetables. Phil and I were about to bite into our rinds when we realised that the preparation was not yet completed. The next thing was to gouge the pointed red pips, which contained the fatty oil, out of the rinds, knead them and put them in a big oval

86

basin made of tree-bark where they were then mixed with water into a thick sauce. Whilst some of the men were occupied with this process others were chewing at their fruit rinds, after which they slapped them on their bellies. Then at a signal they all began to gobble the sauce. Leaves served as spoons, and soon all around there was nothing but the sound of smacking lips. Slowly all the faces became red from the sauce, though I dare say my own was more green than red because I found the taste revolting. But there was nothing for it, from time to time I had to swallow a little of the stuff, which I did with great difficulty. A guest is granted every right but one, and that is to turn up his nose at what is offered him. The Papuans wouldn't have liked that at all. When they had finished they wiped their fatty hands on their swollen bellies until the skin shone like glass.

In order not to cause the Danis to become distrustful I didn't want to exploit the festive spirit for further inquiries about "the source," but I am quite certain that in the end I shall find out what I want to and that before long I shall witness them shaping and sharpening their stone axes.

March 18

Nine days have passed since I last made up my diary. Nine days in which I picked up a few remarks about the site of "the source," noted them down, and made use of them. From what I have learnt the site must be somewhere in the neighbourhood of Kangime. Phil and I propose to fly there and then go on by foot. As far as I could discover, Kangime would be the shortest way to the quarry. But I still don't know exactly where it lies, which means that we shall just have to search for it. It is also unclear whether there is only one quarry there, or whether there is another one north of Ilaga. The Danis provide contradictory information with extraordinary persistence.

Bert Huizenga arrived five days ago and brought letters. News from Frankfurt told me that the fabrication of our deserter Danis had in the meantime gone round the world and that our friends were worrying about us, fearing that we really had been swallowed up by an avalanche. I hope that by this time the false report has been corrected.

Yesterday was our final pay-day. Axes and matchets were distributed, and those who had been with us to the mountain, or had done the journey between Ilaga and our base camp at least twice, were given a watch each in addition. Watches are in great demand among the natives. They represent something incomprehensible and therefore magic, so, of course, anyone who owns one is a very proud possessor. Everyone who had taken part in the expedition was also given a coloured necklace, a handful of beads and a Tirolean whetstone for his axe. The natives had cast eager eyes on our small knives with the fixed handles, but we only had a few with us and with the best will in the world we could not afford to part with them.

Today Phil returned on account of lack of time from another unsuccessful attempt to climb Kelabo, so it is still unconquered.

March 20

Bert brought the news that it will be possible to carry everything away by plane tomorrow or the day after. Over a ton of baggage is here waiting to be flown out. I shall need about six hundredweight or so of it for my expedition to the quarry of the stone axes, so this is to be flown to Kangime. The rest of it is to go to Wamena.

Mulia   *March 21*

Wherever I go and no matter to whom I happen to be talking there is only one subject that really interests me—Ya-Li-Me, as the Danis call it, the source of their stone axes. Today I had various wireless talks with Kangime from the station run by the American missionary Mr Larson here, but no one—no European that is—in Kangime knows anything at all about the whereabouts of the quarry, though some of the people I questioned have lived there for a year and even longer. Perhaps it's just an *idée fixe* of the Danis? A sort of fairy tale in keeping with their magic? However, I didn't give up and I had a discussion with Ilu. Finally I was told there that they had, in fact, heard something about a mysterious quarry near Mulia. I immediately got in touch with Mulia, and there I was told: yes, there was a

88

quarry in the north, and the two missionaries had once been within a few days' march of it.

At last all my doubt and anxiety about the existence of the quarry —never mind its site—was dissipated. The quarry did exist. It was not just a fable. It was a reality.

Johanson, the pilot, arrived at midday to fly Phil and me to Mulia. Bert Huizenga had got permission from the Mission for us to land and we touched down in brilliant sunshine, welcomed by the whole European colony.

The colony was larger than one would normally expect because there is a goitre research station in Mulia run by the Dutch Government.

Once again, the rest of the day was taken up with what now chiefly interested me: Ya-Li-Me, the source of the stone axes. The American missionaries Dillinger and Scovill had already been half-way there and they were able to give me valuable information. I was shown some of the wonderful green and blue stones from which the natives make their blades.

In the meantime I have discovered that it is between five and six days' journey from here to the mysterious quarry; and from what I could understand there is a river there, with a great rock face towering above it. The natives are said to build scaffolding against this rock and then split off the stone with big fires. No white man has ever seen this, of course, and here too the natives remain obstinately silent, with the result that I have only a very hazy picture of the whole thing. The uncertainty naturally makes me all the more eager to clear up the mystery. It seems quite certain that the stone is not just taken from the river bed, as was observed to be the case in Ormu on the north coast at the beginning of the century. Because of the expression "source of the stone axes" I had at first thought—feared, in fact—that this would turn out to be the case here too. It would have been too ordinary and everyday a procedure. But now I know that a romantic secret is really behind it all, probably with some cult significance, but in any case a method of splitting and shaping stone which is unknown to us today because it is a process belonging to the Stone Age.

Habits and customs from the Bronze Age are also said to exist in the neighbourhood of Ya-Li-Me; and some Danis say that farther north there are natives who possess axes made of a soft reddish-yellow metal. We shall have to make some further inquiries about this and keep our eyes and ears open for anything we can pick up. I simply can't understand how it comes about that amongst all these missionaries, district officers and geologists no one has ever taken advantage of this unique opportunity to study the last vestiges of neolithic, probably even paleolithic, civilisation still existing on earth. Just imagine the situation: there is no need for excavations and conclusions drawn from fragmentary finds—the Stone Age actually still exists in our time! Since I have been here in New Guinea it has often seemed to me that the moon and the planets have come closer to us than we are to our own pre-history. But that, too, is a bit of luck for me. I hardly dare to believe that within a few days from now Phil and I will be the first modern men to witness a truly primeval past still in existence. At the same time we shall probably be more or less the last, too, because it certainly won't be long now before the natives learn to use steel crowbars—and perhaps even explosive charges—to split their rock. They'll probably soon be using machinery and selling their products to eager tourists. This sort of thing is already going on around the airfields in the Australian part of New Guinea.

March 22

The day passed in collecting information about the quarry, and in recruiting porters. We have now obtained a good deal of information about the route we must take, but so far we have got only four porters. And we want to make a start for Ya-Li-Me tomorrow.

March 23

The first day's march is now behind us, and I really ought to be well satisfied with matters so far. But I am in a very strange and almost eerie situation: whilst I am engaged in writing up this diary one might almost say that a dead native is watching me.

Shortly before we started off early in the morning there were suddenly twelve porters available instead of four, so no one had to carry any extra weight and we could start on the easy rise up over the pass. After about an hour we had reached the first village in Yomo Valley. As in all the native villages, there were cooking holes in front of the huts for braising meat and vegetables. Next to them were heaps of the stones which are heated in the fire to serve as cooking ranges and chafing dishes, so to speak. No geologist should miss those stones; they represent treasure trove for his purposes.

Not far from Mulia the limestone ceased, and now there is only slate with quartz.

The way became more difficult and we made only slow progress, climbing over fences and stone walls, crossing over fields and passing more villages, and all the time descending lower and lower into Yomo Valley. Our side of the valley was particularly steep and the paths were often hardly visible. Our approach to the bed of the valley was therefore slow work, and, in addition, we often had to stop to rest. Deep silence was all around us, broken now and again by the alarmed fluttering rise of a bird of paradise. The flight of these birds is short, clumsy and laborious, and when they settle down again the noise is dull and heavy, almost menacing. Only very rarely did we get a glimpse of one of them through the thick foliage.

It was late afternoon when we came to our first camping site. Quite suddenly the forest ceased and we came into an extensive clearing. It must have been uninhabited for a long time because tangled wild sugar-canes were growing to a height of ten feet everywhere. The porters used their matchets to cut a space free for our tent.

In the centre of the clearing stood a sixteen-foot-high tower of wooden poles, and on top of it was a cylindrical hutlike shape made of tree-bark. I noticed that our porters stood a little in awe of this erection and I soon discovered the reason: there was a dead man crouched in the bark hut. The Danis confirmed my observation by putting their heads to one side, closing their eyes and sticking out their tongues.

They explained that in all probability the dead man was the last owner of the clearing, and that he had left no successors. Friendly neighbours from a near-by village had therefore built him this traditional last resting place, and there he sits cross-legged and can still watch over his fields without the wild dogs being able to get at him.

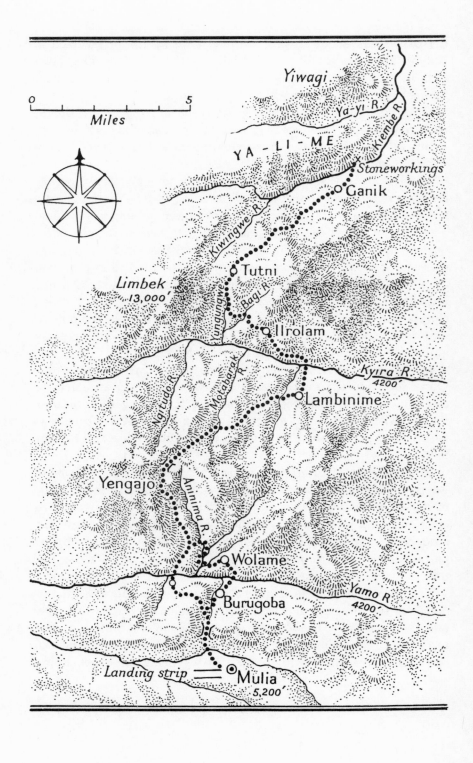

Yiwagi

Ya-yi R.

Kiembe R.

YA - LI - ME

Stoneworkings

○ Ganik

Kiwingwe R.

○ Tutni

Limbek
13,000′

Ungungwe R.

Bagi R.

○ Ilrolam

Kyira R.
4200′

○ Lambinime

Ngitudo R.

Motabarak R.

Yengajo

Aninima R.

○ Wolame

Yamo R.
4200′

○ Burugoba

Landing strip ━━━ ◉ Mulia
5,200′

0   5
Miles

At first I was a bit worried, thinking that perhaps it might be regarded as a bad omen, but I've got used to his presence now, and my ideas are going off in a different direction. Supposing he could still see us. . . . He would be absolutely amazed. His unripe bananas were being slashed from his trees. A tree stem was hacked open and the soft pith removed and chewed like sugar-cane. And this was done with a gleaming matchet, a thing he had never seen in his life. And the shining steel axes would have flabbergasted him as they bit into the wood of his trees after his death. He had never known anything but stone axes, and to cut through laterally to the centre of a tree with a stone axe would be the work of hours, and hard work at that. And now he had sat there and watched a Dani cut down a tree with only a few blows of this new magic axe. He was witnessing a tool that could clear his land in a few weeks. In his lifetime the same work would have required years of hard labour.

I noticed something else of interest in this macabre camping site. It was very hot and our Danis were very thirsty when we arrived, so I distributed a little salt. Salt is such a rarity for them, and therefore such a treasure that they went down on their knees in the dirt to lick up every grain that had fallen.

They accepted the "Tuan salt," as they call it, with loud shouts of "Wa-wa-wa!" and words of thanks, and proceeded to turn it into "Dani salt." For this purpose they first begged for a few roots of ginger, which I had bought from a village on the way in exchange for coloured beads. Armed with salt, ginger roots and banana leaves they went into the sketchily repaired hut of the dead man on the tower, and there they dug out a small trench. Others were in the meantime holding the banana leaves to the fire until they were quite soft. And now the actual process began. The small trench was laid out with the banana leaves and our four oldest porters sat round it. They poured water on the banana leaves and taking the ginger roots, still covered with dirt, into their mouths they chewed them into a paste. When this was done they spat the result onto the banana leaves in the little trench, sprinkled it with "Tuan salt," chewed more ginger roots, spat them into the hole, added more salt, and so on, and finally they chewed up the stems and spat them into the mixture too. The whole was then carefully stirred and "Dani salt" was ready.

Now the others were allowed to get at the mixture with sticks and leaves as spoons, and within a few minutes the whole ginger and salt concoction was gone.

We started off at eight o'clock and, now, at half-past nine, we are taking our first short rest. In the meantime I have discovered that there are not twelve but thirteen porters with us. The confusion comes from the fact that their broad-nosed faces all look so much alike that it's simply impossible to tell them apart. Thirteen porters are better than twelve. In any case, I like the number: it was the thirteenth of last month when we climbed the Carstensz Pyramid. Who isn't glad to be reminded of a success? After a few minutes rest we went on again.

Another four hours march is now behind us. Although it isn't raining we are all wet through, but from within. The oppressive humid heat is taking it out of all of us. Phil therefore proposed that we should have another short rest and a bathe as soon as we came to a fairly clear stream. This we did, and once again the Danis saw their two Tuans with naked torsos, and once again they were so astonished that they could hardly close their mouths: people with white bodies always seem to belong to the sphere of magic and miracles for them.

The bathe did us all good. We are feeling fresher and there is laughter heard again. The Danis are chattering away excitedly and happily. I'm still lying on my belly, resting, and watching them with interest. They are always good tempered, almost never tired, and here, incidentally, they don't seem so inquisitive as they were in Ilaga Valley. They smoke a great deal more though, and they light their tobacco spindles with a proper lighter, though one which belongs in the Stone Age: a short bamboo stem in the hollow of which there is a stone and tinder. When the stone is smartly driven along the bamboo stem several times in succession the tinder begins to glow. This method of producing fire is rainproof, and so when our civilised matches won't light, as they never will after hours of marching in the rain, we fall back on this prehistoric lighter, which the Danis always carry with them.

94

Here in Yomo Valley there is tobacco growing in front of almost every native hut. Incidentally, the Danis don't always wait for it to ripen and be cut and dried; they just tear off a green leaf, twiddle it about a bit by the fire till it's dry and then smoke it like that.

Hollandia   *March 28*

I'm afraid that as so often, the unexpected has happened. I thought to be at the "Source of the Stone Axes" long ago, but instead of that, here I am bandaged up like a mummy and lying in a modern hospital bed made of steel tubing. Everything around me is white and antiseptic, and the mountain Papuans, the streams and the jungle are all far away now. This is the hospital of Hollandia, and I am one of its patients. Walking is out of the question, and it's as much as I can do to write. When I think of that old long-dead Dani in his funerary tower above the clearing where we halted on our way to the "Source of the Stone Axes" I am beginning to wonder whether he wasn't a bad omen after all.

All the same, I've been luckier than anyone normally has a right to expect at the hands of fate. And the aches and pains I can feel all over my body make no difference to that though my spine and my left knee are particularly painful. I haven't been properly examined yet so I don't really know what's only bruised and what's actually broken. But the mere fact that I can think about it, and even—though with difficulty—write about it, makes it quite clear that I have escaped. I'm still alive!

Let me now try to reconstruct everything that happened in the four days since March 24, the day we took our refreshing bathe in that stream.

First of all we gradually made our way upwards through fabulously beautiful jungle scenery. It was a mossy area, and delicately woven lichen, a symbiosis of fungus and algae, hung like fine veils over everything. But otherwise this mossy landscape didn't offer much that was worth closer examination or photographing, and there were no picturesque streams or romantic waterfalls.

But at last, early in the afternoon, we once more heard the familiar sound of a waterfall ahead. I quickened my pace because I wanted to

95

get there before the others, and then I came to it. Masses of water plunged into the depths in powerful cataracts, hurtling on to stone terraces and sending clouds of spray up to the tops of the trees, continuing its way down, sweeping thunderously through narrow gulleys in the rock, and shooting out in a great sheaf of water beyond —a tremendous sight. And dangerous as well, but I noted this only incidentally. At the moment I was interested only in filming it.

First of all I directed my camera towards the porters making their way up by the side of the fall. Then I clambered past them, still keeping perforce very close to the tumultuous mass of water, to film the next group of porters making their way up.

I saw Phil standing at a spot that looked ideal for my purpose so I clambered down quickly to join him, but when I got there he had disappeared. He had gone into the jungle after a bird of paradise he wanted to shoot. It was then I discovered another spot which I thought would offer me an even better view. It was a pile of rubble right on the edge of the fall. Without hesitation I jumped towards it. This was the last deliberate decision I was in a position to make, because it was at this point that the disaster occurred. The moment I landed on the heap of rubble it shot away from under me and I found myself in the water! Later on Phil told me that the heap had collected on a piece of slate without any firm foundation. To have thrown a stone at it would probably have been enough to set it in motion. And I had jumped on it with all my weight!

At first I was in possession of all my senses, and I tried desperately to find something to cling to whilst at the same time bracing myself on the bottom with my feet so that the water should not sweep me away. Today I know that any such attempt was ridiculous: the water rushed with incredible force against my body, and the rocks under my feet had been worn smooth and were very slimy. I hadn't a chance—at least, not here. The water picked me up and swept me on. For a moment, head first, I looked down into the depths, and then I closed my eyes. In such situations there is nothing to be done at all. Nature takes no notice of any attempts to resist.

When and where I let go of my camera I don't know. From that moment when I saw the abyss before my eyes I can't separate the times at all. Water, gasping for air, a dull blow, more water, a

96

falling body, gasping for breath . . . I can't even remember the order any more. Later on the porters told me that I brushed against a jutting rock over which the water was shooting into the air before falling in the next cataract. If I had struck that rock full on I should have been hurled into the air over the fall on to the smooth, almost vertical dividing slab that ended some 160 feet or so farther down. There really isn't much doubt about what would have happened to me then.

Seconds, hours, eternities? I don't know any more. All I can remember is the feeling of absolute helplessness that suddenly came over me. I tried to hold my arms protectingly before my head and to roll myself up like an embryo. I think you do that sort of thing instinctively in such circumstances.

And now, although I was only half conscious by this time, it seemed like a miracle when my helter-skelter rush into the depths suddenly ceased. I couldn't see anything because blood was pouring down from a head wound into my eyes. Gropingly I sought to find my whereabouts, and I had enough sense to realise that I mustn't try to work my way out of the water at the edge of this natural pool where it led over to the next fall, since the cascade plunged down three times as far as before and ended on a slab of rock against which a human body would just have been smashed to a pulp.

I couldn't breathe properly, and I heard myself groaning. From a distance I thought I could distinguish the porters shouting "Tuan! Tuan!" That brought me my first ray of hope. At least they realised what had happened to me. And Phil—good old Phil—would soon be there.

In between clawing at the rocks I desperately kept trying to wipe the blood out of my eyes so that I could at least see what was happening to me. I could see light as though through a veil, but I couldn't distinguish any details. Then I must have managed to wipe the blood out of my eyes sufficiently to see the pool I was in. I must already have lost a great deal of blood because the whole pool had an ugly reddish tinge.

I clung desperately to my rock and waited. Above, below and all around me water gushed and roared. And then—I don't know how much time passed in between—I heard Phil's voice. He had our

97

medicine chest with him, and he bedded me down on the rock as well as he could and gave me first aid like an experienced doctor. Not that there was very much he could do for me. He disinfected my head wound, cut away hanging strips of skin, and bandaged me. Only then did he examine my general condition, which was very poor. I didn't know which way to lie, my whole body was painful. And now that the worst danger was past the effect of shock began to make itself felt. I was trembling all over as though with ague. My teeth were chattering not because I was cold, but because the delayed excitement was shaking me to the core. I groaned. Now and again I felt dark waves of vertigo rise up in me, but I exerted all my will power to remain conscious. I had the feeling that I simply could not afford to lose consciousness now, and that at all costs I must keep my shaken psyche alive. Phil had sat me up to make it easier for him to examine me, but now I asked him to help me to some place where I could lie down and husband my strength. With his help I crawled along the edge of the pool, which was still reddish with my lost blood, clambered over a tree and got to the bank on all fours, and then went a little way down the path up which we had come. The whole time the porters had not come near the water at all. As I laboriously dragged myself along I realised at every movement that it was not only my head I had injured. My body was painful all over. It also struck me that I appeared still to be losing blood. I also noticed that the difficulty I had in breathing was nothing to do with the shock I had had but came from my ribs, well back in the neighbourhood of the spine. And every time I bent my left knee it was as though a steel spike were stabbing into it. I could hardly use my right arm at all—head, spine, ribs, left knee, right arm. . . . But apart from that, as they say, I was all right in myself. A manner of speaking, but all the same, by comparison with what could have happened to me there was something to be said for it. After all, I had plunged only about one-third the way down the waterfall. But what would have happened beyond that pool if I had been swept any farther didn't bear thinking about. There would have been no question of any sort of life, however painful.

I continued to crawl downwards, and Phil helped me as best he could. The porters now eagerly removed everything from my path that was at all removable, but every foot of the way was sheer torture. Finally Phil found a place by a little stream which was big enough for him to set up the tent. I crouched there in misery and watched him at work. When the tent was up he helped me take off my dripping clothes, and then he bedded me down on our air mattress. I still had the feeling that I was living behind a misty veil. This was partly due to the shock of my fall and partly to the powerful analgesic tablets Phil had given me against the almost intolerable pain in my whole body. However, I had got to the tent site almost under my own steam. One of the porters had offered to carry me, but what could a little man like that do with nearly thirteen stone live weight on his shoulders, plus the weight of my sodden clothes? He probably didn't realise how heavy I am. And if he had fallen over one of the numerous treacherous roots in the path and dropped me the renewed fall would certainly have meant my losing consciousness at the very least. I therefore preferred to drag myself along as well as I could despite the pain. And when I came to a tree-trunk I couldn't climb over I just dragged myself through underneath it.

I now lay in the tent in a sort of semi-conscious trance. As I could hardly move my limbs Phil was able to do no more than pull my sleeping-bag over my feet. And now I felt that another wave of unconsciousness was welling up in me. I had never experienced unconsciousness in my life, except asleep. I had never before been even half unconscious. But now the tablets, the shock and the great loss of blood together threatened me with unconsciousness for the first time. Grimly I fought against that unpleasant preliminary feeling of vertigo and pain. Once again I succeeded, and the wave died away. I lay there staring at the roof of the tent, and my thoughts began to whir. First there was the memory of that old Dani in his funeral tower. And then it was replaced by the thought of Ya-Li-Me. Oh Lord, I remembered, that was where I wanted to go; but I will too. I just must. Then the idea occurred to me that I might die, that I might lose consciousness and never recover it—just slide over like that, without knowing anything more about it, without waking up again. Then I thought of the missionaries in Mulia. Only a few days ago they had prayed for me. Had their prayers helped? Had their prayers perhaps saved me from a worse fate? After all, I was alive, and where there's life there's hope. And then rose the question: when did you last pray? A prayer of thankfulness perhaps? Or a prayer in extreme danger? My memories were unclear and faded before I could recognise them clearly.

Once again I felt a wave of unconsciousness creeping over, worse than before, apparently irresistible. Was this going to be the end? Blood was oozing through the bandages. So I was still losing blood and growing weaker. A little weaker still. And then unconsciousness. My whole will revolted against it, and I managed to raise myself up a little. It was as though I had drunk too much and was trying to sit up—everything swayed, and a feeling of sickness welled up. But I wasn't drunk, and this time there was the pain as well. With a groan I sank back. But in the last resort I think it was the pain that kept unconsciousness away. And as painful as it was I was glad. Just keep conscious!

As soon as he had got me out and realised that it would not be possible to transport me before I had had a thorough medical examination Phil sent off two porters with a message to the mission in Mulia. We now hoped that help would arrive within three days at the latest, perhaps even the day after tomorrow.

In the evening Phil gave me more tablets, but they brought me no relief—even the most powerful drugs can't help much against such pain.

March 29

The x-ray examination this morning revealed the fact that three of my ribs are broken, and towards the back too, a hand's-breadth from my spine. The front ribs are still whole, and heart, lungs and kidneys are all right. I have had injections and I can write more easily now. There are two days to make up, so let's go back to the waterfall, to the day after that unlucky Saturday of the accident. I had had practically no sleep at all properly speaking, but I dozed through the Sunday fighting alternately against the pain and the waves of threatened unconsciousness. The time went by incredibly slowly. I must wait here at least twice twenty-four hours I kept thinking— perhaps three days. But Sunday finally passed, and the night to

Monday. Phil renewed my bandages and gave me more tablets, which didn't seem to do much good. I tried to sleep, but I was constantly on my guard against unconsciousness and in consequence I didn't sleep a wink even in the second night.

Philip Temple proved to be a wonderful nurse, calm and reliable, and careful without being squeamish. He talked to me encouragingly, and kept reminding me that by tomorrow at the latest we could expect help from Mulia. The longest part of the waiting was certainly already over. . . . And all the soothing sort of things you say to a man in my condition. I'm not saying this in any depreciating way—if you aren't able to give a badly injured man morphia then you have to do your best to keep his courage up by talking nonsense if necessary. It did help a bit, and even a bit of help was something in my state.

In the afternoon just as Phil had renewed my bandages —"That's better. It's looking quite promising. Better than I expected."—there was a disturbance outside the tent. A moment or two later the two messengers Phil had sent to Mulia appeared in the entrance. When they saw that I was still alive—they had probably doubted it—their broad-nosed faces broadened even further into cheerful grins. They were both breathing heavily and covered in sweat. At first they could hardly speak, but then they gasped out the almost unbelievable news: the two Tuans weren't far behind them; they would be here a full day before we expected them!

And it was true: very little later the younger of the two missionaries, Scovill, turned up, also out of breath, and informed us that Dr van Rhijn of the Goitre Research Station, would be here any minute. Our runners had arrived in Mulia the previous day in the middle of the Sunday service, and Scovill and Dr van Rhijn had started off at once. It is quite amazing that they managed to cover the distance in such a short time. After all, neither of them is trained for such ordeals, and it was so hot down there in Yomo Valley that even the porters, who rarely drink anything, immediately rushed to the stream.

Scovill and Dr van Rhijn had brought a stretcher and a big medicine chest with them. They were still a bit doubtful as to what was the best thing to do for me, but after a thorough examination Dr van Rhijn decided that I should be moved at once. Heart and lungs seemed to be in order, and he could fix up the broken ribs with sticking plaster for the time being. So they got me on to the stretcher and off we went.

The journey, as I experience it again in retrospect, was a nightmare. When the way went upwards I slipped back on the stretcher until my head touched the knees of the rear bearer, and when the way went downwards I slid forward so that my feet rested in the small of the foremost bearer's back. And when the bearers were on level ground the way was hampered by the inevitable fallen tree-trunks. The little natives had to raise me up over them, but as my spine with the broken ribs was the lowest part of me they invariably scraped it against the trunk as they lifted the stretcher over. And if it wasn't a tree-trunk then it was a rock that had to be negotiated. I lay there helplessly and endured it all. Now and again I groaned, and the only other thing I could do was swear under my breath. Now and again I slid sideways into the cords on which the stretcher was suspended, and then I wasn't lying on the stretcher at all but lolling helplessly against the cords. Or I tried to hold myself in place by the cords on one side, only to find myself sliding over to the other side.

My bearers didn't seem to bother in the least about these mishaps, and I couldn't understand their callousness, but I was soon to learn the reason.

I don't know how long we had been going in this way before Scovill found a piece of ground smooth enough to allow the bearers to put the stretcher down for a short rest. By this time I was quite exhausted from my efforts to cling on to the cords. It seemed to me impossible that I could survive even another hour of this—not to mention two whole days.

But the solution was at hand, and it also told me why the natives were apparently so indifferent to what happened to me. Before we started off at all they demanded that the method of transport should be left to them, and that they should be allowed to do what they thought right. They didn't want to use the stretcher Dr van Rhijn and Scovill had brought with them; they wanted to make one of their own, but that had been forbidden. However, now they kicked up such a fuss that Scovill as interpreter finally agreed that they should be allowed to carry me the way they thought best. I was quite in agreement when I was informed; it seemed to me that nothing they did could possibly be any worse.

Satisfied at last they went to work. They laid out six rope-lengths across the ground, on top they put the deflated mattress and my sleeping-bag, and then me. One porter then got into position at the head and the other at the foot, and on their shoulders the others placed a thick pole they had quickly cut out of the jungle. Thus this pole ran in the same direction as my body and right above me. Six Danis now took up their positions on either side and carefully lifted up the rope ends raising me slowly and gently until my nose at one end and my feet at the other touched the pole. Then they tied the rope ends round the pole so that I was wrapped up beneath the pole like a mummy. At the head-end they padded the pole with a towel so that if my head should knock against it the blow would be softened.

More tablets helped me get through the following hours, and perhaps I was too exhausted to feel the pain so clearly. And in any case this native method of transporting an injured man seemed to work. The pole, the rope ends and my body formed one piece, and so I no longer slid around painfully at every jolt. The fact is that our own form of stretcher is not made either for jungle conditions or steep paths.

Nothing was now too much trouble for our porters. The bush telegraph had spread the news of my accident far and wide, and at least a hundred natives had arrived—probably from sheer curiosity, but at least they did their best to help. There was always a group of them ahead clearing the path and removing every obstacle that possibly could be removed, and building crossings with trunks at a tremendous speed. There were always about twenty of them with me. In their enthusiasm they were trotting, there was no question of walking. Now that they had been allowed to do things in their own way they were obviously anxious to show the Tuans a thing or two. Every few minutes the bearers changed and new men took over with renewed energy. Whether we were going up hill or down dale, the chain of porters was there; everyone was ready to lend a helping hand, everyone did his best to make my situation as easy as possible.

But even the transport method of the natives didn't improve matters all that much. The ropes began to work loose, the one more than the other, and my whole weight pressed into six ropes, and before long my poor ribs were banging against tree-trunks, rocks and tree-stumps as before. Desperately I held on to the pole with both hands. My arms were bound inside the ropes. I was so wrapped up that I could hardly see anything at all—only the pole just above my nose and an occasional glimpse of the sky between the tree-tops. There I lay, thoroughly packed and tied up, and waited anxiously for the next jolt. When it invariably came I groaned and cursed under my breath. When a relatively long time passed without a jolt I encouraged the bearers: "*Op, op!*" for those who spoke the Mulia dialect, "*Pano!*" for those who understood only the Bokondini dialect. Both words mean more or less "Good, good!"

The greatest advantage of the native method of transport was that when we were going steeply either up or down I no longer slid backwards or forwards so badly, but sometimes the way was so steep that I was almost hanging head down, and then instead of the sky I could see the porters bringing up the rear. Phil and Dr van Rhijn were with them. Scovill was usually ahead.

After a while the ropes had loosened so much that I was swaying from side to side like a hammock. Because of the constant up and down gradients in this difficult terrain it had to happen sooner or later. I don't recall it with any pleasure.

Once again we came to the clearing with the funeral tower in the middle where the dead Dani peasant kept his endless watch, but I was so exhausted that I took very little notice of it. However, I did remember that on the way before we reached the clearing we had had to go up a very steep slope. Now we went down it. My feet dropped and the ropes on which I was suspended scraped down the pole, as we descended almost vertically towards the river.

It had been raining steadily since Monday and the river was very swollen. At the sight the Danis seemed doubtful about the advisability of attempting a crossing, so Phil organised a living chain of the toughest men he could find, and with linked arms they stood across the river in a chain to break the force of the current whilst my bearers got me across below the chain.

That passage across the river was the worst patch for me, and for the first time since my tumble into the waterfall I was scared, because now I was not only in danger but absolutely helpless. My arms and legs were both firmly tied, there were ropes round my whole body and I was attached to a pole. It was a very disagreeable feeling indeed. Supposing the strength of the current—and it was strong!—flung my bearers into a panic. What would be the first thing they would do? Why, let go of me, of course.

But they didn't fall into a panic; they stuck it out, those brave chaps—although they could see how violently the current was surging against my body and although more than one of them lost his footing. Their faces were hard and set, and they even marched quite a good way down stream in the centre of the now much broader river bed. At least the water made a refreshing change for my poor back: no tree-trunks and no rocks to grate against my broken ribs.

No sooner had we crossed the river than it began to grow dark, and now my bearers accelerated their pace to such a tempo that the Tuans Scovill, van Rhijn and Phil could hardly keep up with them even without loads. The Danis obviously wanted to get to the nearest village before it got quite dark. As they negotiated a bank my back scraped for the last time against something hard, and then my bearers just put me down in the pouring rain and left me there.

Whilst Phil set up the tent, Scovill and Dr van Rhijn pre-pared soup for the four Tuans. And as a "special bonus" there was a glass of brandy for each of us, from the supply the doctor had brought with him, though Scovill wouldn't touch it.

Soon all was silent, and everyone slept. Even I slept now and again with the help of tablets. In between whiles I lay awake listening to the gushing of the near-by stream.

At daybreak I was feeling pretty wretched, but I told myself that it wouldn't be long now before we were in Mulia, and this kept my courage up.

I was packed up in Dani fashion once more, and when everything was ready we started off again. Crossing a mountain ridge we reached a suspension bridge across the Yamo River. Phil said we had been on the way only two and a half hours, but it seemed to me more like two and a half days. And now we had to cross the Yamo. The bridge was made of plaited liana. It looked very frail and, of course, it was too narrow for me and my bearers. Dr van Rhijn looked worried, but I didn't mind—at least it offered me a good excuse for getting out of the package I had been imprisoned in. The Danis carefully released me, and after I had made a few tentative movements with my arms and legs, I made my way slowly and cautiously across the swinging bridge. Phil went over walking backwards in front of me in order to catch me if I should fall. I protested against what looked like excessive caution, and I didn't realise how necessary it was. Every movement I made was painful, but nevertheless I regarded with horror the prospect of being packed up again when we got to the other side. Being tied up like that simply made me nervous, and I had already had to fight against one or two minor attacks of claustrophobia.

But there was no escape; my freedom lasted only until I got to the other side of that liana bridge, and then I was tied up into a package again. It was no use even to curse, and so I tried to induce a mood of fatalism in myself. There's nothing you can do about it, I told myself; everything that must be will be. But I wasn't very receptive to this form of argument, and the hours that followed were terrible.

Now and again I did doze off a bit though, but it was only a cat-nap and so near the surface of consciousness that I could still feel the steps of the bearers and even now and again the approach of a new wave of unconsciousness. The first time I felt clearly that I was already unconscious, and it was only with the power of the subconscious that I dragged myself out of it until I was thoroughly conscious again. The second time the wave got no farther than the preliminary feeling of vertigo. It woke me up and with my last remaining energy I raised my already drooping head and remained conscious.

The chief cause was, of course, my fall, but I take it that the frequent and heavy drugging had something to do with it too. Throughout this period I swallowed several packets of tranquilliser pills, and—at Dr van Rhijn's advice—antibiotic tablets as well, in case the broken ribs should tear the lungs. The antibiotics were to ward off a possible attack of pneumonia.

On the last day the bearers were particularly careful with me, and I think this was due to the fact that the previous evening Scovill had read them the Riot Act and told them to remember that I was in great pain. Fortunately there were now only short stretches through the jungle so that at least I didn't have to suffer so much from the tree-trunks. But as against that, whenever we came to the village limits I had to be lifted over fences that were over three feet high. However, not once did my poor back have to scrape against any of them.

Finally, early in the afternoon, Mulia lay beneath us in bright sunshine—Mulia, the small Mission Station we had set off from so hopefully only a few days previously. I found the sun in my face too strong so I asked Phil for my old hat, but Phil informed me with regret that it had been a victim of the waterfall, so now I had lost two hats: the Carstensz expedition had cost me one, "the Source of the Stone Axes" the other, both in the water. They were both old friends of mine, and they had been with me on many expeditions in several continents. Now they were lost for ever in the torrential waters of New Guinea. That was a pity!

Despite the seriousness of my condition I couldn't help seeing the comic side of our entry into the village. As we reached the first houses I became aware of an unusual shoving and pushing around my pole. I turned my head to one side as well as I could and realised what was happening. Every man in my escort, which had now grown to at least two hundred, wanted to take hold of the pole to show everyone in the village that he had done his share too. And the actual bearers went forward now with almost indescribable enthusiasm, as though they had only just started on the job. The final obstacle was the wall around the airfield at Mulia, and when they had climbed over this Dr van Rhijn was at last able to give the signal for them to lower me gently to the ground. The long ordeal was over.

But I wasn't out of the wood yet. Now we were in Mulia the tremendous tension relaxed and my remaining strength threatened to ebb. I was aware that the moment was dangerous and I fought against my weakness. I remembered Hias Noichl. He had smashed his hand on the North Face of the Eiger, but he had managed a descent which would have been a fine performance for a man with two uninjured hands. But then in the comfortable seat of my car on the way to hospital he had lost consciousness.

Once again my battle was successful and I remained conscious, but now at the last moment, after hours and hours of patience, I almost panicked because it seemed to take such a long time to release me from the cords that bound me. I felt that I was going to suffocate—right now in a matter of seconds. And when I was finally out of my mummy case I was quite convinced that I could not have stood another hour in that close constriction.

But I must praise my helpful bearers all the same. After all, they had had to carry me, the pole, the air-mattress, the sleeping-bag, the ground sheet and my clothes, something like a couple of hundred-weight in all. And through extraordinarily difficult terrain at that: over mountains and through valleys, through trackless jungle and across rivers and streams. In addition, they had done it at a speed a European would have found great difficulty in emulating even with a light pack. Of course, for their childlike temperament it had been a sort of circus, and at the same time a welcome opportunity to show the Tuans what they could do if necessary, an opportunity to demonstrate their strength and agility. The white man with his civilisation had made their lives monotonous. As warriors they had once been accustomed to using bows and arrows and spears: either to make war or go hunting. And now they had at last been given an opportunity of showing their paces. My accident will undoubtedly remain in their minds as the happiest incident of the whole expedition.

In Mulia I was already beginning to wonder with dismay whether it would be possible to organise a second expedition to Ya-Li-Me, since the Danis would probably interpret my accident as a sign that their Gods who protect the quarry from interlopers were displeased. After all, the flat, elongated stones used for ceremonial and magic purposes in the Long Houses in which the Papuans hold their orgies also come from this quarry. Those stones represent a sort of phallic and fertility rite symbol. On the other hand, we certainly succeeded in establishing good relations with these Danis just as we had done on the Carstensz expedition, so perhaps we might be able to count on the "Old Guard" to come with us again after all.

I spent the night in Dr van Rhijn's house in Mulia, where a room had been prepared for Phil and me. There was a good deal of discussion that evening, and the Professor from Leyden gave me a new and thorough examination. Pulse and blood pressure proved to be normal, my broken ribs were well plastered up, and for the pain there were more tablets.

For the first time we heard something about a new invasion by Sukarno's troops and the situation was said to be serious. The nurse then gave me a stiff injection to make me sleep and I went off gently.

But it didn't last long, and at two o'clock I was wide-awake again. I felt around for pills, but there were none within reach so I had to wake up Phil, and he got me something from the medicine chest. God knows, he's had a lot to put up with these last few days. In my sleep I was still jolting against tree-trunks and groaning aloud.

Yesterday morning at nine o'clock I was able to sit next to Dave Steiger, a MAF pilot, and fly here to Hollandia. Before leaving I said *au revoir* to my friendly helpers in Mulia, not good-bye—I intended to see them again. A night during which I had a certain amount of sleep reinforced my intention of returning to Mulia and having another shot at reaching the source of the stone axes. I'd sooner give up the idea of exploring Baliem Gorge than that.

We had the most wonderful flying weather conceivable. In brilliant sunshine I was able to look down on my own particular Golgotha. Not a very enjoyable memory, but at least I was already looking forward to my return at some time in the future. Then we passed over the enormous meandering Idenburg River. It must be very difficult if not impossible to explore it thoroughly from ground level —except that you should never call anything "impossible."

After an hour's flight we touched down on the airfield of Sentani, the capital of West New Guinea. Whilst our machine was still taxi-ing to a halt a white painted ambulance raced out to meet us. They were obviously prepared to receive "the patient from Mulia."

On the drive into town we stopped at the post office and I was able to send a telegram home. This time, when I really have met with an accident, I hope to get my blow in before the reporters. Even if the report of the accident was published yesterday, my reassuring news will have got there first.

By midday we were driving into the bungalow colony of the local hospital. Each hospital bungalow is known by the name of some well-known doctor. I was delivered into "de Rook" bungalow and put in a ward with five other patients.

That was yesterday. I began to write up my diary at once, but I didn't get so much done as I have today. First of all my pains and aches were more troublesome, secondly, I was still tired, and, thirdly, towards the end of the afternoon I had another medical visit. All the doctor could do was to say that nothing further could be done until I had had an x-ray, but by the time he had gone I felt too tired to write any more. I had a good, long night's sleep, and this morning I was x-rayed.

March 30

I couldn't get any writing done almost all day, because there was an almost uninterrupted procession of visitors. There are flowers all over the place, and fruit and other presents. The sympathy of the Dutch is really quite touching.

Yesterday when I was wheeled back into my ward after the x-ray examination the heat generated under the sticking plaster caused big blisters to form at the place where the ribs are broken, and I had to get them to take the plaster off. My head wound has been rebandaged but they're not paying much attention to my knee and shoulder injuries—the broken ribs are the thing.

I hope to be able to go back to Mulia by April 18. But that's only three weeks ahead.

This morning the doctor made another examination of my ribs with the help of the x-ray photos. He said they were simple fractures and that there were no complications. My other injuries are regarded as relatively unimportant. And that's right. If I hadn't broken my ribs, and my very painful and almost immovable knee were my only injury the doctors would concentrate all their attention on that. And the same is true of my head and shoulder injuries. Any one of the three injuries apart from the ribs would be enough to put a man in hospital, but as it is the doctor knows that they will all have healed long before the ribs, and there you are.

I have determined to follow the instructions of the doctors and nurses very conscientiously, because only if I do can I possibly hope to keep my next dateline—April 18. And I must keep it, because by

April 30 I must be in Wamena or Bokondini, and before that I want to have cleared up the mystery surrounding Ya-Li-Me, the Source of the Stone Axes.

Professor de Bruijn visited me today. He has the reputation of being one of the leading Dutch experts on New Guinea and his name is well known. I told him about my exploration of the Carstensz area. Some of the information he had already, but some of it was new to him. He seemed particularly interested in my Baliem project.

A number of other visitors came to see me, some of whom I had never met before. In any case, the result was that my hope of being able to do a good deal of reading in hospital proved ill-founded—at least it did as far as today is concerned. But I take it that in a few days when the first excitement has calmed down a bit I shall just be another "patient," and I shall have more time to myself.

Indonesian parachutists have been landing again along the south coasts, but no one is greatly exercised about it here in Hollandia because the invasion area is a long way away.

I weigh only 150 pounds, which means that I've lost about thirty pounds—very agreeable news!

Sunday. Perhaps to celebrate the good day all my bandages have been taken off, and the doctor says my ribs will knit just as well in a hotel as here. I need no longer remain immobile, so from tomorrow on I am discharged.

The Head Surgeon of the hospital, Dr de Vries, paid me a farewell visit and chatted to me for about an hour. It appears that he is a specialist in fractures, and he gave me a few words of advice on my way: for example, that I should start doing joint exercises straight away to prevent stiffening and in order to ensure that, if possible, my knee, arm and shoulder are in perfect order again at the same time as my ribs.

Since then I have moved into a hotel and have a very nice room with a shower attached. The hospital has lent me a chaise-longue, so everything has been done for my comfort, and apart from the fact that I'm still in a certain amount of pain everything is going well.

Whoever has had the good or bad luck to have had one foot on the other side of the divide as I have had—more than once—knows that in escaping death you experience the joy of rebirth, and you learn to appreciate life more. And naturally such experiences lead one to think more intensely about the significance of life and its many aspects and complications.

I am lying back now in my chaise-longue with my diary on my knee, and doing my best to analyse the extent of the dangers and the depth of my experiences, and to weigh one against the other. It's altogether an odd business: what happened to me at the waterfall would not have happened to an altogether inexperienced person—he would never have thought of treating the waterfall so contemptuously.

On the other hand, of course, experience gives greater security and more confidence in one's own ability and in one's own possibilities, but, naturally, this same confidence involves greater dangers such as never threaten the inexperienced. Without self-confidence there can be no achievement, so much is clear. But the desire to achieve something out of the ordinary necessarily increases the element of danger. An example taken from another field will perhaps help to make this clearer.

A poor swimmer, who, in consequence of his inexperience, will hardly trust himself to swim more than a little way out into the sea, is not likely to encounter any very great dangers: jellyfish can sting him, he can gash himself on a coral reef, but if he runs into any real danger rescuers on the shore will not have far to swim to save him. But a man who knows himself to be a good swimmer will—quite rightly—have confidence in his own ability, and he will swim out very much farther. He won't find any jellyfish to sting him so far out, but he might well fall in with sharks. The danger of coral reefs will be less for a powerful swimmer, but there may perhaps be a greater

13. The children were delightful—they are everywhere
14. Cowrie shells protect this little fellow from evil spirits (OVERLEAF)

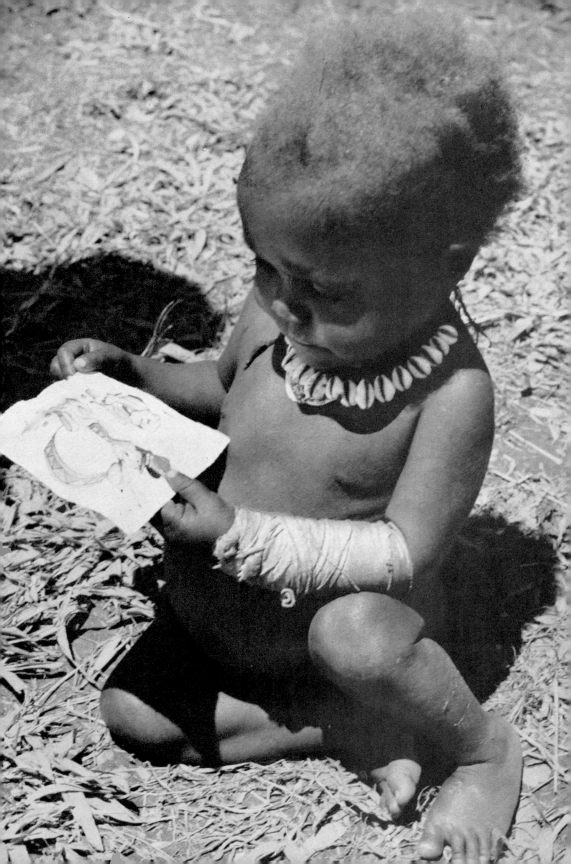

danger of some treacherous undertow farther out. And if he does get into difficulties a would-be rescuer will have that much farther to swim before he can come to his aid. On the other hand, a poor swimmer will never cross the Channel; that achievement is for the good swimmer only.

Of course, you can say: well, who wants to swim the Channel anyway? Who wants to climb Nanga Parbat? Who wants to climb the North Face of the Eiger? Or, in my own particular case now, who wants to go to "the Source of the Stone Axes."

Or to put it differently: many people might like to, and some people might want to. But very few people would dare to. But this is a question of outlook and temperament—and experience. And so we find ourselves back where we started from.

Thanks to this realization that experience can involve greater dangers, I am all the more thankful that things went as well for me as they did.

April 3

At last I've got time to attend to my correspondence, to read, and to think about my future plans and my immediately past experiences.

It is strange how desires can change. How often in the loneliness and the dull, oppressive heat of the Yamo Valley with Phil Temple did I dream of the joy of a glass of cool beer! It was the first wish we thought we would realise when we got back to Hollandia. But now I have been here in Hollandia for a whole week, and I haven't drunk a single glass of beer. I just haven't given it a moment's thought. But perhaps that has something to do with my condition: a healthy body has altogether different desires from those of a battered one.

Isn't it a pity that they don't give you *hors d'oeuvres* in hospital? Isn't it a shame that all waterfalls rush downwards? And wouldn't it be fun if for a change you fell upwards in the mountains?

April 4

Dr Valk turned up here today—the Dutch doctor who was coming with us on the Carstensz expedition and was then prevented by tummy trouble. We discussed the unconfirmed reports that to the north

113

of "my" quarry, in the neighbourhood of the lake plateau, there is a tribe which makes its axes out of some soft reddish-yellow substance. If the reports are really true then the substance can only be bronze. Or perhaps copper. In any case, it's a question that can't be resolved from a sickbed. I propose to go to the neighbourhood again, and I will keep my eyes and ears open and ask around.

April 5

Phil has written to tell me that about a week ago he set off in the direction of Tiom. I take it that he couldn't get a plane and that he's making for Wilhelmina Top. A very good piece of news: I shall be able to fly back to Mulia on April 11, a good week before I had planned. Even the doctor seems to have no very serious objections, even if he did shake his head doubtfully. I can take a 350-lb pack with me.

Today I was in town—if one can call Hollandia a town. I visited the Geological Institute and looked up the nature of the stone from which the natives make their axes. The greenish stone, which is regarded as the best and which comes from "my" quarry to the north of Mulia, is epidote, degree of hardness: 6 to 7. The bluish stone which is obtained in the same neighbourhood and used for small chisels is called glaucophane, and belongs to the better known hornblende group. The black stone which is taken from the Yamo River, and isn't very popular with the natives, is flint sandstone.

April 7

Fourteen days have now passed since I tumbled into the waterfall. The stabbing pain in my chest has gone, but I still have to sleep on my back. I find this very disagreeable and it causes me many sleepless nights. I am still taking tablets day and night. Rather to my surprise my left knee is as stiff as ever. It looks as though it will take longer than the ribs, and in any case it is taking longer than expected. My right shoulder has improved, but part of the nerve fibres seem to have been severed because my upper arm is almost without feeling. And I can't move my arm as easily as I would like to.

However, when I consider that at this time just a fortnight ago I was lying very much battered on a rock with the water around me reddish from my lost blood I can't grumble. On the whole things have gone well. I'm still alive, and when I think of that I feel very thankful indeed. At the same time it makes me feel that perhaps it would be better not to swim out so far in future, to live a quieter life, not to chase after so many dangerous ambitions. After all, there are other things in life I'm very fond of, too: my books, music, ski-ing and golf, for example. I also like to hear and read about what other people have done. And there are quite a lot of books I could write: a Tibetan encyclopaedia, a Tibetan guide book, a history of Lhasa. But would it really be much good? You get to know your own temperament in time, and the fact is I prefer first-hand experience to reading about it second-hand in books. What usually happens is that you set yourself an objective, and when you've reached it you find it wasn't an ultimate objective at all, but merely a stage on the way to the next—long ago secretly determined—objective. It's like slalom ski-ing—whilst you're sailing through one gate your eyes and your mind are already on the next.

In addition, you often have a number of objectives in mind at the same time, and very often you're not in a position to choose your next objective of your own free will. The things themselves take command, and suddenly "your" decision is made for you by character and temperament in circumstances perhaps favoured by chance or influenced by other people's decisions.

April 10

Yesterday evening I spent a few hours with René Wassink. He was young Michael Rockefeller's companion last December when Michael lost his life. Wassink is a very knowledgeable fellow, and at the same time a very agreeable and amusing one, and I have to thank him for a lot of good advice in connection with my planned tour to the south coast of the island. As an experienced ethnographer he was able to tell me about very many interesting places it would be worth while visiting. Despite the loss of time caused by my accident I haven't given up hope of penetrating as part of my third expedition into the area where young Rockefeller disappeared. Numerous stories have already appeared about it in the newspapers, some of them true, others invented. As yet no one really knows what actually happened. For example, a couple of weeks ago there was a rumour that Michael's watch had been found. Now is that true or isn't it? No one seems to know. A further report has come in from a Missionary Station about a native found to be in possession of a bone knife made from a human thigh bone, the sort of thing that can be made only when the bone is still warm. Perhaps I shall have a chance of investigating on the spot how much is true and how much isn't. Wassink feels sure young Rockefeller was drowned while trying to swim ashore. Wassink himself hadn't much hope of survival, but he decided to cling on to the wreckage of their catamaran and hope that help would come.

Michael Rockefeller's father has promised Wassink to put up the money to found an ethnological museum in Hollandia. This is the project he's engaged on at the moment, and it takes up all his time. He is devoted to his work, and is fortunate enough to be amongst those few happy men whose hobbies and occupations coincide.

Tomorrow I am flying back to Mulia with Steiger. My left leg is still stiff, and my ribs still give me a bit of trouble when I'm lying down, but I hope to be able to reach the quarry in short stages. Another point: Mulia is cheaper than Hollandia, and I can read just as well there as here.

April 11

The flight to Mulia is off for the time being. I was already getting my things together when Dave Steiger arrived to tell me that the Mission Station won't give permission for him to land. They don't want "visitors" in Mulia. No one can understand it. I'm honestly puzzled and my friends here are quite indignant.

Everyone in the hotel knows about the landing prohibition, and one or two of the pressmen are so angry they want to write exasperated attacks on the decision. I am saying as little as possible. After all, I'm a guest here.

It is easy to see that there is tension between some of the Mission Stations and the Dutch authorities. This has to do with the whole history of Dutch colonisation here. Probably it's because the Dutch

116

authorities made the mistake—which the Australian authorities in the other part of the island did not—of allowing the Missions to establish themselves before the administration. In consequence a certain struggle for power has developed.

But there are probably also other reasons for the disinclination to welcome "visitors"—there have been people who have made a nuisance of themselves from the point of view of the Missions, who have hampered their work and stirred up trouble amongst the natives. Nothing of the sort is true in my case, of course. I always live in a tent, and I have never asked, and certainly never demanded, any assistance from the Missions. And no one can say that I have ever done anything to upset the natives. It is possible though that the Missions don't like to see members of their flock going off as porters for strangers, because on longer journeys the natives get into the area of some other Mission Station, where perhaps they get to know things their own missionaries would sooner they didn't—even missionaries are not always above resentments and jealousies.

This morning I was examined and x-rayed again. The doctor says I should do exercises, but I think the best sort of exercise for me would be to get going on my expedition again as soon as possible.

April 13

Yesterday the *New Guinea Courier* published an article about me with reference to the incomprehensible landing prohibition. The writer is good enough to express the hope that I shall soon be given permission to land, since, as he writes amiably, I'm not "just an inexperienced newcomer."

I'm very interested to see what happens, and in the meantime I'm staying on here in Hollandia and getting fit under medical supervision. This further delay is at least made tolerable by the fact that life in this little town on Humboldt Bay is quite agreeable. The position alone, on the bay with its many small islands, is particularly attractive. Between the islands there are native villages built on piles. You can reach them only by boat. And the beach of Hollandia is so wonderfully beautiful that I have no hesitation in comparing it to the beach of Tahiti. There is a good deal of life on the bay, boats are sailing everywhere, and brilliant colours enhance the general picture. There are memories of the war here, too, though. You can still see the wreckage of sunken American and Japanese landing craft on the shallow bottom.

Serpentine roads meander up the steep slope to the villas and the modern bungalows of the European community up above, and there are always cars driving around. In the evenings you sit on the terraces with the scent of frangipani in your nostrils. It is released only after sundown. Fishing goes on at night and native craft are dotted over the surface, their lights reflected in the dark water. Sometimes there may be a big freighter lying at anchor a little way out, interrupting its voyage for a call at Hollandia; or perhaps a Dutch naval vessel with all its lights on.

Quite suddenly after dark, as though at a secret signal, the crickets start up, and their chirping fills the whole air with a tremendous chattering. It is almost deafening and it is difficult to believe that such fragile creatures can make such a noise merely by rubbing their hind-legs together. And as suddenly as it starts this concert stops. The quietness after the air has been full of their noise is almost funereal, almost oppressive. It is as though the world had suddenly ceased to exist. But then there is very often another noise: the rain falling on the corrugated iron roofs in a steady drumming. In the upper town people have long ago retired to their bedrooms: social life ends earlier in the evening here than anywhere else in the world, because office work starts in the morning at 7 a.m.

The Papuans down there along the beach and in their pile houses behave differently. Perhaps they remember their forebears, who held their orgies at night and slept during the day. In any case, from time to time they let loose blood-curdling shrieks. Theirs is a strange kind of life in this otherwise lifeless night. Now and again you think you can hear the sound of a jet plane, and only when you notice that the powerful but subdued roar is neither coming any nearer nor stopping do you gradually realise that it isn't a plane at all, but the river pouring over the coral reef into Humboldt Bay.

Everybody feels a bit embarrassed that the question of the landing prohibition has created such a furore, and the excuse is that they feared that I wouldn't be able to get enough porters. It was really all a misunderstanding. Well, perhaps it was, perhaps it wasn't—the real thing for me is to get to Mulia. They can leave the question of finding porters or not finding porters to me.

It seems that people here are gradually getting used to the idea that before long New Guinea will have to be ceded to the Indonesians. The Hague has already agreed to the U.S. plan for an evacuation of the Dutch part of the island over the space of two years. Conditions here are exactly the opposite to conditions in Algeria. In colonial days New Guinea was always a sort of stepchild of the motherland, and only when it was, so to speak, "left over" did people to begin take an interest in it.

I find evidence again and again that the Dutch are extremely generous to the native Papuans, and that they are doing everything possible to guide them painlessly into the process of civilisation. The people who really hate the natives are the half-castes, the Eurasians. A good deal of the racial prejudice comes from them. The reason for their attitude is clear enough: they don't, or don't yet, count as Europeans, but they actively resent being classed as natives. The Eurasians are also the first to take flight in face of dangerous political developments. They have already fled from Indonesia because of Sukarno, and now he's coming after them here too. There is a general fear that when he takes over the country will fall back into its old state, and particularly the highlands, which have not yet been properly opened up to civilisation. It is feared that the country will once again be a stepchild, but of another mother.

For the same reason the Papuans themselves don't want any change in the existing political situation, and their attitude is a real compliment to the great efforts the Dutch have made in recent years, and are still making, to help them. If there is to be a change then the Papuans would prefer to be independent and look after themselves. But, of course, anything of that sort could only be a matter for the future since at the moment they are just not in a position to do so.

It's true that they already have a Papuan flag, and it gives them a good deal of satisfaction, self-assurance and pride, but apart from this there really is nothing on which real independence could be based. A young State needs experienced officials, and so far there aren't even schools everywhere. Many more will first have to be built before there can be any great change. Not only this, but a great many other things would be necessary and they would have to be very carefully thought out in advance. There is no magic solution. How to please everybody is the problem: the whites, the Eurasians, the Papuans, the missionaries, the United Nations—and the various political parties way back there in the Dutch motherland.

Wamena   *April 18*

Today I had the chance of flying here to Wamena on a special flight in a Kroonduif machine. Apart from myself there was a Papuan policeman, a teacher going on Easter leave, two nurses, and Dr Le Roux, who is going on to Bokondini to inspect the hospital there.

The flight, over great forests and lonely native villages, right down to the landing in the magnificent Baliem Valley, was without incident.

Phil Temple was waiting for me at the airfield, and I was delighted to see my old friend and companion once more. I was less delighted with the news he had for me: namely, that owing to the Easter holidays we should have to wait until the Tuesday of next week before we can fly back to Mulia.

I spent the evening with Phil and José Veling, the Assistant to the District Comissioner here, who had some interesting yarns to spin. During the enforced period of waiting in Wamena for our plane to Mulia I was anxious to go with him to the local source of native salt, but he explained with regret that for the time being this was out of the question because there was trouble amongst the natives in the valley.

Only quite recently José himself had been involved in a dangerous incident in which he might well have lost his life. Whilst out on patrol he and his men had been ambushed by Danis armed with spears. A so-called "white" spear hurtling past his head had been the first indication that anything was wrong. He and his men had been compelled to open fire, and in the subsequent affray three of the attackers had been killed.

These "white" spears are about sixteen feet long, and are made of a light-coloured wood. They can be used more swiftly and accurately than the heavier type of myrtle-wood spear, which is known as a "black" spear. More than one Dutch official and quite a number of missionaries have lost their lives at the hands of natives armed with these light "white" spears. This, José explained, was the reason why he and his men had had to shoot at once. Only a little while previously the Danis had murdered a young native preacher, a so-called "Guru," despite the fact that he was attached to the Mission and wore European clothing. This wearing of European clothing is—or was—of considerable importance, since at one time the Danis all thought that some sort of magic resided in the White Man's clothing and made the wearer immune from attack. Obviously the Danis do not believe this any more, or, at least, not since the murder of the young native missionary. They realise that our jackets and trousers are not some magic kind of armour against their spears and arrows, and this not unnaturally encourages their aggressive instincts.

In the afternoon I went for a walk as far as Baliem River, chiefly in order to give my still stiff knee a little exercise. Unfortunately there had hardly been any improvement at all in it, and I am gradually giving up hope of being able to bend it without trouble again in the near future.

April 20

Today is Good Friday. We spent the morning packing, and in four days' time at the latest we hope to be able to make a start. We are already separating the baggage: one part for me for the journey from Mulia to the source of the stone axes, another part for Phil for the way from Mulia to the quarry and on to the Bo-Ko-Yan tribe and Tiom, a third part for Phil for the journey from Tiom to Wilhelmina Top; and, finally a, fourth part for me for the journey to my last great objective: the south coast through Baliem Gorge.

I used the afternoon to have a closer look at Wamena. This collection of aluminium huts has often been criticised on account of its siting. It lies right in the middle of the plain, on ground as flat as a pancake, and it would certainly have been better to site it against a hill. The fact that it lies on the boundary between two hostile tribes has also given rise to criticism, but I am inclined to think that this particular objection is unjustified, since if it had been sited in one territory or the other it would have been surrounded by one homogeneous tribe, and therefore the danger of a large-scale attack would have been greater.

April 22

Easter in Wamena. I'm not feeling in the best of spirits at the moment. Influenza is rife throughout the highlands. A radio message has just come in from the District Officer at Mindiptana to say that owing to the influenza epidemic it is doubtful whether porters can be sent at the moment.

I had my attack in Ilaga, and now I hear that sixty-two people died there in that epidemic, and another thirteen in Bokondini. Wamena seems to have been more or less spared, at least there have been no fatal cases as yet.

I shall need my porters by May 10; that's almost three weeks ahead, so I'm hoping that they'll all be well again by that time.

Johanson brought two passengers into Wamena today. The pilots of the Christian Missions are really first-class chaps. Their performances are often quite astounding, and they're always extremely helpful. Very often they have to land in semi-darkness without landing lights on narrow strips of ground because they have to fly a sick man away for treatment, a man whose life depends perhaps on the speed with which they can get him there. Pilots like Johanson, Steiger, Bader, and whatever their names are, need a good deal of courage and experience, and often aerobatic artistry. Landing on a freshly tilled field is always a hair-raising experience. Very often there's a steep precipice at the beginning or the end of a very bumpy landing strip. And quite frequently they have to touch down or take off on an incline, irrespective of where the wind lies.

Wamena is rather a dismal place to spend the Easter holidays in, particularly as the hotel managers don't bestir themselves in the least to make the festive days a bit more pleasant than usual. There weren't any flowers on the table, and the food was as dull and monotonous as ever.

Mulia   *April 24*

This morning I got back here at last, with Bob Johanson in his Cessna 180. As we have eight hundredweight of baggage again we could take only half of it with us. We went back for the rest in the afternoon. Phil Temple is now there too, so before long we shall be able to make a start for the source of the stone axes. This time we've just got to do it.

April 25

My fear that it would be difficult to find porters has turned out to be only too well founded. The natives still have a lively memory of my tumble into the waterfall, and they are now quite convinced that the spirits are against me and my expedition. And there's no help to be expected from the Mission. They are quite friendly, but reserved. I can only hope that—like last time—the porters will turn up on their own at the last minute.

April 27

The problem of how to get porters is still our main worry. Whenever we try to sound the natives on the point they get hard of hearing and clearly unwilling. But I must start in three days at the latest, and so far we have only two men. Phil is going with them into Yamo Valley today to see if he can rustle up some more. If he doesn't succeed then we'll have to make do with just the two, that's all. This is the first time in my experience that the missionaries haven't been positively helpful. In the ordinary way whenever I came to a mission station I could always be quite sure that my porter troubles were over with their assistance.

123

But although the Danis are reluctant whenever I try to get them to come along with me, they are now at least perfectly willing to give me information about the source of their stone axes. According to them the "blue" axe is called *wang-kob-me*, whilst the "black" one is called *ka-lu*. As I think I have already said, the "blue" axe of glaucophane is more highly valued than the "black" one of flinty slate. Then there is a "green" axe, which is called *andiba*, and this is made of epidote or chloromelanite. And all three kinds come from Ya-Li-Me. That is "our" quarry. I am wondering whether there are three different sites there, or whether perhaps the place is one big valley. I'd really like to start straight away and get the answers to all these questions as quickly as possible.

April 29

A ray of hope! Phil sent back a message yesterday saying that he'd managed to recruit five more porters. In addition, I haven't been idle and I managed to persuade four more fellows here to come with us. We still haven't enough, but far more than just the two we originally had to reckon with. As a precautionary measure I am distributing better food than usual and paying higher wages. In this way I hope at least to keep those we have got.

I hadn't time to write up my diary yesterday, since the time was taken up by a small excursion into the upper Mulia Valley. On the way we came across the calabash bushes which provide the pumpkinlike fruits whose outer rinds serve the male natives as penis sheathings. The fruits are as might be expected, elongated, and take on very many different forms. The bushes are grown under cover in a kind of pergola and are tended as we tend grapes. Here and there a tree is used as a support, so that at first you get the impression that the calabashes are its fruit.

There are three carp lakes along the northern edge of the valley, but there aren't many carp there. It may be that the water isn't fresh enough. The carp ponds were established on the advice of the Dutch authorities who were anxious to supplement the native diet with a little more protein, and thus help to stop the spread of goitre, which is particularly common hereabouts.

On this excursion I also came across a hut of particularly interesting construction. It belonged to a chief, and was more roomy than the usual round huts with their conical roofs, and it had double walls. You hadn't to climb over the usual fence to get into the vegetable patch; opposite the entrance was a second hole through which you could go direct into it. Generally speaking you can't get at the vegetable patch direct from the hut. There were beetroots, turnips, cabbage, beans, and, of course, tobacco growing there.

On the way back I also came across two splendid orange-coloured rhododendrons, one of them with enormous flowers, and the other with small delicate flowers something like our alpine roses. But when the flower is in full bloom it is more like a primrose. I also saw white rhododendrons as tall as trees, of the kind I had already seen on the way to the Carstensz.

In the meantime a second message has arrived from Phil. He has now six porters and is on the way back with them to Mulia. Splendid fellow! So tomorrow we'll be able to start.

The Mission held a service to-day. It was attended by about six hundred natives. It was an impressive sight. They were gathered under a great spreading tree, the men on one side, the women on the other, strictly separated. In between them stood the two missionaries. Small cirrus clouds were sailing across the mountains at the end of the valley, and all around in a great circle were the huts of the natives with their dark, conical grass roofs, weighted down with stones to prevent the wind from carrying them away. They were no ordinary stones though. They were "magic stones," and the natives hoped that their presence would keep away evil spirits. The contrast struck me forcibly during the service: here Christianity, there, a stone's throw away, heathenism. It was a fabulous picture, as though some talented artist had designed it and then put it straight on to canvas with swift, powerful brushstrokes.

"Have a plan and stick to it."   *April 30*

Double cause for celebration today: it is the Queen of Holland's birthday, and we are at last about to leave for Ya-Li-Me. Something like two thousand Danis will stream into Bokondini today to take part in the celebrations, and about three hundred into Wamena, so the Dutch tell me. The Government has granted money to provide them with amusements. There will be football, sack races and climbing the greasy pole. Whoever gets to the top will be rewarded with a prize in the form of a steel axe.

I shan't see any of the celebrations, because in an hour we shall be leaving for the quarry.

I spent a week in Mulia making all the necessary preparations, and now we can start at last. Phil and I now have twelve porters who, in return for good wages, are prepared to carry our baggage, which has been reduced to the absolute minimum.

The first day's march is now behind us. In Burugoba, a native village high above the river Yamo, whose rushing water can be distinctly heard, we found an empty hut, which saved us the trouble of spending the night in our little tent.

I feel tired and quite exhausted. I didn't find it easy to clamber upwards with my still stiff knee, but going down through the wet forest over slippery moss-grown ground was not much better, so after an hour and a half I had to rest. Owing to the constant extra strain on my right leg I've developed muscular cramp. Two old Dani women had accompanied us part of the way and when they saw me massaging my painful calf they came up at once to show me what to do. They picked nettle leaves—I'd never seen such big nettle leaves in my life before—and indicated that I should rub my leg with them. This I did until my skin felt as though it were on fire. Before long it was red and inflamed and blisters began to form. It was a real horse cure, but at least it did the trick—after about ten minutes the cramp had disappeared completely.

After that we went down the east side of the valley to Burugoba. It was the same route over which they had carried me "pig fashion" on March 26, but up instead of down. Incidentally, the method is well named, because I had been bound to a pole in exactly the same way as they carry a pig. At each halt now the Danis came up to examine my healed head wound, and to marvel. I explained to them that the *tuan ingen*, which is what they call our tablets, had worked this miracle, and they were duly impressed.

The porters stopped constantly on the way to collect bananas,

126

peanuts, spinach, sugar cane and sweet potatoes to take along with them. I pay them with cowrie shells, and the children get a few bright glass beads for their trouble.

It's a great relief to me to be outside a hospital ward and on my way again. Phil is happy about it too, and we are both in the best of spirits.

On the way one of our porters explained to me how the mountain Papuans manage to trade with members of a tribe with which they are living on hostile terms. The traders meet in a clearing which is a sort of No-Man's-Land between the two hostile tribes. The man who wants to sell puts his goods down in the clearing and retires out of sight into the jungle. From his hiding place he informs the enemy by bush telegraph that he is willing to trade. A prospective purchaser arrives and examines the goods. The two then haggle about the price by shouting to each other. When they come to an agreement the purchaser puts down his cowrie shells and goes off with the goods.

Even their blood feuds are not always conducted with utter ruthlessness. If it starts to rain, for example, the warriors engaged will hurl one last flight of imprecations at their enemies and turn tail to seek shelter from the rain. If the next day is fine, hostilities can begin again.

May 1

What a night! A very mixed company was sleeping in the small hut. At least, some of them may have slept. I certainly didn't—or hardly.

After dark several Danis came in, and, in addition, rats and mice, and they seemed to be playing hide and seek amongst us. They flitted around eerily, and they fell quiet for a moment or two only when some pig outside, plagued by vermin, scratched itself against the side of the hut. But the cockroaches, which were of phenomenal size, and the mosquitoes did not allow themselves to be disturbed even by the scraping of the pigs against the hut wall. However even apart from all these things I should hardly have slept because the Danis made up the fire in the middle of the hut too much. The poor devils were probably shivering with cold, but all the same the fire

127

had to be kept down because the straw roof of the hut was as dry as tinder, and one good spark would have turned the whole hut into a flaming torch. I had seen that sort of thing happen too often on an expedition and I didn't care to lose our baggage that way, including my camera, which was the only one I had with me now.

In consequence I only dozed, sometimes with my eyes closed, sometimes open. Now and again I took a swipe at a rat or a mouse, or waved my arms in the air when the mosquitoes got too bad. Time seemed to go very slowly, but at last it got to midnight. And then I witnessed a scene reminiscent of Caliban in *The Tempest*. I was blinking at the fire when suddenly one of the Danis rose silently from where he had been lying. In the dancing light of the fire he looked like a grotesque giant, and little shadows danced over his face. He stood there in a crouched position, his arms hanging down by his side. There was no difference at all between his appearance and what you would imagine to have been that of a cave-man in prehistoric times. He was quite naked, and he looked more like an ape than a man. Everything was perfectly silent for the time being, and even the rats and mice seemed to be intimidated. For a moment or two I thought I was dreaming, the thing was so unreal. Then the man turned away and went out of the hut. After only a short while he was there again, crouching in his corner, where I could see him now only as a dark shadow. What he was doing I couldn't make out, but it was something or other, because I could hear his movements and his breathing. Then without warning he came back to the fire, and crouched there for a few seconds. I could see him more clearly again now. He seemed in a kind of trance. Suddenly he lifted his hands to his head, loosened his hairnet and began alternately to scratch his head wildly and hammer on it with his fists. When this was over he took a corncob and put it on the fire. Perhaps we'll get a bit of peace now, I thought. He just wants some supper. But no, because with a swift movement he seized one of the thick supports of the roof and began to shake it like a madman. My curiosity now turned into anxiety: if he went on like this he'd have the whole hut around our ears. But no sooner had I become aware of the danger than he fell quiet again, sank into himself, folded his hands and began to mutter something. A prayer, an exorcism formula? I've no idea. But his

128

18. The stone axes take three months to sharpen

19. Every reason to be happy—a steel axe (OVERLEAF)

20. But he has to be contented with his stone one (OVERLEAF)

breathing grew heavier and heavier, and then suddenly with two loud reports, two wads flew out of his nostrils like corks out of bottles and landed in the glowing fire. Quietly the man now got up, went back to his place, and composed himself to sleep.

Peace at last, and I hoped to get a bit of sleep, but I had reckoned without the local natives. I was just dropping off when there was a burst of loud shouting. Through the entrance of our hut I could see flickering flames. I crawled outside, and there in the darkness of the night a hut some little distance away was going up in flames. We heard shrieks and our own Danis replied to them in kind. I watched the villagers desperately pulling off the burning roof, and they worked so swiftly that they actually succeeded in saving the walls of the hut. A few minutes later the flames had been beaten out, and there was again peace in this disturbed night. The smell of burning hung on the air for hours afterwards. At last I dozed off into a not very refreshing sleep, and when morning finally came it was raining again.

There was corn on the cob and sweet potatoes for breakfast. I take it that this will be my main staff of life for the next fews week. It's odd: I have eaten corn on the cob in a New York restaurant, and I found it wickedly expensive, but here amongst these "savages" I can get a whole netful of them, twenty cobs, for one cowrie shell. I wouldn't get a crust of bread for that in New York. It must be the point of view. With food it's like everything else in the world: if you have it in superfluity then it has no value; if it's rare you're prepared to sacrifice time, money and labour to get it.

Throughout the journey today we have been trying to get some more porters, and therefore we haven't got very far. It's evening now and we're camping in the small settlement, Bolame, where I spent the night five weeks ago in a very bad state after my tumble.

The way here was delightful. On our way down to Yamo River the clouds disappeared and there was bright sunshine. It gives me a very strange feeling to be making my way along these same paths I was carried over under my pole, half bemused by drugs only a few weeks ago. I knew every gnarled root, every rock on the way. A rock you've scraped your broken ribs against most painfully is not easily forgotten. And I certainly remember the swinging liana bridge,

129

21. *You need a good head for a bridge like this* (INSIDE)
22. *Armed to the teeth*

every inch of it. I insisted on crawling over it under my own steam without Phil's profferred assistance, though I realise now that under the influence of the drugs and because I had lost so much blood I could easily have lost consciousness. That is a disagreeable thought. But I didn't lose consciousness, and nothing happened, and now I'm on my way to Ya-Li-Me again. I'm thankful, and that's that.

May 2

After marching for hours through the pouring rain we reached Yengayo, the big bivouac hollow, this afternoon at four o'clock.

Our route went through the romantic valley of the Aninima River which we had to cross and recross. Finally we came to a very narrow path and had to go up something like a thousand feet very steeply. Once again I couldn't help admiring the catlike agility and confidence of our porters.

The spur that was hacked out five weeks ago to make my return easier came in useful now. The Danis were very proud of it, and they gaily shouted their "Wa-wa-wa!" call. But when we came to "my" waterfall, they fell quiet, because, of course, it was here that an evil spirit had frustrated my first attempt to reach the source of the stone axes. Film and photograph will show clearer than words what I managed to survive here. Shortly after we arrived at the waterfall it started to rain, and then went on without stopping.

And now, wet to the skin, we are crouched in the bivouac cave. Its special characteristics? Very little room and lots of dirt. And the word "cave" is a flattering exaggeration; to be quite accurate it's no more than an overhang which offers us very little protection against the rain. It gave us a great deal of trouble to get a fire going. One of our Danis had to climb up about eighty feet into one of the thickly mossed oaks which grow around our bivouac together with mountain bamboos in order to hack off branches thin enough to start our fire.

On the way we managed to recruit another couple of porters, so we're a party of about twenty now, and we are all huddled up as closely as possible to the fire we have at last succeeded in getting

130

going. There was roasted corn on the cob and sweet potatoes and we shared the meal in a brotherly fashion.

May 3

We got off to a particularly early start this morning. The wet and the cold got us moving at the first light of dawn. We are ascending through fabulously beautiful mossy woodland now. After about an hour of this we reached the pass. Then we went down a narrow path into the Kyira Valley. Wherever you look there are waterfalls hurtling downwards into the valley with tremendous force. Their size and power is something altogether difficult to imagine if you have never seen them and "my" waterfall was child's play by comparison with the waterfalls we are meeting today. Very often our path goes along so close to the tumbling masses of water that one false step would be the end of anyone who slipped in as I did a few weeks ago.

Towards midday we reached a bivouac site with an old round hut and a gloomy cave. The site is right on the edge of a gorge, and to look down into it is almost as though you were looking into Hades itself. The sides are so steep and go down so far that we were unable to see where the water gushing out from the side actually hit the ground below—not that I went all that close to the edge, because I really am like the proverbial burnt child who dreads the fire.

On the whole way the Danis treated me with quite touching care and consideration. They were constantly telling me where to place my feet, and if I happened to slip or slide a little they would cry out in alarm. Perhaps they were only anxious to avoid having to carry me back again; if so I can sympathise with them.

It was about five o'clock when we reached the first Kyira village at last. It is called Lambinime, and like all the villages in this area it is small and isolated. The valley through which the river runs is very narrow here and lies east to west. The falls are eastward.

May 4

Quite early this morning our Danis informed me that they do not intend to go any farther today than the village on the other side of the descent, explaining that Missionary Scovill had instructed them "to

131

make church" there. Naturally we made no attempt to dissuade them.

We reached the gorge about half an hour after leaving Lambinime. A suspension bridge sweeps steeply upward across the river, which roars and tumbles about 180 feet below.

It was easily the wildest landscape we had yet come across. Slowly and cautiously we made our way forward over the slippery boles at our feet, looking down in some trepidation at the yawning depths beneath us. The gorge was even wider down below, and the sound of the roaring river came up to us in a hollow, menacing rumble.

On the other side of the river we found we had to negotiate a steep rock face, but fortunately there was a ladder of plaited liana to help us up. At the top the jungle began again, and the ground still rose steeply. It took us a good hour before we finally reached the round huts of Ilrolam.

We are the first white men these villagers have ever seen, but they turned out to be very friendly, and as an earnest of it they prepared us an enormous banquet of welcome. The whole population gathered to meet us, and in accordance with native custom we had to shake hands with each villager—about thirty in all. Now a Papuan "shakehands" is a bit different from ours. You first clench your hand, but for one finger, which you crook round the other fellow's, after which you snatch your hand away so that a slight snapping noise is produced. To fail to greet a single one of the Papuans in this fashion would be regarded as gross rudeness—no matter whether there are three, or three hundred of them.

Before long the smell—by this time quite familiar—of bananas, maize and spinach cooking in the usual pit came to our nostrils. To mark our appreciation of this friendly reception, and as presents from guests to hosts, Phil and I distributed shells to the natives after we had all eaten.

One of our porters, a man from Bokondini, is called Yigana. By the way, the Papuans have no family names, only what we would call Christian names. There is nothing fixed and immutable about their names either: if a man doesn't like his name, or gets fed up with it, he just chooses himself another one. Or perhaps his clan will do it for him. There was one porter who took part in our Dugundugu expedition. What his name was I can't remember, but on his return he changed it to Dugundugu.

But to come back to Yigana. He was one of the first to join us in this expedition and I have the impression that he is an adventurous type. Also he seems to have been up to something for which he now fears punishment, because he was particularly anxious to get out of Bokondini, and then out of Mulia, as quickly as possible. His personal appearance confirms this general impression—he is horrible to look at. His whole body is covered with scars, and one hand and one leg are crippled, but this doesn't stop him from carrying his load with the rest. His voice suits his appearance. It is sullen, hoarse and strong. Despite all this he is the one who leads the others in prayer and pronounces the gospel for them.

There is wild ginger growing around our village camping site, and our porters are taking advantage of it to prepare their "Dani salt," spitting the chewed ginger stems into a banana-leaf basin and finally consuming the concoction with evident signs of pleasure as a great delicacy.

May 5

Our porters were laughing uproariously and singing loudly until past midnight, and neither Phil nor I could get to sleep properly. At first Phil was a bit annoyed—until we discovered this morning why our Danis were so elated last night, and then he was mollified. It appears that we both have to be given names, and the Danis had great fun choosing them for us. An hour ago we were solemnly informed that henceforth I am to be known to them as "Ya-Tuan," whilst Phil is to be known as "Ya-i-Tuan." *Ya* is the word for stone axe, and *Tuan* is the Malay word for "Sir," or foreigner, or stranger, whilst *i* is the word for river. In the course of time *Tuan* has come to convey much the same as the Indian word *Sahib*, which originally meant merely a stranger, or a foreigner, but now means someone in authority. For example, in India today a policeman is addressed as *Sahib*, and in the same way a policeman in Ilaga or Wamena is addressed as *Tuan*. So I am now the Stone-Axe Gentleman, and Phil is the Stone-Axe River Gentleman.

Once you're on friendly terms with the mountain Papuans you soon realise that they have a very definite sense of humour.

We had expected to move off in about ten minutes, but in fact it was nearly nine o'clock before we finally did get moving. It wasn't long before beads of sweat began to form on my forehead. The whole time we had to climb over slanting, slippery tree-trunks. There was no other way: left, right, underneath. One river I crossed by straddling a tree-trunk, whilst our Danis, light-footed and elegant as usual, just danced over it.

For a good deal of the way this morning I felt very much like a clumsy elephant compared to them. I did my best to tread in their footsteps, but a branch usually broke under me, or my foot went down into the brushwood that often covers the marshy ground like close network. I'm probably too heavy, and in any case they possess an extraordinary agility. With a hop, skip and a jump they clear all obstacles like mountain chamois.

On more than one occasion we had to negotiate absolutely vertical gnarled root faces. My bones are still aching and I must confess that this was the most difficult jungle passage I had yet met. New Guinea is notorious for having the wildest jungle landscape anywhere in the world. Even Africa and the Amazon valley can't compare with it.

Towards midday a tropical downpour started, and it certainly lived up to its name. The Danis put on the picturesque pandanus leaf hats I had brought them—they are always very anxious to protect their matted locks from the rain. I made no attempt to protect myself from the downpour because I was wet to the skin from sweat anyway, and I wanted to have full freedom of movement for the difficult clambering we had to do. I think I've experienced just about everything now and very little could surprise me: almost five months of New Guinea, downpours practically every day, almost impenetrable jungle, and a variety of tumbles—at least it's good training.

We found it impossible to stay by the river all the time; sometimes it had gouged out deep gorges which were just impassable, and from their steep sides one waterfall after the other thundered down to join the river. On one occasion we had to climb up over a ridge in order to circumvent a gorge. It meant a detour and additional effort.

Finally about, 150 feet above the river, we found the small bivouac hole in which I am now lying and writing this. It isn't an ideal site by any means, small, low and damp, but nevertheless we were glad to have come across it. The porters are moaning about the never-ending rain, but it hasn't really spoiled their spirits, and they once again showed their best sides: when they heard Phil and me grumbling about the damp they immediately built us a little raised terrace of boles and brushwood on which we can now lie and be half-way dry. Not that it's particularly comfortable even so—the water constantly dripping down from the roof sees to that. The smoke of the two fires is curling around in thick, damp swathes over us, and only when we're lying down can we find a place which is not quite so smoky for our heads.

It is still just pouring down. The normally small stream flowing below us is now a brown, gurgling torrent, of primeval force. It's almost a bit too much in the way of romantic savagery. But it's a new experience, and we've never seen anything quite like it before, so that offers some compensation for our discomfort.

Unfortunately it has been so gloomy all day that it was impossible for me to do any filming. And what films I could have made! Just the picture of the Danis clambering up the other side of the river to get wood for our fires. Almost like birds, and as though they had the help of wings, they spring lightly and elegantly over a vibrating tree trunk that reaches only three-quarters over the swiftly rushing water.

May 6

We left our eyrie very early this morning, and once again we have put a day behind us that demanded the last ounce of our strength and endurance. We were clambering over trunks and gnarled roots all the time, and hardly once could we make a normal step. My knee is still causing me a good deal of trouble. However, we made good progress, and by midday we had reached the mountain crest, but, as is the case with most of these passes, we couldn't see very far. We were unsighted by enormous oaks, rhododendrons and pandanus palms, and in between them there is an almost impenetrable confusion of dank jungle vegetation.

135

The pass represented the end of our way through "the valley of waterfalls," and we now began to descend gradually. We were making progress only with difficulty. One of the mountain Papuans had to go ahead all the time with an axe to make a passage through the undergrowth for us, and he often had to work very hard. We were constantly hoping to reach the next village, but each time our hopes were dashed. Only later that afternoon after we had passed a number of bivouac holes, did we finally get there. Suddenly our Danis stopped, whispered to each other and pointed forward. Phil cocked his rifle as a precautionary measure, and then we both spotted the village. But there wasn't a soul to be seen, and the round huts looked quite deserted. It was a very disagreeable feeling—in such places you never know whether the natives are going to greet you with a shower of arrows or a cheerful babble of welcome.

Slowly and cautiously we approached the little settlement, and then quite suddenly we spotted them, about forty men crouched together in a clearing and staring at us silently. I didn't feel too happy at the sight of their black painted faces and their forbidding head-dresses of animal skins. The women were crouching beside them, just as silent and motionless, but with averted faces. They are the precious and carefully protected possession of every tribe. Rapidly I counted the heads; there were seventy-five souls in all.

I was aware that these were men and women of the Vano tribe, and the story goes that they first like to lick a stranger to see whether he tastes all right. This sounded rather disagreeable, but it turned out not to be true. Slowly I approached the silent villagers and extended my hand to one of them after the other, taking good care not to leave a single one out. That would have been, as I have said, a mortal insult.

When I had greeted them all I distributed salt and glass beads amongst the women and children, whilst Phil gave the men tobacco. At that they began to thaw a little, but it took us two hours before we could extract permission to pitch our tent in their village.

In the last light of the day I went for a short walk, and suddenly I found myself looking out over an open valley which ended in an enormous broad plain. That was the most beautiful sight of the day for me, because I was undoubtedly looking at the lake plateau and

136

the famous marshy plain which is only about 150 to 200 feet above sea level. It is formed by the rivers Rouffaer and Idenburg. I had always wanted to see this plain from an eminence, but I hadn't thought that we were already so near it. Scovill had said something about its being at least five days' journey from here. And how near we must be now to our real objective! There is no further mountain ridge between us and the quarry, which can't be very far below us now. Ya-Li-Me, the source of the stone axes, lies at the confluence of the Kimbe and Ya-Yi rivers.

Phil is beside himself at the news. We really feel like going on through the night instead of staying here. Our spirits are too high to allow us to bother much about the rain which is still constantly pouring down, or about the first high wind I have experienced here in New Guinea. It is so strong that the rain is beating in almost horizontally under our tent roof.

May 7

Instead of marching off straight away to the source of the stone axes we have been compelled to put up with a rest day here. The rain is too violent for our porters, and, in addition, they want a big and nourishing meal. So we stayed in the Vano village for another day. The name of this village is Ganik. All the mountains, valleys and rivers in the neighbourhood have names; only the big river far out there hasn't one yet.

This morning for the first time the good spirits of our porters seemed in danger. The wind was driving the rain at us in fierce flurries, and they crouched together miserably, shivering under their pandanus bonnets. I then bargained with the Vanos for a pig weighing about sixty-five pounds, offering them a steel axe in exchange. The haggling took hours, and whilst it was going on I watched coloured parrots and cockatoos flying over the clearing, flapping their wings and setting up quite a din with their shrieking. After a while they all perched together in the crown of a tall tree and began to peck at its red berries. Finally they were joined by three brilliant birds of paradise. Far away towards the valley soared a pair of eagles.

When the haggling was over and the pig was mine, and the preparations for roast pork were well under way two of our Danis went off on a mouse hunt. They actually caught one and ate it just as it was. Now and again mouse heads are dried out and the teeth used to make necklaces. Rats are just killed and flung away.

In the meantime the other porters cleaned out one of the cooking holes which are several feet deep and perhaps five feet wide, and always to be found in native villages, and then they slaughtered the pig. Their way of doing it is a torture for the poor beast. First of all a cord is fastened round one hind leg and a Dani holds the other end of the cord. Then a second Dani takes a bow and arrow and shoots the pig from a distance of about twenty feet—at least that's the way they killed our pig. But the first arrow did not penetrate the pig's heart, and the wretched beast kicked and struggled and rolled over and over in its blood until the haft of the arrow snapped off. The Dani then shot a second arrow into the struggling pig, but this did not penetrate the heart either, and the terrified squealing became almost intolerable. Having used two arrows the Danis now stood around a little helplessly waiting for the pig to die. I couldn't stand it any more and so I suggested that the pig should at least be stunned with an axe blow first and then have its throat slit. After a certain amount of argument the Danis carried out my proposal and the wretched pig was put out of its misery.

A great pile of wood was built near the cooking hole and set alight, and large stones were placed on top of it to get hot for the roasting. Whilst the fire was burning some of the Danis singed off the pig's bristles. With their knives they scored two deep cuts from the chops down over the belly to the tail. Then they inserted an axe haft into the pig's throat and gutted it, extracting the whole innards in one piece, which they carried off to the river to wash.

They made no attempt to collect the blood, and just let it drip to the ground where it formed a disagreeable slime with the grass and sand. Those parts of the pig's innards for which they had no use were thrown around on the ground, whereupon the other village pigs rushed up and cannibalistically devoured what fell to their share of father, grandfather—or whatever the relationship of their dead companion was to them. Now a number of lean and even emaciated village dogs joined the savagely grunting horde, and soon there was a general mêlée of pig against dog, pig against pig, and dog against dog, as each fought for its share of the feast. It was nightfall before it was over.

But back to the preparations for the feast of roast pork. In the meantime the Vano women brought sweet-potato leaves and sugar-cane, advancing in single file to our tent and laying their offerings at our feet.

The cooking hole was lined out with banana leaves as usual, and then came the hot stones, which the men removed from the fire, using pieces of wood as tongs. The women then put in spinach and sweet potatoes with their leaves, placing more hot stones on top of them, and unripe bananas on top of that. Only when the hole was filled almost to the brim came the pieces of pork, which were wrapped in ginger leaves. Further hot stones were placed around them, and then the whole was covered with freshly-cut grass turves which closed up the mound like a kiln.

So far the various preparations had taken about three hours, and now the final ceremony took place. The men and women assembled round the cooking hole, the sexes strictly segregated, and began to say grace. It was interesting to note that these Vanos also closed their eyes and put their palms together in the approved fashion as learned from the missionaries. One or two of the men went on smoking it is true, but most of them were deeply concentrated on their prayers.

A further hour passed, and then the kiln was opened up and the steaming vegetables distributed. Phil and I were served first, then the Vanos, and, finally, our porters. Phil and I were first because we were the hosts, even if the vegetables had been provided by the villagers. Phil and I took one of the legs and half the liver, but the liver was so dry as a result of the long baking that you could hardly get your teeth into it. However, the pork itself was very tender, and it was enjoyed by all the men with obvious and audible pleasure. No one wasted any eating time by talking. Night had fallen by the time everyone had eaten, and then a great palaver began.

Phil and I are now lying in our tent enjoying the cool night air. Storm clouds rolled up on the horizon and in the meantime the storm has thundered itself out over the lake plateau. A crescent of moon is now shedding silvery light over the landscape. Silhouttes show up clearly everywhere, and it's almost as though one were looking at a film. Quite wonderful.

I lay awake until one o'clock. A second storm rolled up, and this time the rain extended from the lake plateau to us. It poured down by the bucketful, and the rain came into our tents, and nothing was left of the previous romanticism. Phil and I lay there and just cursed.

However, when I woke up this morning the sun was shining. It is something like the mountain slopes in Assam here: you get tropical rain at night, and in the morning the sky is clear again. But not even the most beautiful sunshine was sufficient to compensate us for the laborious difficulties of negotiating wet and slippery tree-trunks. I remember that at school I was one of the best on the horizontal bars; here I was definitely one of the worst.

After about an hour we reached the bed of the river Kiembe and tried to ford it by wading, but after trying for a long time it became clear that it was impossible. We had to build a bridge across, and that took up a good deal of time. The natives felled enormous trees and pushed them with great skill and experience over to the other side, where there were rocks in all shades of blue and green.

I was beginning to wonder whether we had already reached the quarry the Papuans call Ya-Li-Me, the source of their stone axes, but it didn't look much like a quarry: just rocks lying along the bank of a river. On the other hand, when I came to think of it, the Papuans had never said anything about a quarry; they had just talked about the source of the stone axes.

It was Ya-Li-Me after all, and we have reached the goal of our expedition at last. It is certainly a romantic place of almost indescribable fascination. If it is still possible anywhere on earth to feel the breath of the Stone Age it is here in this tropical, rocky valley through which a great river thunders wildly, pouring down its waters in great cascades on to the near-by lake plateau.

And now I watched Stone Age men without tools splitting the hard rock to get their stone axes. A scaffolding of twenty-foot-long poles was built up against a big green rock face, and stones were then laid out on a wooden platform to serve as a hearth. Wood was piled on to this hearth and set alight, whilst the men used grass turves to push the fire up as closely as possible against the slightly overhanging wall of rock. These naked savages clambering around like monkeys on their scaffolding were an improbable sight. When they had finally got the fire going to their satisfaction they lowered themselves to the ground and sat or stood around silently watching their primitive handiwork. Whenever it was necessary they would climb back on to the scaffolding to tend to their fire. Some of them used the time of waiting by attending to their matted hair and removing some of their lice. Others vigorously hammered cold stones to form the first axes.

For the time being I had forgotten the nuclear age I had left behind to come here and watch these savages enacting an incident from man's prehistory. I had forgotten the petrol-lighter and the Swiss timekeeper in my pocket, for such technical devices are just inconceivable here. I had returned not merely to the source of the stone axe, but to the source of mankind itself. Never in all my life have I felt myself so near to nature as I did here in Ya-Li-Me, the Source of the Stone Axes, surrounded by naked savages who, until quite recently anyway, knew nothing at all about our material progress, and were nevertheless quite content with their lot.

May 9

The fire burned all day, and was made up from time to time. Though the Danis kept warning us that at any moment now pieces of rock would start flying through the air, nothing in fact happened at all. After a while one of them decided to try a little magic, and he began to exhort the fire with tremendous fervour, obviously urging it to do what we were all waiting for. But perhaps he wasn't very good at magic, because nothing happened and there was no sound apart from the crackling of the fire.

A heavy downpour of rain now forced us to take shelter in a cave a little way up river, but from time to time the Danis ran back through the downpour to keep the fire going.

The fire was kept going throughout the night, but when I woke up in the morning nothing had happened, and the rock face was still uncracked.

In the meantime the Danis have sought out a different rock, carefully examining its structure and its veining. Apparently they were satisfied that this was a more suitable candidate, but unfortunately it was actually in the river with the water sweeping round it, which made the job of building the scaffolding much more difficult. However, they succeeded and soon a fire was burning there too, and the procedure started up all over again: the Danis waited, made up the fire, waited again, and so on, exactly the same as yesterday.

The rock with the water swirling round it naturally offers wonderful possibilities for filming, and I have decided to stay around here all day. As most of our porters are still patiently tending the other fire and hoping for the best there are only three men here with me. Incidentally, I lit this particular fire. One of the older Danis asked me to light it, saying that as I was now called Ya-Tuan, the Stone-Axe Gentleman, the spirits would certainly look favourably on any fire I lit. When I had done so the Dani put on a most mysterious air, and taking me by the hand, he produced a small, greasy bundle which he carefully unwrapped to reveal a small piece of rancid pork fat, or *wam*. This he stuck on the end of a stick and then went back with me to the fire. I then had to push the fat into the fire with the stick whilst he murmured magic incantations.

Shortly after midday what was left of my fire was thrown into the water, where it made a tremendous hissing and went out. The Danis now got to work, attacking the rock face with stones, wedges and bars and bit by bit they actually succeeded in splitting away pieces of the rock, which were then carried to safety by wooden tongs and worked on feverishly. The porters from the other fire had joined us now, having observed that we had had greater success.

Everyone sought to secure a piece of the precious rock, and the younger ones immediately began to work it into the shape of a knife. The bigger the piece that broke away the more delightedly they yelped. It was like an enthusiastic celebration.

Our rock is glaucophane of a wonderfully blue colour. The Danis call it *wang-kob-me*. The splinters which break away during the workings are as sharp as razors and there have already been a few cuts which Phil has had to bandage. But in the general excitement no one is worried by such "industrial accidents."

The great lentil-shaped stones are already being roughly hewn. The Dani children find this wonderful, and scramble for and squabble over the falling pieces in order to make themselves small knives and axes.

From all sides now there is a high metallic ringing, and it really sounds as though you are in a forge in which iron is being worked. You can tell from the high-pitched ring how hard this *wang-kob-me* must be.

A small gathering of lively wagtails watched us from the other side of the river, obviously wondering at the unusual noise in their usually so peaceful neighbourhood. Sometimes a cockatoo would shriek. And now and again a pigeon would pass over us with a slight whir of wings. The main background noise was, of course, the roaring and rushing of the river on its way down to the plain and the sea. Everywhere there were tropical flowers, and the sun shone almost all day. Small wonder that I felt as though I had been enchanted. This day in Ya-Li-Me will remain an unforgettable experience for me.

I realise that we are the first white men who have ever had a chance to glimpse this incident from the earliest history of mankind. At the same time we shall probably be the last, because it obviously won't be long now before the natives start breaking off this rock with modern tools, and the resulting stone axes will be sold to tourists as souvenirs. This is, in fact, already taking place in the Australian part of the island with the splendid Hagen stone axes.

This afternoon a number of Vano women came along with their menfolk bringing us sweet potatoes and sugar-cane. As a reward I gave them some of the much desired cowrie shells. There were a few women around yesterday, but they soon disappeared. Phil and I assume that the men drove them off. Perhaps here at one time the mysterious magic stones were quarried for the men's houses, and they are absolutely taboo for women, though in this respect a good deal has changed under the influence of the Missions. The men still don't let the women come close, but they don't mind their sitting a little distance off and watching. The women who arrived today looked strangely "lighter and cleaner" than those who were here yesterday. We discovered that the cause of this was the pork fat with which they had rubbed their skins.

The roar of the river has been in our ears for two days now and occasionally I feel as if I were deaf. Since yesterday, however, the high ringing tone of the rock has been added, and it is a sound that will stay with me for a long while.

I have had ample opportunity to study how the rock is hewn, and again and again I find it astonishing that the rough form of a stone axe is produced in such a relatively short time. Incidentally, this is all the Danis do here. The "final touch" is given to the axes after they have been taken back to the villages, and when they are finished they are so smooth and shiny that you can see your face in them as in a mirror. However, according to size, this final stage lasts anything from a few days to a few months.

The great number of new and interesting impressions here in Ya-Li-Me during the past couple of days has made me quite forget the trouble with my stiff knee. Sometimes I feel like a man who has discovered paradise. When I look out of the tent the first things I see close at hand are red and white begonias and in between are the glowing colours of stem orchids standing out magnificently against a background of hissing white spray from the tumbling stream.

Almost all the Danis are engaged all day long hewing stone at the river's edge. Only the two who carried our heavy rucksacks this far are still lying exhausted by the fire. Their heads are resting on a few rough-hewn stone axes. One of them has wound a length of spoilt film strip round his forehead. The Danis we have with us this time also have the habit of hanging things on to their persons or sticking them through the holes in their noses as ornaments. The length of film strip comes from my accident: the film in my camera got wet and was discarded as unusable.

Between the two resting men is a whole pile of chewed out sugar cane, and they are still chewing as they lie there. I think I'll take a few film shots.

144

Once again it has been impressed on me how much fire means to these primitive people. It not only warms the cold body and drives away the evil spirits, but it also helps them to split the hard stone they need for their knives and axes. It is thus obviously an element of magical power. When I went down to the *wang-kob-me* rocks once more early this morning the fire was already burning again. My early appearance made the Danis realise at once that I was gradually beginning to think of moving. They immediately began to behave like children interrupted in their favourite game when it's time for something else, and they protested vigorously. They are in their element here and inclined to forget everything else, including particularly the fact that by their own agreement they are my porters. They are crouched grimly around between the rocks hammering away with stones at their stone, working almost fanatically, silent and most unwilling to be disturbed. In the meantime, at least, they have discovered that the evil spirits that dragged me into the waterfall and almost put paid to me have got over their dislike and have now no objection so that I am obviously entitled to bear my new name of Ya-Tuan. But this makes it all the more difficult for them to understand how I could possibly want to leave Ya-Li-Me so soon. The fact is, however, that apart from anything else our rations are running short.

During the night I was awakened by loud rumbling thunder. I turned over on to the other side and hoped that the storm would soon pass over. But an hour later it still hadn't stopped so I crawled to the tent entrance to watch the enormous flashes of fanlike lightning you get in these parts. But to my surprise the sky above me was perfectly clear and I pursued my investigation further. I discovered that the rumbling was being caused by great masses of rubble which were being carried down to the valley by the rushing water. Satisfied that I had solved the mystery I went back to the tent and slept.

The time has come. It is almost twelve o'clock, and most of the porters are still crouching amongst the rocks and hammering away frenziedly, but, all the same, we must go now. But in the end the only solution was to start off with a few of the more reasonable ones

145

26. *The magic didn't work* (INSIDE)
27. *The beard came off as soon as I got back to civilisation*

and hope that the others would follow. Phil is going to stay behind, and he feels fairly confident that he will be able to persuade the rest to start off at some time today.

We are now resting in the native village of Ganik again. Our journey was made more difficult by the fact that the old Ya-Li-Me bridge had been swept away in the meantime. However, our porters immediately set to and built another and better one. On the other side the inhabitants of the Vano village where we had stayed the first time on our way to Ya-Li-Me were already waiting for us. Shouting happily they plunged into the water and thereby gave me an opportunity of filming a bathing scene for which any producer of a nature film would have given his eye-teeth: unposed pictures from the early days of man: brown, naked bodies leaping around in the sun, the water running off their muscles like glass beads. Their faces are radiant with childlike pleasure, and the noise they are making almost outdoes the roar of the near-by waterfalls. You would hardly believe that this old world of our could still offer such a picture.

Phil did soon come up with the main body of porters, but he told me he had to threaten to shoot them before he could get them to start. And there are still a few missing. I wonder whether we shall ever see them again.

After another half an hour or so we reached Ganik. It was oppressively hot, and our porters' leader made it dramatically clear to us with gestures of his almost fingerless brown hands that rain was on the way and that we could expect a storm. The only way to protect ourselves from it, he insisted was to stay in the village overnight. The porters had arranged all this amongst themselves beforehand, of course, but there was nothing for us to do but agree.

Towards evening I took a long walk. In the twilight at the end of the day the lake plateau lay before me in a pearly haze, calm, untouched, and without a sign of the threatened storm.

When I returned I had a look at the huts of these mountain Papuans. Unlike all the other native villages, we have been in, some of these huts are four cornered. You go into the round huts up two inclined ramps beneath which the pigs have their entrance hole. Some of the huts don't offer much in the way of comfort. They have

146

only the one room, which is divided in the middle by a partition: on the one side sleep the natives, on the other their pigs.

The particular feature of this village is that a thick bundle of grass, something like a horse's tail, is fixed to the highest spot on all the roofs.

In the meantime I have realised that we are in a *cul-de-sac* here. There is no path leading on in any direction. The lake plateau lies ahead of us, of course, but there is no more opening in that direction than there is to the Toli Valley. The only way to get at it is to go back to Kyira Valley and make eastwards from there. The Bokoyan tribe is said to live there, and Phil wants to visit them anyway, so he'll have to go on with me at least to Kyira Valley. There are pretty terrible tales current about these Bokoyans, and they are also said to possess reddish-yellow metal axes. Is it possible that we shall be able to go back to the Bronze Age too?

May 11

I have to get my bearings gradually. We are on the way again. We spent four days and nights in the legendary Ya-Li-Me Valley, and I am not exaggerating when I say that what we experienced there was as deeply impressive as anything throughout all my voyages and expeditions. Nothing in that valley—the tropical fauna, the tumultuous river, the rare and suddenly appearing birds—has any connection with civilisation as we know it, does not even remotely suggest it. And in particular the sight of those naked men and boys, from the youngest to the eldest, all ecstatically concentrated on their hammering, gave us a perfect picture of the Stone Age. With triumphant shouts of "Wa-wa-wa!" they pounced on each stone that broke away and worked with grim persistence until they had given it the rough form of an axe.

And with what matter-of-course friendliness the Vanos sent us food every day. Their women, always freshly rubbed all over with pork fat, brought it regularly to us from the village. In our honour the men had decked themselves out with coloured feathers. Phil and I frequently felt like interlopers, but the natural friendliness of the Danis and the Vanos helped us again and again to overcome such feelings. All this and the fact that we were the first, and would in all

147

probability be the last, white men to visit this world untouched by time and progress, contributed to our elation.

Again and again our porters did their utmost to delay our departure from the village, and to some extent their tricks were successful. One of them complained of having trouble with his feet, another was quite certain that the spirits were not on our side at the moment and that it would therefore be better to delay our start. Once we did get them going we had to press on in forced marches in order to make up for lost time.

And now since midday we have been sitting in a cave our mountain Papuans call Tu-Vo-Vit. When we arrived it began to rain as usual, quite heavily, in fact, and this was a welcome excuse for our porters to insist that we should bivouac here. After they had assured us eagerly that we should be able to get to the Kyira from here tomorrow Phil and I finally allowed ourselves to be persuaded. My original intention had been to press on to the Tutni cave, which is much higher up and about three hours farther on, so that we should have had those three hours to spare tomorrow, but I find that I have to reconcile myself again and again to the fact that these natives are the real leaders of the expedition. They just weren't willing to go on any farther, and you can't do much with resentful porters.

Shortly before we got to Tu-Vo-Vit they came across two cockatoos and asked Phil to kill them. I could see that he wasn't very keen on the idea, but he compromised by shooting one of the birds. He missed the second one, and I am sure he missed intentionally, though he denied it. The dead cockatoo was an enormous bird with splendid yellow and white feathers. I felt sorry for it, but the Danis were beside themselves with delight. First of all they plucked the bird and shared the feathers, and then they drew it and cut it up. The youngsters got the meat. On the whole they are very well looked after and always get the best pieces.

I have had to describe so many new experiences and impressions that I can't remember whether I have already said that some of the porters had their sons with them—quite young fellows, almost children still. The idea is to make them into good warriors, so from very early on they have to learn to endure hardships.

The Danis are still hammering away industriously at the stones they have brought with them from Ya-Li-Me, and it is a picture that never fails to fascinate me: these primeval men in a cave hammering away at stone axes just as our own forefathers did in their caves ten, twenty and thirty thousand years ago. There are cockatoo feathers in their hair, and around their necks and arms are bands of plaited liana. You sit there watching them and after a while you find yourself wondering why you're wearing boots, trousers and a shirt, and how it comes that you own a pocket-knife, a lighter and a Leica. Incidentally, these primitive natives have developed an extraordinary manual agility in plaiting bands from the liana that so often blocked our passage to Ya-Li-Me. They plait them straight on to arm or neck so that the ornaments are in place for good.

Some of these mountain Papuans wear their hair half long, but without any attempt to give themselves any particular hair style, though it is in any case so bristly and curly that it would hardly be possible to do anything with it. However they wear hair nets just like their long-haired brothers of the valleys, whose hair would come down over their shoulders if they released the dirty, greasy net. It's certainly neither an aesthetic nor a beautiful sight when, as they occasionally do, they lift the whole matted bundle a little and scratch away like mad at their scalps. You just have to remind yourself that they have lived in this way for many thousands of years. Sometimes they will drum away furiously with their fists on their craniums, apparently to persuade the verminous inhabitants of their hair to give them a little peace. When they have finished they roll up their hair again, tuck it under the greasy net, and just sit there happily as though nothing had happened.

Another of their habits I find it just as difficult to get used to is the way they grind their teeth. They will often sit there quietly watching your every movement, and the whole time they will be grinding their teeth.

Apart from one or two things like this I have got quite used to them and their ways, and I think they have got used to us too, though maybe they don't like some of our habits either. The way they express their sympathy is sometimes quite touching: for example, when I slip. As soon as it happens a groan goes up with one accord and they all look like children who are about to burst into tears.

They have an ejaculation which must mean something like "Sorry!" and this they use almost as though it were their fault that I slipped. The ejaculation is always used when a leech, a *mu-li*, fastens itself on and begins to suck blood. And, if they observe one of those dreadful stinging flies that are so common here, one of them will spring forward and flap the great insect away. When everything is all right again they drum on their penis-sheaths with their fingernails in delight and break out into a joyful "Wa-wa-wa!"

On the way here I have had to fight a losing battle with leeches. Whenever I put out my hand for support against a rock I always had to look at it at once for leeches in the hope of being able to remove them before they got a chance of sucking themselves full. They really are a truly terrible pest. I had to keep looking at my legs too, but nevertheless, as soon as we stopped I would always find a few of the loathsome creatures ensconced between shoe and sock and sucking away at my blood. In the hope of being free of their attention whilst asleep at least we would clear away the undergrowth in a circle around us.

Leeches like darkness and gloom, and it is still a mystery how they manage to live when they can't suck blood. And how do they manage to find their unfortunate victim, man, with such extraordinary celerity? Do they hear him, smell him, or sense his vibrations? It would really be a good thing if our biologists and physiologists would have a systematic go at finding answers to these and similar questions. It is said that leeches increase in numbers when they can find blood, but until we arrived these leeches—and there was no shortage of them—lived in this jungle solitude without ever having known man. There aren't many animals here either, so how does the leech get on without blood? We don't even know how they reproduce their loathsome species.

To see them move at all is a revolting sight, but it's still worse to see them wriggle when you try to wrench them out of your flesh. What's more, if they are present in large numbers they can be dangerous too. I remember a British officer telling me about two men of his Gurkha company who got lost in the Assam jungle. Their bodies were found two days later—with every drop of blood sucked away by leeches.

Our Danis are already asleep, and Phil and I are lying tired and exhausted in our tent. At least my wounds have been cleaned and dressed. The rain is pelting down monotonously on the canvas of our tent. Before long I, too, shall be asleep.

We got moving quite early this morning, and after a brisk march we reached the pass at about midday. It was the "eyrie" where we had spent the night on our way here the first time, and the stream still gushed tumultously into the valley. We had a short rest and then we set off again, reaching the village of Ilrolam by late afternoon as expected, and wet through with sweat. The last of our porters arrived a couple of hours later. Two of our Danis had, it appeared stayed behind at the pass. The pace seems to have been to hot for them. One of them called Igane comes from Bokondini, and I have noticed him more than once. Whenever we come to a village where they don't know him he immediately starts to deliver long and boastful speeches. But as soon as the pace is stepped up on the way he begins to flag and fall behind.

I rather feared yesterday that our mountain Papuans would be unwilling to go on today, and so it has turned out. They are always full of excuses, of course—particularly if we happen to be making a halt in a village which they don't want to leave. This time it was because we must wait for the two missing men to turn up. When they dig their toes in like this we usually have to give way, and we did so this time again, but we sent off a runner to Mulia to tell them to get a message through to Wamena for us to say we shall be a few days late.

The evening before last the wireless broadcast a long report about our expedition to Ya-Li-Me, the "Source of the Stone Axes." Phil and I lay in our tent and listened to it on our transistor. At the same time we learnt that we are expected back in Wamena after our return from Ya-Li-Me, and that the Geological Institute proposes to pay for the cost of flying in ten Muju porters for our subsequent Baliem expedition. The Dutch geologist van der Wegen is to come with us, and a police-boat will be waiting for us on the Catalina River to take us back. This was naturally all very good news.

Owing to the frequent delays my schedule is now getting a bit tight, and I have already more or less made up my mind, though with great regret, that I shall have to forego the visit I had promised myself to the Dalai Lama on the way back.

Yesterday the "chief" of our porters once again allowed me to witness some more of his "magic." We were crossing one of the many wild forest streams. On the other side we had to negotiate a sheer rock face fifteen feet high. Liana served us as rope and bamboo as poles. Before we crossed the stream the "chief" hurried up to me excitedly and importantly and invited me to touch his stone axe, during which he muttered a mysterious incantation, which, naturally, I did not understand. Then he told me that his incantation and my touch as Ya-Tuan, the Stone-Axe Gentleman, would help us. It wasn't quite clear just how it was going to help us, but never mind. I take it that his axe is a sort of amulet as well, and that he was using the opportunity of our crossing to lend it new magical properties. Our "sorcerer" is already quite an old man by Dani standards—no less than forty-five. Owing to constant grinding his teeth are no more than stumps now.

Almost every Dani has scars on hips, knees and shoulders, usually caused by burns. It took me some time to find out what lay behind it: at nights, because it is so cold, they get as close to the fire as they possibly can, with the result that sparks, and even pieces of burning wood fall on to their bodies and cause burns which heal only very slowly. An abnormality which is quite common amongst Danis is projecting hip-bones. Two of our own Danis suffer in this way. I take it that it comes from some sort of dislocation. Another of our Danis has burnt off all his fingers, and has only thumbs, but on the back of his hands new finger stumps have grown complete with fingernails.

Amongst the Vanos we came across several cases of Cascado sickness, which is quite widespread in these parts. A twelve-year-old boy in Kyira was obviously suffering from leprosy. It was recognisable at once from his moon-shaped face and corroded legs, though it might possibly have been framboesia, or yaws. One way or the other, there is a useful field of operations amongst the mountain Papuans for our

European doctors. The Mission Stations are doing what they can, but they cannot manage it alone. We saw one or two cases in which they had cured natives of yaws, but some of the cured patients no longer had noses, just two holes.

May 14

Phil and I separated today. He is going to try to make his way through the valley from the Kyira to Toli, and from there he will go back to Tiom. It cost us a good deal of time because we had to find new porters for him, and by the time we had recruited them it was almost midday. Then we said good-bye. I didn't find this parting easy. After all, we have been together for weeks on end, we have climbed previously unclimbed mountains, we have toiled our way through the jungle, and we have sweated, frozen, cursed and laughed together. And throughout Phil Temple was always a fine and reliable companion. But there you are, the time for parting always comes sooner or later.

My first day without Phil is now behind me. It wasn't an easy one. For one thing I had my first really serious clash with my porters. But let me put the incidents down as they occurred. First of all we went again across the narrow bridge over that sinister valley, and after an hour we had reached the village on the other side. All the Danis were crouched together in a hut and showed no signs of moving. It soon became clear to me that they intended to do what they had already done on the outward journey—spend a lazy, carefree day in the village. I had put up with it then but I wasn't prepared to put up with it now. I just lost my patience and temper and I bawled them out so violently that I was surprised at my own thunder. The Danis weren't used to that sort of thing from me, and they were a trifle intimidated by my bawling. But only to the extent of finding excuses. First of all they tried to persuade me that they had too much to carry, and in order to help out they had thought of a truly splendid plan: they would stay here for a while and eat some of the food, which they then wouldn't have to carry. When I refused to be persuaded by this wonderful scheme they explained that they had to carry too many stones for me. That wasn't true either, because for myself I had

153

chosen four loads and two nets of stone axes only. I now had the whole baggage opened up and the rough-hewn stone axes laid upon the ground. Each porter now had to contribute a stone axe from his own collection. Nevertheless about three times as many rough-hewn axes were left over as I had reserved for myself. The cunning knaves had simply taken far more for their own use. Of course, with these extra stone axes they were overloaded because in addition each man had five red pandanus fruit, each of which weighed between eighteen and twenty pounds. And on top of all this there was spinach and sweet potatoes. When I saw the situation I told them that they would have to leave their own stone axes behind and go back for them later. At this they fell silent and played deaf. They just refused to listen to anything more I had to say. Finally I turned all the cockatoo feathers they had given me for safe keeping out of my camera-case, packed my rations in a rucksack and set off on my own. That did the trick. As soon as their leader saw that I was serious and had no intention of giving way this time, he came running after me to assure me that they would come along too. I knew that they were as incalculable as young puppies, but I was certainly relieved when they caved in. And at the same time they showed me again what they could do when they set their minds on it. Despite the pouring rain they set a pace which even gave me some trouble to keep up with, and by five o'clock we had reached a cave we knew from the way here.

I am now lying in it on my belly writing up this diary. It is an ideal camping site protected by an overhanging rock. Below us the river is thundering downwards in great cascades, a kind of wet hell. Once again the roaring water fills me with respect for its enormous force. You can't see where the waterfall ends; it just plunges down between wet, green walls. In the growing dusk it is an eerily impressive sight.

In the meantime my Danis have recovered their good spirits, and they are now busily engaged preparing a big evening meal. Two are digging out the inevitable cooking hole, and others are in the cave preparing pandanus fruit. With a bone knife—a steel knife isn't strong enough and the Danis reject it with contempt—they cut into the fruit lengthwise and then drive in a wedge until it splits. Inside is a whitish yellowish pith which is scraped out with a piece of tin. After that they divide the two halves lengthwise once more and then put the pieces into the cooking hole. Our meal has been gently braising between the hot stones together with green bananas and sweet potatoes for over an hour now.

Supper is over. Almost every time I get to know a new method of preparation. This time the oily mass inside the pandanus kernels was kneaded with water. A little of my salt—a great delicacy—for the Danis—is then added, and in a very short space of time the whole meal has disappeared. At the moment two of the Danis are engaged in filling up the cooking hole, and when they have finished I shall make myself a warm place for the night on it.

May 15

Our bivouac cave was ideal. There were hardly any drips from the roof and I slept wonderfully. Now I'm lying here awake and refreshed with time to enter a few more items about Ya-Li-Me, "the Source of the Stone Axes."

The methods the mountain Papuans use to break away the rock and work the stone up into their axes is more or less the same technique that was used in later Palaeolithic times—say between ten and thirty thousand years ago—by our own forebears. Although they have learnt to grind their stones, the rest of their way of living is even older. For example, even now they don't have any form of vessel apart from perhaps a scraped out fruit or a hollowed tree-trunk. Metal and its working is altogether unknown, and so even is pottery.

They make their choppers and axes in two different ways. They take either a piece of wood as a haft or a branch splayed at one end and angled like a crutch. This angled end is hollowed out so that it will take a correspondingly worked stone to about half its depth. The hole is previously lined with some soft material like plant pith. The idea of this is that a blow should cause the stone to give a little and prevent the wood from splitting. With the other kind of axe the haft is straight and at the conical big end it is pierced through horizontally. The stone, which has been worked into the shape of an axe, is thrust into this hole. Stone chisels are used to work the hafts.

In our part of the world silex stones were generally used for making axes. Silex is a generic name for stone that breaks into layers

155

when struck and thus lends itself more easily to the desired shape. But the mountain Papuans haven't such stone at their disposal. They break and split crystalline and granular mountain stone that naturally breaks in certain definite directions. In my collection, which led to trouble with the porters yesterday, there are green and blue stones, most of them are lentil-shaped and already roughly hewn, but there are also asymmetrical forms, and these are used primarily as blades for axes with angled, crutchlike hafts.

Incidentally, carefully polished stone axes are never used for working purposes; they are employed as means of payment, like the pigs, chiefly for wife purchase, and they remain in the family.

In the meantime my Danis have got themselves ready to move off, and so it will be evening before I can get at my diary again. We are going to try to reach a village for the night.

As I have already mentioned, on the way from Ya-Li-Me to the Yamo, the leeches were a terrible plague, and today was particularly bad. I waged an endless struggle against the treacherous little creatures. Often they let themselves fall from trees as you pass beneath, and fix themselves to neck, hands and feet. Whilst we were resting one of the porters removed one from my forehead which I hadn't even noticed.

Whilst we were resting at another spot I discovered a brown snake about three feet long and as thick as my thumb nesting in a crevice on the overhang behind us. One of the Danis followed my glance, spotted the snake and began to drum away in alarm on his penis-sheath. When the news got round there was tremendous excitement, but the snake was either too lazy or too peaceful; it just stayed where it was without moving.

My outburst of anger yesterday continues to have its effect. At seven o'clock in the morning when I was still lying on my belly making entries in my diary my Danis were already prepared to move off. The whole way, upwards as well, they did faster than many a descent. They simply flitted along the waterfalls, performed like monkeys on the tree-stumps, and didn't utter a word of complaint. They were also prepared to put up with a much shorter midday rest than usual, and so it wasn't long before we reached the waterfall which was the scene of my dangerous tumble seven weeks before. I

156

had another look at that rushing, spraying mass of water and could only shake my head. At least I had survived.

After a march that took nearly ten hours we came once more to the village at the bottom of the valley, and here I am lying on a sprung bark floor in a native hut together with the Danis, an indefinite number of mice, and innumerable ordinary cockroaches. I don't know whether I would succeed in going to sleep here in ordinary circumstances, but after ten hours' heavy going the body demands its rest and isn't too particular about the circumstances.

May 16

We are in Mulia once more! In the worst of the midday heat we had to ascend something like three thousand feet, and then at last the small collection of ugly corrugated roofs lay below us.

I found a mountain of letters waiting for me in the tent I had left behind. My Leica has also arrived; unfortunately without film.

The prospects of being flown out to Bokondini are no better than our original prospects of being flown here from Hollandia. I am therefore resigning myself to a long wait. I have bought vegetables and borrowed a lamp from the missionaries in order to be able to read my correspondence and write up my diary at night.

The long wait doesn't suit me at all, of course, but as there is nothing I can do about it I will at least use the time to record one or two observations concerning the life of the mountain Papuans. For one thing, as far as housing is concerned there is strict segregation between the sexes, and the women are strictly forbidden even to enter the men's houses. A mysterious magic aura is supposed to surround these houses, and it refuses all entrance to females. I am told that there is no known case where this taboo has been ignored. As a result, family life is lived, and sexual relations take place, always in the open air, usually in the fields. Incidentally, it seems doubtful whether the Danis realise the connection between sexual intercourse, which they regard merely as the satisfaction of their physical desires, and pregnancy. I certainly heard no word at any time to suggest that they did.

157

Their marital and family relationships are based on a very different ethic to ours: if the man whom a woman allows to have sexual intercourse with her happens to be of the same clan as herself then according to the rules of tribal cohabitation this is enough to make her his wife.

PART THREE

Baliem Gorge

LIFE's like that. You can hardly contain your feverish impatience that something should happen, and it just doesn't happen. But you possess your soul in patience, as I made up my mind to do yesterday in Mulia, and then things go far more quickly than you had dared to hope. Yesterday I was lying in my tent between the native huts of Mulia and trying to work out—without much success—when I should be in Wamena and able to start my preparations for the third part of my expedition, the exploration of Baliem Gorge, and today I am already in Wamena, sitting in a real room, with a real bed behind me, and my diary lying open on a real table. And I'm well washed and well shaved, and I'm wearing a clean shirt. The Stone Age has given me short-term leave to return to civilisation, and I must say it's very pleasant.

The area around Wamena is the only flat land in the central mountain area of the island. But it won't be long before I shall be leaving here for the mountains again, first to the south-east into Baliem Gorge, then to the south-west and the south coast, where there are still cannibals, and where the Indonesians have tried several times to land parachute troops, but not very successfully.

But let's go back to yesterday. Quite unexpectedly the Mission pilot Dave Steiger turned up and to my great delight he asked me whether I could be ready to fly in an hour's time. I could indeed! Whilst Steiger was making his regular flight to Bokondini and back I got my things together, including my tent, at lightning speed. Amongst other things I had no less than forty or so stone axes from Ya-Li-Me in my baggage. The vegetables I bought yesterday in Mulia, thinking that I would have to stay there some time, and a quantity of other things I now no longer needed, I gave to my porters as a parting gift. By the time Steiger touched down again I was ready.

161

29. The Stone Age is a reality here

I got into the plane with my baggage, and my porters were lined up on each side of the runway to see me off. Their dark, broad-nosed faces looked sad. But the parting was not so easy for me either. The natives don't wave good-bye, they don't shed tears, they don't utter any regretful words—in fact they don't seem to have any way of deliberately expressing emotion of such a kind. But if you have lived with them as long as I did then you learn to read the expressions on their faces.

Steiger took off: a final circle over Mulia, and then we set course for the watershed of the Yamo and Toli rivers. It wasn't long before we landed in Bokondini, which is as clean and neat as a new pin. How different from Mulia, and how much more agreeable! The houses with their neat thatched roofs looked almost cultivated by comparison with the corrugated iron roofs and the aluminium huts of Mulia.

I changed planes and was flown to Baliem Valley, a magnificent and orderly neighbourhood clearly showing the influence of the Mission Stations and the Dutch Administration. The villages are much more spaciously planned, and all around there are tilled fields with watercourses between them, which is typical of the whole Baliem area. My pilot circled and then we touched down safely in Wamena.

May 18

It was not only a great pleasure but also an urgent necessity to be able to wash properly again. It was no less agreeable to be able to sleep in a good, clean bed. It is only here that I have really noticed how many festering places I have on my body to be cleansed, treated and healed. Thank goodness I started taking antibiotics several days ago. They are now beginning to have their effect, and the swelling in the glands has been much reduced.

May 19

It is Saturday. I am staying in the government hotel Pasangrahan. It's a fine sounding name, but unfortunately that's about all there is to it. We should call it a tin hut at home. The outside walls and the

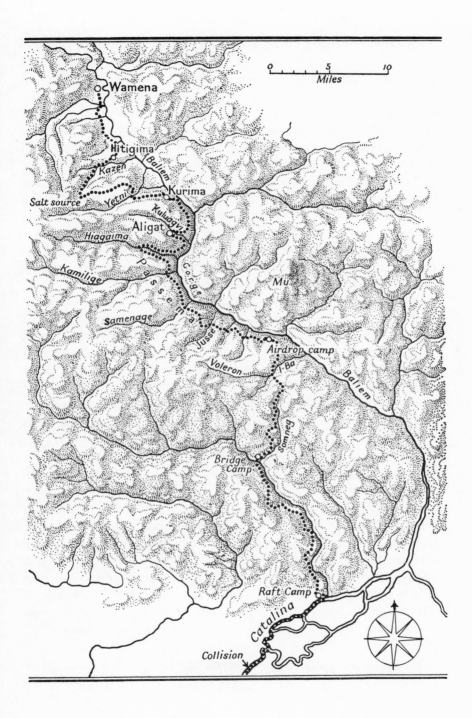

roofs are of corrugated iron, and it looks dreadful. And the concrete flooring and the precast interior walls don't improve matters in the least, rather the contrary. In addition there is a disturbing background of some noise or other day and night. During the day the hot sun causes the tin roof to expand to the accompaniment of clanking reports; and at night when the temperature drops you get the same thing in reverse as the metal cools off. An altogether different kind of noise is provided by the scurrying and squeaking of myriads of rats and mice—it's either a love joust or a sports meeting. At irregular but frequent intervals they race in pairs over the floors and along or between the walls. They are obviously enjoying themselves hugely, which is more than I can say for myself.

About an hour ago there was a heavy downpour of rain, and the din it made on the tin roof was so terrific that any normal conversation would have been rendered altogether impossible.

A bath is not one of the pleasures available here. There is a shower and a W.C. outside the house, and the equipment looks all right, but there is no water. There's also a washbasin in my room with a nicely polished tap, but again there's no water, and it doesn't look as though there ever was or will be. But these minor privations don't upset me—at least I'm dry, and my room has a balcony. And if there's no water where it ought to be, at least there's beer—cool, clear foaming beer. The food never varies, but, after all, that helps you to get used to it. I'm even beginning to feel at home—after all, this is the third time I've been here. Each time I found there was a new housekeeper, but the ideas of each on the subject of food were exactly the same.

However, I have my room, a table, a chair and time to write up my diary. On the whole when I compare my situation during the past few months, in a tent or in a dripping wet cave, then I have every reason to be satisfied.

The people here in Wamena are particularly friendly to me. Not only are they prepared to see about the remainder of my baggage, which is still in Ilaga, but as an extra sign of their willingness to help they have presented me with a new pair of stout boots. I have already worn out four pairs.

My favourite occupation is studying the stone axes I collected in the Ilaga and Mulia areas, the old ones that I bargained with the mountain Papuans for, and which could, if they had tongues, tell of family histories going back over many generations, and those freshly quarried axes I brought back with me from Ya-Li-Me. During the next few days I propose to list them and pack them up ready for transport to Europe.

My first talks with the few Europeans who live here in Wamena were almost exclusively about my finds in Ya-Li-Me. In this way I discovered that there is no quarry in Ormu, the well-known stone-axe source on the north coast of the island, and that the stones from which the axes are made there are simply taken from the river bed, or just found on the ground in the neighbourhood. Such "found" stones are already more or less the shape of axes. According to the natives there are other sources of stone axes up in the mountains, but they find it easier to get what they need from the Ormu neighbourhood. At one time each chief had, so to speak, the prospecting rights over a certain area, but in the meantime this has become a mere tradition without much meaning, particularly as in the already largely civilised coastal areas stone axes are rarely used as supplementary bridal payments nowadays. And, of course, in these areas the natives obtain some of their tools from the Europeans, and these tools are naturally of metal.

In areas where the stone axe is still used as a bridal payment a reasonably good one is valued at between fifty and two hundred florins. If a particularly rich native peasant marries then he is expected to pay up to a thousand florins for the axe which he symbolically gives in payment for his bride. But such an axe is then, of course, bigger and more carefully polished and altogether an outstanding example of its kind. To be able to afford such a splendid axe as bridal purchase price is a matter of prestige.

Old stone axes are important possessions in Ormu too, particularly in questions of inheritance. They are carefully and mysteriously kept under the pile houses until they are required. But although it is highly interesting for me to learn what I can in retrospect about these stone axes, it is still more important for me at the moment to find out as much as I can about Baliem Gorge and the route I shall have to take there. During the first couple of days that I was in Wamena

I learned quite a number of new and interesting details. One of the things I was told illustrates once again the great difference of outlook between us and the Papuans. It appears that right at the entrance to the Gorge there is a 130-foot-high rock face which falls away vertically into a raging torrent beneath. This, it appears, was a favourite suicide spot for women newly widowed, the Papuan version of the widow's immolation. I have already mentioned that a Dani marriage can hardly be compared with marriage as we know it. All that is necessary for a couple to be regarded as married according to mountain Papuan tribal custom is that a man and woman who indulge in sexual intercourse should belong to the same clan. Where men of substance and power are concerned there may well be quite a number of such "wives"; and in the old days when a prominent man, say, a chief, died, quite a number of his "widows" might spring from this rock into the rushing torrent beneath. Not only this, but sometimes they would even drag their children with them, as many as three at a time. The very youngest would usually be sleeping peacefully in the net in which Papuan women carry their belongings on their backs.

The paramount chief of the area around the entrance to Baliem Gorge is reputed to be particularly rich and powerful, which means that he will have anything up to a couple of hundred "wives." Tribal warfare is very frequent in these parts, and about a week ago there was a new outbreak. Mountain tribes were apparently revenging themselves for a defeat suffered at the hands of the valley tribes a couple of years previously. The same thing now happened in reverse: the mountain tribes surged down into the valley and took a bloody revenge for their previous defeat. At such times they know no mercy, and the same men who can be as playful and good-tempered as bear cubs turn into bloodthirsty, brutal and fierce warriors once they are on the war-path. Their weapons are no less cruel than their behaviour. For example, their arrows are made with two-way barbs so that once they have penetrated into flesh they can neither be pushed through nor withdrawn without tearing the flesh and causing terrible injuries. The vengeful warriors from the mountains of Baliem Gorge killed the paramount chief of the valley tribes, raped his women, and burned down his villages, a total of several hundred

166

huts. They then retired in triumph to their own villages in the mountains. Next year, or the year after, or perhaps in three, five or even eight years' time, the long-memoried valley tribes will organise a similar punitive expedition into the mountains, and, if they are successful, they will take a similarly brutal and bloody vengeance. One thing they certainly won't do is forget.

The Dutch District Officer of the combined Baliem and Bokondini districts immediately sent a Papuan police detachment under a young Dutch police officer to restore order. But the age-old spirit of vengeance was too strong to be subdued, and the raiding mountain tribes refused to allow themselves to be pacified before their work was done, and they even attacked the police, who were then compelled to open fire.

Such revenge raids always take place in the night when the victims are fast asleep in their huts, protected only by boards across the entrance. They sleep like logs, as I more than once had good reason to discover. Even a great deal of noise won't wake them. No raiding party therefore has to be particularly circumspect when attacking a sleeping village.

The Dutch authorities do their best to prevent the natives accumulating weapons, and their problem is in principle much the same as that of the various disarmament conferences in our more civilised part of the world, if on a smaller scale. Spears are regarded as permissible for purposes of defence but not for attack. If a police inspection reveals the presence of, say, five hundred spears in a Dani village then three hundred of them will be confiscated. And if a native is found with a spear far away from his own settlement the spear is immediately destroyed.

This afternoon I paid a visit to the police inspector of Wamena in his office. The local police lock-up consists of a couple of Dani huts surrounded with barbed wire. The prisoners incarcerated there at the moment are all murderers, and they are led off to work chained together, three at a time. The conditions under which they are held are terrible by European standards, but, in fact, the difference between the conditions under which a Dani is ordinarily housed and the conditions in these police lock-ups is no greater than that between an ordinary European dwelling and a prison cell, if as great. In the store-room of the police station I saw piles of confiscated spears, each eighteen to twenty feet in length—unlike the light arrows these weapons are deadly.

Dusk has fallen. All my leg sores have got worse and developed into typical tropical ulcers. I shall obviously have to get expert medical treatment; so far I have been attending to them myself, bathing them carefully, smearing them with ointment and keeping them covered up.

I can't help thinking how worthwhile it would be if someone could be found to finance a well-equipped archaeological expedition here, to investigate, for example, the mutual relationship between the Stone and the Bronze Ages, because, as I have already mentioned, there are persistent reports that some natives are in possession of bronze axes.

When I returned from my visit to the police station I met my Baliem Gorge partner, the Dutch geologist Gerard van der Wegen. He is in the middle thirties, not very powerfully built, but wiry, and probably tough. He has certainly had a good deal of practical experience on this island. We got together to discuss the plan of campaign for our journey into Baliem Gorge. Both he and his assistant, who was with us, felt it would be a good thing if we arranged for provision by plane half-way along the route. We'll discuss this in detail later after we've had a chance of talking to the pilot. Van der Wegen produced air photographs showing fields of sweet potatoes growing about eight or ten days' march away. According to these photographs the route goes from Baliem River over a pass and then through an uninhabited area into an inhabited area again.

May 20

This morning the local doctor returned from a professional visit to Vollo Valley, where tribal warfare has been raging. He told us that about a hundred villages had been burnt down, and that something like two or three thousand natives had been involved in the fighting. A good deal of damage has been done to the sweet-potato fields it appears, with the result that there is famine and sickness amongst the natives who got the worst of it, and to survive at all they have had to submit to a neighbouring tribe if they are to get food until they can put their own fields in order again. The question of taking revenge on the attackers is already being discussed, it seems. It is assumed that a certain powerful chief, who refuses either to be guided by the missionaries or to submit to the authorities, is behind it all. A great number of such raids is already put down to his account.

There is a tendency to compare these tribal conflicts with the Sicilian blood feud, the vendetta, but the comparison is not very accurate. Although Dani tribal warfare is a very cruel and brutal thing, it can always be peaceably settled by the payment of pigs to redeem the blood guilt, though this has to take place solemnly and publicly. The confession of guilt has to be manifest, and also the repentance.

More police stations from which permanent patrols could scour the countryside are necessary if these tribal wars are to be prevented. And in particular those tribes and clans which have been converted to Christianity and have destroyed their amulets and their weapons are in urgent need of protection at the hands of those who have so per-suaded them, since, naturally, natives in the adjoining areas who are not so minded and are not under the control of the authorities, are always inclined to find pretexts to attack such of their neighbours as have rendered themselves defenceless. Such a case occurred only a little while ago—also at the entrance to Baliem Gorge—and many peaceable Danis lost their lives in consequence, which can hardly be encouraging to the others.

May 21

Monday. We're to start on Wednesday, and the expedition baggage, including medicaments, is beginning to pile up on the floor of my room. But I have to interrupt my preparations frequently to attend to my leg sores. The tropical climate is proving a greater hindrance to the process of healing than I imagined. What would in the ordinary way have been just harmless thorn scratches, are more like gouges, and hardly visible spots where leeches have sucked are like pits in the flesh.

The rain has been beating down on Wamena for hours now, but I've got used to the sound and I hardly notice it any more. Our project is beginning to take on tangible shape, and thanks in parti- cular to the help of the Geological Institute my idea is becoming a reality: a proper expedition. The Coastal District Officer has agreed to fetch us out of the wilderness in a motor-boat after three weeks— provided, of course, that the threatened invasion by the Indonesians doesn't completely upset the apple-cart. In that eventuality he has promised to let us know by wireless what has happened in our absence.

My Baliem Gorge companion, Gerard van der Wegen, doesn't want to go with me to the south coast. His idea is to explore the Baliem Gorge and then return to Wamena. All I can do is to tell him that as far as I'm concerned he will be able to please himself in the matter, and be at liberty to turn back whenever he wants to. For my part I am still quite determined to pass right through Baliem Gorge and come out on the south coast. Sailing tackle is part of my baggage on this expedition, and if an invasion should take place I want to be able to sail across the Arafura Sea to Australia.

I sorted and packed all day long. In all probability I shall not return to Wamena from this expedition. When I have completed my project my intention is to fly back from Merauke on the south coast direct to Hollandia on the north coast, from where I started, crossing the whole of New Guinea. It was only when I started my sorting and packing that I realised how many odds and ends I had accumulated.

I am waiting for the regular plane from Hollandia now because I need films. The atmosphere during the past twenty-four hours has been a bit feverish, what with the packing, the differences of opinion concerning the likely difficulties to be met with on an unknown route, and the continuing uncertainty of the political situation. I shall be glad to get on the move again and have other things to bother about.

I'm really in very good fettle now that the third and last part of my expedition into the Stone Age is about to begin. Thanks to expert treatment by Dr Smit here my sores are also much better and my glands are no longer swollen. The injuries I suffered during my tumble have left me with a certain amount of trouble with my knee and my shoulder, but I'm getting used to it and I don't let it stop me. With the aid of a stout stick I'll manage all right.

It's agreeable to know that it's pretty certain that there'll be a boat to pick us up on the south coast when we get there. Gerard van der Wegen is still pessimistic, but together with my unlimited confidence that makes a good mixture for such an expedition. This evening I propose to distribute my final parting gifts. The policemen from Bokondini who were with me on the Carstensz expedition will get the watertight watches they were promised.

May 23

Gerard van der Wegen went off at ten o'clock this morning with our porters, ten Mujus. I remained in Wamena until just after midday and then I started off too. We have arranged that van der Wegen shall wait for me with the porters at the last Mission Station before the entrance to the gorge.

Shortly before I left, when I was at Dr Smit's for his concluding treatment for my sores, a native of about forty came in supported by his son. His hand was bleeding, and it appeared that he had cut off two of his fingers that morning because his wife had been stolen in the night. I think I have already mentioned that this demonstration of sorrow is quite common amongst the mountain Papuans of New Guinea. Later on I saw father and son sitting on the police inspector's doorstep. They want to persuade him to send police after the thief to secure the wife's return.

After the few rest days I quickly got into the swing again and found myself making good progress. The way was fairly level and went alternately between tall wild sugar-cane and casuarina groves. There was no mud this time, and my progress was about the same as one would expect to make on a tour in the Alps.

The two Papuans who are with me are native teachers of religion, so-called "gurus" from the north coast. Their job is to convert the natives of Baliem Gorge to Christianity.

Gerard speaks good Malay, and as some of our Mujus understand

171

Malay he has taken charge of the porters. We have equipped them with a light blanket, a pullover and a pair of shorts each, so that they all look fairly respectable. Apart from the question of appearance in that sense it is also very necessary that they should obviously belong to us because we shall be making contact with tribes who are in an excitable state on account of the warlike activities which have been going on, and they might well immediately attack, and perhaps even kill, native strangers if they were naked. Our porters already have Christian names like Johan and Antony, but their leader is just addressed as Mandur, which is the Malay word for leader.

May 24

Today I saw a natural source of salt for the first time here and I was able to see how Papuan women get their salt.

But let's take things in order: I hadn't slept very much, and I was awake before sunrise. Gradually the stars paled as dawn broke. Gerard was up early too, and I think curiosity concerning what lies ahead of us is affecting him as much as it is me.

We set off striding vigorously up a broad valley named Kazen. There are many tilled fields and a great number of particularly fine coniferous trees. I have also been told that there is a valuable source of salt in the neighbourhood. After we had gone for about an hour, the local Dani who is with us pointed out a rather dirty watercourse divided up into pools by stones. The actual source lay about a hundred yards farther on. It was romantically situated in a narrow clearing surrounded by pandanus palms and banana trees. The natives had dammed the source with stones and built fifteen small basins in descending terraces. There was a good deal of activity going on when we arrived. About a dozen women were standing in the water working away at pieces of dried banana-tree bark to make sponges to hold the salt. They were vigorously kneading, biting and pummelling the bark to make it as porous as possible so that it would soak up the water. I also noticed that they were using other kinds of vegetable matter in the same way.

At the source of the Stone Axes it was the men who did the work whilst the women sat around and looked on. But here it was the men who sat together away from the work in progress, warming themselves at a cheerfully burning fire. We noticed, however, that they did not let their wives out of their sight for one moment. We were approaching the area of tribal warfare here, and an unexpected attack could therefore take place at any moment. The men who sat there quietly enjoying the sight of their womenfolk hard at work had their weapons with them for instant use if necessary. In the meantime they looked with approval as each new batch of bark was soaked in the saline water and then laid out on the rocks to dry. When it is dry the bark is burned, and the result is a porous, cellular, pumicelike salty stone dust which the Papuans chew with obvious pleasure. It tastes of salt and has a smoky smell.

Like the quarrying of stone, this salt production is a real undertaking for the Danis. It is always done in groups. The women do the work, and the men are there to defend them if need be during the days they spend at the salt source.

Incidentally, this salt source belongs to the local chief, who behaves like any mediaeval landowner with a sinecure: anyone who wishes to take salt from the water must pay dues for it. In kind, of course: pigs or sweet potatoes, stone axes or other weapons. It is all grist to his mill. On payment of these dues, the person concerned has the right to take away as much as he can carry in a net—that is to say, as much as she can carry; the men carry nothing except their weapons, and they must be able to use them at a moment's notice.

Going on our way we came to a large tributary of the Baliem called Yetni. It has a huge bed and its waters rush along powerfully over it. The Danis told us that in rainy weather it becomes quite impassable, but we were lucky with the weather and we were able to cross it without a great deal of trouble. However, as the water came up to our waists we took the precaution of holding hands and crossing in a chain, which gave us greater confidence.

Because of its great width and the difficulty of crossing it the Yetni forms a powerful natural tribal frontier. Of course the tribes living along it and separated by it are deadly enemies. Indeed, it is the general rule, confirmed now and again by exceptions, that tribes whose territories adjoin live on bad terms with each other. Conversely tribes are usually on good terms with tribes living in perhaps the

173

next valley but one, whose territory does not adjoin theirs, and they will exchange wives and trade with goods and cowrie shells.

Two of the natives who were at the salt source happened to want to go to Passema Valley, which is on our way, so they took advantage of the opportunity to join us. In this way they can hope to pass safely through hostile tribal territory, something they would never have dared do alone.

The Yetni divides the Hitigima and Kurima valleys, and we have now reached Kurima and halted.

Last spring there was bloody warfare between the inhabitants of these two valleys. One of the tribes had embraced Christianity and burned their amulets, bows and arrows and spears. As soon as the neighbouring heathen tribe learned of this it attacked, and a great number of unarmed Christian Danis were killed. After this unfortunate affair the manning of the police station in Kurima Valley was increased to six Papuan policemen from the coast. So far they have managed to keep the peace, but whether they will be able to do so indefinitely is another matter.

Kurima lies on a broad terrace about 160 feet above the wild Baliem River, and it is the last outpost of civilisation. Shortly before we came to the police station we rested on the suicide rock previously mentioned.

In order to get to the villages on the other side of the river we had to cross a very long suspension bridge of plaited liana which swings in an elegant arc over the 180-foot-wide river. The porters told us how such a bridge is built. The first length of liana is shot across from one side of the river to the other attached to an arrow. Once this first line is over thicker ropes of liana and rattan can be hauled across and the bridge built.

Despite this bridge—or because of it perhaps—the crossing was an adventurous business, because the platform over which you have to cross does not begin and end at ground level since otherwise the middle of the bridge would be submerged, so first of all you have to climb up a high scaffolding before you can get to the swaying bridge at all. Its first half now sweeps down steeply to the middle of the river, after which the second half sweeps up just as steeply to the other side. In addition, the catwalk itself is not level, and as you cross you have to be very adroit indeed to compensate for the often quite violent swaying under your feet.

Shortly before Hitigima the Baliem River passes through rapids, and as far as we have been able to see, its gradient is fairly uniform. Every few yards downstream big rocks jut out of the water, and the swift current forms great whirlpools around them. The water is yellowish brown and quite warm.

I was particularly impressed in this area by the skilful way the Danis make their fields. There are tilled fields as far as you can see, often rising steeply up the hillsides and going over the brow into the next valley. And the only tool the Danis have to do all this with is a long piece of wood in the form of a spade. In fact this primitive digging instrument is both spade and plough for them. Nevertheless, although they are built with such primitive means, these Dani terraces remind me of the steep vineyards in our more civilised alpine valleys at home.

Some of the villages here are quite large, and they are built just like those we encountered in the Wamena plain. For daytime use there is a long rectangular hut where the cooking is done and the pigs are kept. The huts of the men and women, which are round in shape, are quite separate from this daytime hut.

Tomorrow will be an important day for us: the first couple of hours will take us over known paths, but after that we shall be in virgin country into which no white man has ever previously penetrated.

May 26

Yesterday I didn't get a chance of noting down anything in my diary. We were on our feet all day long, making our way along the Baliem all the time. Once again it was raining in torrents and by the time we reached Aligat in the Kuluagvi valley that evening we were wet to the skin. On our arrival we were immediately surrounded by a great crowd of natives, and secretly I was hoping that we would be able to recruit a few porters from amongst these fellows to supplement our Mujus, but when I crawled out of my tent this morning there wasn't a sign of an inhabitant to be seen anywhere. As far as eye could see there wasn't a single Baliem Dani in sight; the houses were empty and the fields were deserted. It was like a strange dream, I might have been in some deserted valley of the moon.

We were disappointed, but there was nothing to be done about it and we started off with our Mujus. They had no easy job today. For nine hours we followed the course of the Baliem along difficult tracks. Up and down we went and there was often hardly a path to be seen. When the jungle undergrowth ceased the rocks started. Finally a narrow pass in the Baliem Gorge forced us to climb for hours in a side valley. By the time we got to Hiagaima Valley, tired and exhausted, it was beginning to grow dark. Our two native preachers have a hut here so we will make a halt. We are at least two and a half miles from the Baliem. There is a liana bridge here spanning one of its wild tributaries. Coming from Kurima the two native preachers reached this place over a mountain ridge in a few hours, whereas we took two days for our route along the Baliem. But at least we know what the gorge is like there.

Thanks to the constant up and down and the many twistings of the valley we have marched something like ten miles over very difficult terrain, but as the crow flies the distance is only about a quarter of that.

However, when we got into the Hiagaima Valley something particularly agreeable happened: twenty natives immediately volunteered to help us and carried our loads to our camping site.

Tomorrow we are going to enter Baliem Gorge again from the other side of the valley.

Like all the mountain Papuans I have met so far, the men of this neighbourhood wear no clothing at all—unless you can call their penis-sheaths clothing. The women wear a short loincloth woven of pandanus strips. It is interesting to discover that this valley tribe intermarries with the natives of Ilaga and understands the dialect spoken there.

May 27

Porterage difficulties all day! It's always the same: when we come to a village a horde of natives surrounds us only too anxious to carry our loads, but as soon as we leave the immediate neighbourhood of their village they abandon their loads and go back without a word.

Our progress over narrow, slippery paths was unusually difficult. We went along the slope all the time, negotiating one steep spur after the other, and once, deep down below, we saw a bridge spanning the torrential Baliem. We had only four supplementary porters for the last stage of the way and we made only slow progress. Finally we found a place to bivouac on an isolated ridge.

We find ourselves repeatedly faced with a strange mixture of heathen traditions and the first influence of the Christian missions amongst these natives. The mountain Papuans often retain their old magic stones, but they don't really believe in them any more. In some villages the natives have burned their amulets or thrown them into the river; in others they still retain them but are quite willing to sell them. I was therefore able to buy a bridal thong and a family axe for a little salt and some cowrie shells. With Christianity comes civilisation and its achievements: a piece of sheet iron here, some glass beads there, and perhaps even a steel knife. There are villages which still live wholly in the Stone Age, whilst neighbouring villages are already in a transitional period. But one thing is common to them all, and that is their method of clothing themselves: in the case of the men it is a complete absence of clothing except for the penis-sheaths, whilst all the women wear loincloths woven of plant fibres.

I made an interesting observation yesterday: I had often noticed that in addition to their stone knives the Papuans often have bamboo ones. The blade is made of split bamboo, and it is quite incredibly sharp. Amongst other things such bamboo knives are used to sever the umbilical cord on the birth of a child.

May 28

The day began with a disappointment: when I lined up the porters to start off in the morning I discovered that overnight another fellow had made off. The two natives who wanted to go from the salt source to Passema have long disappeared.

The first part of our day's march would have taken us up steeply into open terrain of limestone but we should have to climb. As climbing was quite out of the question for our Mujus we chose a much more laborious way through thick jungle. When I say it was more laborious, I mean it was more laborious for me—our porters clambered like young apes over the masses of knotted and gnarled roots and tree-trunks that caused me so much trouble. From rising ground we now saw for the first time what I knew from native descriptions to be the Passema area. We stopped for a rest on a particularly high spur, and the natives told me that during tribal hostilities it is used for making smoke-signals. The place is called Le-u.

After our rest our way went downwards again through a forest of oaks which was wet and dank from so much rain, and infested with leeches. In the afternoon we reached the valley of the Moki. Owing to the constant fighting between the natives the tracks are seldom used and difficult to see, and the going was therefore difficult. Here and there along the Baliem the track had been swept away altogether by landslides, and we therefore had some difficulty in finding our way at all. The water of the Moki, which we had to ford, was fairly clean, and we used the opportunity to bathe and wash out our wounds.

Throughout the day we haven't come across a single village, but I'm not too sorry about that, because at the moment we are in an area where tribal fighting is taking place, and in such circumstances you never know how the excited and nervous natives will receive you. However, late in the afternoon we realised that our presence had been discovered and that eyes were watching us from the cover of the jungle. Our natives from Hiagaima began to tremble with fear, and when finally the natives of Passema rushed on us with wild shouts we could hardly keep our own men together. To our great relief we realised that "the reception committee" was unarmed. With joyful shouts of "Wa-wa-wa!" they now escorted us to their village.

The first thing we did was to pitch our tent near their primitive huts, which were surrounded by sugar-cane. It took us some time to recover from our ten-hour march. Although these natives are very friendly, the situation is by no means altogether satisfactory. For example we can get no answer to our repeated question as to who is chief here, and one or two men ornamented with boars' tusks and cowrie shells have suddenly disappeared. It also took a great deal of bargaining and urging before we could finally persuade them to let us have a few sweet potatoes.

Our fears were not confirmed and the night passed peacefully. All the same, I was not sorry when we left the village the next morning. This was at eight o'clock, and our way went first through sugar-cane groves, and then steeply upwards along the course of a mountain stream. After about an hour and a half the broad Passema valley lay before us. But we still had to go through several side valleys. Signal fires were burning on the ridges in between, and this gave us a disagreeable feeling since we already knew that such fires were used by the mountain Papuans to communicate with each other in times of tribal warfare. In one of the first villages we came to we discovered a further sign of how dangerous the situation was at the moment. There was a hut which had been built, we were told, by a native preacher who had turned up here about a fortnight ago. But the very next day the right-hand man of the chief told him that it would be better for his own security if he left the valley at once and came again some other time. That doesn't sound too good.

From village to village our caravan increased in size, and by the afternoon there were several hundred in all. A native, a representative of the big chiefs, was in the lead, of course.

At about four o'clock in the afternoon when we were once again in the neighbourhood of a village, we found, to our great surprise, Vahasuma, one of the two most important chiefs of the neighbourhood, sitting with six of his guards on a rock and waiting for us. He greeted us with a twisted smile that would have looked false at once a mile downwind. Our Danis from Hiagaima kept themselves nervously in the rear and breathed an audible sigh of relief when the chief and his companions shook hands with us. After this greeting we continued our way to the village together.

We were allowed to pitch our two tents on an open space in front of a particularly fine men's house. We were still engaged in this task when the other powerful chief, also accompanied by his guards, approached us. Proud, and conscious of his strength and power, he made a fine if somewhat alarming sight, and it was very easy to credit him with the cruelties usually perpetrated during tribal hostilities. He was unusually tall for a native, a six-footer, and he towered above our little Danis. His torso was smeared with ochre, but apart from this he was like Vahasuma, naked and without any ornamental feathers. Neither of them needed anything of the kind to underline their importance, their mere appearance was quite enough to convince the beholder of their power and significance. The name of this second chief is Bota, and as soon as either he or Vahasuma opens his mouth all the others falls respectively silent and prick their ears in order not to lose a single word of what they have to say. Officially Vahasuma has four wives and Bota three, but obviously each has a number of pretty young girls as concubines in addition.

Nothing is more difficult in the whole Baliem area than to catch a glimpse of the women. For days we have not caught sight of a single one. Only when I told Bota that I was anxious to give the womenfolk gifts of glass beads was I allowed under his escort to approach the neighbourhood of the women's house.

Today we found only overgrown and hardly recognisable paths— a sure sign that danger is around in the Passema neighbourhood and that the country is in a state of war. This impression is also confirmed by the sight of weapons lying ready for immediate use in all the villages through which we pass. Spears hang from the eaves of the huts, and there are whole bundles of arrows ready on the walls of the men's houses.

Only the children are untouched by the war fever. They run around between the huts waving the equivalent of our "windmills," or they sit quietly against the walls of the huts weaving patterns with plant fibres, colourful ornaments which remind me of Tibetan spirit catchers.

Only late in the evening did I learn that our tents are pitched on land belonging to Chief Bota and quite near the men's house. I had to conduct laborious negotiations with him in order to get anything to eat, and unfortunately I was unable to use my Dani vocabulary because they speak a different dialect here, and only the words for pig and tobacco—*yam* and *tavo*—are the same. First of all I was shown a very small animal for which the chief demanded a steel axe I refused to agree to this very bad bargain. Only over an hour later were two larger pigs brought up and for each I had to pay a steel axe and a handful of cowrie shells.

The atmosphere appears to be reasonably friendly after all, and once again my procedure with doubtful tribes has proved valuable: to arrive preferably late in the afternoon, to distribute presents at once, and—if it is at all possible—to organise a display of strength to impress the natives. It is also important to disappear from the neighbourhood of the village as early as possible the next morning before the natives notice how weak you are compared to them. Once you're over the next mountain ridge and outside the tribal area you won't be pursued. And in the next valley the same game can start up all over again. However, I must confess that I really and truly had agoraphobia for the first time in the village of the two chiefs Vahasuma and Bota, and I was very glad to get out of it.

However, my feelings did not prevent me, now that we could call two good-sized pigs our own, from letting our Danis prepare a roast pork banquet according to their traditions. One or two men held the unfortunate brutes upside down by their hind legs and an archer shot them both dead from a distance of about ten feet. To my relief he was a much better shot and he hit each pig in the heart with only two arrows so that they died at once without preliminary torments.

As our porters were opening up the first of the pigs to gut it villagers suddenly ran up excitedly and declared that the pig must not be eaten. They gave us no reason for their change of mind concerning our roast pork; they just put down one of the axes and half the cowrie shells at our feet. We were completely at a loss, and at first we assumed that the pig was a sow and had piglets and that we were to pay for these in addition. But when I asked whether this was the case they just shook their heads and said nothing. By this time I was beginning to feel a bit uncomfortable. Perhaps without realising it we had done something wrong. But after a disconcerting while other villagers ran up and assured us that everything was now in order and that we could eat our *vam* in peace. Very likely they had consulted a witch-doctor in the meantime and paid him something to switch off the evil spell. Whatever the reason, it was a great relief for all of us and we heaved a sigh. You have to be very careful indeed not to do anything which offends against their ritual habits and customs. As the Papuans are not prepared to talk about such matters it isn't easy to get to know anything about them. However, they live

181

according to them, and with obstinate fanaticism they expect every stranger to respect them. Our situation is made more difficult by the fact that the dialect spoken in Passema is quite different from that spoken by our porters.

Despite the streaming rain we braised our now exorcised pig in the usual cooking hole, but this time without vegetables. As the damp wood had not succeeded in getting the stones sufficiently hot the pork, though juicy, was not quite done to a turn, but at least this time the liver was not hard, and Gerard and I ate it. It was a real delicacy.

May 30

It rained so heavily the whole night through that before long my air mattress was like a life-raft in a deep puddle. I got up in the night and dug a sketchy trench round the tent to draw away at least the worst of the inundation. Obviously we are already far enough along the south face of the Wilhelmina Top range for the tropical south-east monsoon, whose violence is well known, to begin to make itself felt.

The subsequent day was just as exciting as the night. At first things were so depressing that I had the feeling that nothing but driving my stick—a four-foot-long snapped-off spear—into their naked behinds could persuade our native porters to get a move on. But at least the evening made up for all our difficulties.

But let's go back to the morning. Whilst the packing was going on there were about a hundred men crouched motionlessly in their traditional attitude, their arms raised together so that they can entwine the fingers of their hands behind their necks. This is the position they adopt mornings and evenings against the cold. There they all sat watching us, and not one of them said a word. Only when we began to dismantle our tents was there any movement. First of all the two chiefs got up and went off, and then the others followed their example and disappeared one after the other, going in all directions until no one at all was left. But four ancients, as old as the hills, sat as though turned to stone in Bota's hut. One or two youths climbed up quietly and hid themselves in the attic, so to speak. Stout rushes are laid across the round walls of the huts where the conical roofs crown the huts and create this intermediate space between the outer walls and the pointed roof. A tree with notches makes a sort of ladder leading up to this "attic," and there the young natives hid themselves. Only if you poked your head cautiously into the men's house and listened could you hear the soft crackling of the attic floor under their weight.

Neither Gerard nor I felt very happy about the situation. The absence of all the men, the deathly silence, the spears and bows and arrows on the walls of the huts, all created an eerie atmosphere. The Christian missions had not yet succeeded in getting a foothold here. Everywhere there were various kinds of amulets: bird of paradise feathers, pigs' tails and pigs' testicles—those which had once depended from our two pigs were hanging there with them.

We were now reduced to our few Muju porters again. Because there was a lot to carry for so few Gerard ordered them to open up their private bundles to make sure that they were not carrying unnecessary ballast, and it turned out to be a very good idea: before our eyes grew a heap of all sorts of odds and ends: mirrors, pomade— even their old and ragged pieces of clothing were being carted around. We made them throw all this useless ballast away and put on the clothes we had provided them with. It was absolutely necessary for us to discard every unnecessary ounce of weight. There was too much at stake to take chances. This inspection of our porters' kit took up a good deal of time, and it might easily have brought us into still greater danger. During this last half-hour before our departure we saw villagers popping up like shadows from behind the stone walls which surrounded the settlement and disappearing just as eerily. And as though removed by ghostly hands, bows, bundles of arrows, and spears also disappeared. What was in the wind was not difficult to guess.

Our two Hiagaima natives stood a little to one side, and one of them explained to me by signs and throaty ejaculations that they were in a bad way. He explained that he and his companion hadn't had any of the pork the evening before. I can only suppose that the others had just scoffed their share. When we looked for the two as we were about to set off they were nowhere to be seen. I just don't know what happened to them. It may well be that that which they had most feared the whole time they were in the territory of a different tribe had come upon them at last. Perhaps they were killed by the local natives. In any case, there was nothing more I could do for them, and it was high time that we got out ourselves—the hostile atmosphere we could feel around us was unquestionably growing.

I shouldered my heavy rucksack—it weighed fifty-five pounds. I had arranged with Gerard that our Muju porters should make two journeys today: one with me through the next side valley to a village we could already see, and the other with Gerard, who would wait in the meantime with the rest of our baggage for their return. But the porters themselves vehemently opposed this arrangement. They preferred to carry overweight rather than make their way back again on their own. Like our two vanished Hiagaima Papuans, they felt themselves to be undesirable strangers who necessarily had to fear for their lives, and this settled it.

On the way to the next village we noticed again and again that from a safe distance its inhabitants were indicating by signs which way we should go.

We were certainly moving in a mysterious world. What were they up to? Did they want to help us, or decoy us into an ambush? And who was really afraid of whom? It was a source of very real consolation to me to notice that in these parts the Papuans still regarded white men as powerful sorcerers, and our clothing as giving complete immunity from spears and arrows. A very good thing indeed, because otherwise not much thought would be necessary to realise who was really the stronger. If the natives were to attack us their numerical superiority would leave us very little chance. What particularly disturbed us was that the instructions these new natives were giving us were often contradictory so that it was difficult to guess which path was to entice us to our doom. In this situation I recalled my experience with Tibetan robbers in northern Changthang: take no one's advice, just follow your instincts.

By the early afternoon we had obviously left the area directly threatened by tribal warfare behind us. When we came to the edge of a gorge and slowly began to make our way down the slope a few boys popped up from behind bushes and trees, reinforced soon afterwards by men. They followed us for a while without showing any

184

signs of hostility, and before long they started carrying for us to earn themselves a few cowrie shells.

We came to the river Samanage and crossed it over a fairly solid liana bridge. Although I was not now carrying my rucksack I was sweating profusely, and as we clambered up the forty-degree slope on the other side I suffered a good deal of pain in my game knee. To make matters worse, in crossing the bridge I had now injured the other leg. It plunged down between two boles and the rough gnarled wood scraped the skin off my shin.

Gerard and I were pressing forward now, and apart from the Mujus we had with us there were different porters at every village we came to. Not that we minded this very much, the main thing was that we should be able to get porters at all.

We were rapidly approaching the Passema border now. One more valley without bridges, one last village, and then, as at Ilaga, our way went upwards over moss-covered forest terrain and mud for hours on end. And as time passed so our caravan diminished. The strange porters were continually abandoning their loads which then had to be distributed amongst those who were left. I had been carrying my heavy rucksack again for some time.

By the time we finally left the Passema area we were only quite a small group. Funerary poles connected with each other by strands of liana indicated that many Papuans had lost their lives here in tribal warfare and blood feuds. The few natives from Passema who were still with us were getting more and more restive and were obviously on the point of leaving us. Once again the only thing to do was to demonstrate our magic to them. We picked out a fairly dry tree-trunk, and having loaded our only rifle Gerard fired two bullets into it. The wood split away in all directions flying through the air with an eerie sound. This performance created a tremendous impression. At first our Papuans fled in all directions and disappeared into the jungle thickets. They were so panic-stricken that despite their agility some of them barked their shins. After a while they cautiously reappeared and examined the split tree-trunk, joyfully tapping their penis-sheaths at this demonstration of our powerful magic. But only seven of them were left to accompany us on the hour and a half descent into Jessu valley and the first village.

185

At a distance we heard the villagers shouting "*Nabrava! Nabrava!*" which is the usual shout of welcome amongst the Papuans, but their voices sounded a trifle anxious, and for this reason their shouts did not inspire us with any particular optimism. We had already heard the shout too often in the Passema villages through which we had passed, an area in which something like two thousand natives live in fourteen different settlements. It hadn't meant much then and we weren't particularly impressed by it now. But at least there was one good thing here: there weren't many huts, which meant that we should not be faced with any great numerical superiority which might prove dangerous.

A little more tranquil in mind we retired to sleep. The river Baliem is quite close and it seems to me that we have managed to circumvent the rocky spur above the river, which is impassable, by going through the Passema area. It has taken us three days, but as the crow flies we have covered only a few miles. In fact the total result of our laborious progress during the past week amounts to no more than five or six miles in a direct line.

May 31

We are now only four degrees south of the equator, which means that day and night are more or less equal throughout the year. Dawn is shortly before six every morning, and after that daylight grows rapidly.

It was like that this morning too. The first sounds we heard were, as usual, children and pigs. Soon we could hear men prowling around our tent, but whether their intentions were good or evil it was impossible to tell. As a matter of fact it was sheer curiosity that had driven them out so early.

I had become increasingly convinced that the male Dani is a lazy fellow who is quite content to sit around and watch the women work, but after a while I began to realise that this applied only to the minor tasks of everyday life, and that when there was any really heavy work to be done, such as clearing an area of virgin forest, the men got down to it with astonishing vigour and energy. It was they who laid out the terraces on the steep slopes, but once that was done it was up

186

to the women to do the sowing and reaping. That the women should till the fields follows from the belief of so many primitive tribes which regard the woman as the mother and the vessel of fertility, and therefore the fruitfulness of the fields, the sowing and the harvesting are left to women. However, whilst the women are working there are always armed men in the neighbourhood. Whether the women are digging up sweet potatoes or carrying home the harvest in their nets there are always alert men with their bows and arrows and their spears not far away ready to repel any attack. Women are their most precious possession, and the kidnapping of other people's women is a popular sport.

In half an hour at the outside we shall be moving off. The villagers have once again shown themselves from their best side and provided us liberally with sweet potatoes.

At seven o'clock in the morning, as arranged in Wamena, we listened on our transistor in the hope of picking up a message to tell us whether we may expect a food drop tomorrow. But for the first time we were unable to get any station at all.

I must pack up my things now, the porters are ready to move off.

June 1

Yesterday was a record day—despite the fact that just before we started out all our supplementary porters just deserted us. And I had promised the Passema natives a steel knife each, too! So I shouldered my own rucksack and we set off. But we hadn't gone much more than a hundred yards or so before a group of young natives turned up, so I was able to get rid of my rucksack again, and our gallant Mujus were relieved of their burdens and were able to rest a little.

Once again we marched up hill and down dale, and valley followed valley. We also caught sight of the Baliem River again. It had been hidden from us for three days by the spur of rock I mentioned. On the other side of the valley we could see the striking shape of Mu all the time now, and it had impressed us for days. A simply magnificent waterfall hurtled down from its northern face into Baliem Gorge. As you can see the rising spray with the unaided eye for miles I reckoned that the cataract must be at least between six

187

and seven hundred feet high. The sight of it reminded me of young Michael Rockefeller, who always said he would like to discover a really great waterfall, and so I named it Rockefeller Falls.

According to the map we have done about three miles today. This may not sound much, but in this broken country it is an all-time record because it means that we must have gone about twelve miles. We came across very few villages and they all made an impression of great poverty.

We kept on for almost nine hours without much rest. At about five o'clock we reached a village whose situation looked favourable to us for a food drop. Much less agreeable, and in fact quite disturbing, was the circumstance that in all the twenty-two huts there wasn't a soul except two very old men who looked at us with unconcealed mistrust. Overnight there was no sign of the other inhabitants of the village either.

Today the plane should come to drop provisions and letters for us. Perhaps the sight will entice back the inhabitants of the village. Whilst I am writing these diary notes we are listening for messages between Hollandia and Wamena. As we have no transmitter we have to rely on what we can hear from Hollandia. Merauke on the south coast comes in. From there we want to learn whether the boat which is to pick us up has left Agats yet.

The steep gradients of the Baliem River end here and the cataract spreads out into a uniform and slow-moving stream dotted with islands and mounds of rubble brought down by its tributaries and extending out into the stream.

After our successful day yesterday Gerard is no longer so pessimistic as he was at the beginning of our Baliem expedition, and he no longer talks about any early return to Wamena. Our plan is now to go on into the next valley and find out whether we should continue to follow the course of the Baliem or go over a pass to the south to join a tributary. One of the two old Papuans we have met here assures us that in three days from now we can be at the river Moppa. It flows into the river Baliem and its banks are inhabited.

Gerard tells me that on the basis of air photographs the geologists have decided that Baliem Gorge belongs to the Palaeozoic Age and have entered it up on their maps accordingly. But in his view this is not correct, because yesterday he came across red sedimentary rock. Now such stone could possibly belong to a much later period, but the more likely thing is that it belongs to the early Mesozoic age.

Shortly after eight o'clock this morning our transistor started to crackle, and we heard a voice saying: "Hallo! Hallo! Calling the Harrer expedition. A provisions drop will take place between nine and ten o'clock. Please light a clearly distinguishable smoke fire."

Immediately we spread out a strip of yellow stuff we had brought with us from Europe so that it would serve as a marker, then we lit a fire and made it up with damp wood and foliage so that it gave off dense smoke which rose vertically into the air in a thick column. Leaving one Muju behind to keep the fire going we got the others busy cutting down the six-foot-high sugar-cane at the spot chosen for the drop.

I took my camera and clambered up the slope at the edge of the village. By the time I got to the top it was already ten o'clock, but there was nothing to be seen. I was already beginning to fear that the plane had run into bad weather between Hollandia and Wamena, when there was the sound of a plane engine from the great Baliem valley. The weather was ideal, and small cumulus clouds were drifting over the limestone peak to the north. A slight mist was developing way down in the valley, but where we were the weather was perfect.

I could hear the plane but at first I couldn't see it, and then I spotted it far below over the Baliem River. Like a small yellow toy it approached the rocky spur lying to the south of us, which meant that it had already passed us. Then the pilot must have spotted our smoke column, and the plane turned, rose quickly over the mountain ridge and flew direct to our camp site. It described a couple of test circles then its nose sank and it lost height. A moment later we saw the first two loads falling through the air. A third load fell. The plane circled again, and two more loads fell.

Everything had worked splendidly; only one of the five loads had missed the dropping field we had prepared, and after about a quarter of an hour's intensive search we found it amidst the sugar-cane. Unfortunately there was no correspondence apart from one letter from Dr Valk in which he informed us that the political situation

189

had improved a little: the Dutch and the Indonesians had agreed to continue negotiations. For us this meant that a boat would pretty certainly be waiting for us on the south coast.

It is shortly before eleven now and in a few minutes we shall be ready to leave, but there is still very little sign of the inhabitants of the village, though one or two clay-smeared bandy-legged men are standing around and looking at us mistrustfully. But we can hear rustling under the roofs of the men's houses, and we know that other men are hiding there, so that our hope of recruiting a few extra porters for at least a short part of the way is not likely to be fulfilled. In any case, these villagers are so poor that the men are literally too weak to carry loads. At least the hundredweight of rice which has just been dropped for us will tide us over our immediate food worries, but our porters just can't carry the baggage in one, there are so few of them, and they will have to make two journeys. Gerard set off with the Mujus to the pass on the next mountain ridge whilst I stayed behind with six loads.

I now passed four anxious hours. No sooner had Gerard and the porters left the village than movement started up around me, almost silent and certainly eerie. Almost surreptitiously and with their shoulders hunched the men flitted from hut to hut, obviously consulting each other. Gerard had taken our only rifle with him and there I sat, quite unarmed, amidst these noiselessly flitting figures, and, frankly, I felt scared. It wasn't any sudden fear, but a slow and paralysing anxiety that crept up on me. As a precautionary measure I stood with my back against a hut wall on which spears and arrows hung. There I stood and waited for something to happen without knowing quite what.

I could feel many pairs of eyes watching me closely from the bushes and between the cracks of the hut walls, and to show the natives at least that I knew very well what they were for I almost casually drew out a spear here and an arrow there. Slowly the hours passed, and in the meantime my nerves remained taut because I dared not ignore any movement around me, since any one could mean danger for me, perhaps death. I breathed a sigh of relief at the end of four hours when the porters returned. Our Mujus are Papuans too, but for me they are friends whose arrival means the end of my dangerous loneliness. But, of course, even they didn't feel too happy about the situation, and later they told us that they would never again make a journey on their own and without our protection such as the one they had made from the pass back to the village.

It is evening. After negotiating a four-hundred-yard path descending steeply through wet jungle and mossy forest we came to a clearing in which there were two empty huts. A small stream ran through the centre of the clearing and on the other side Gerard had already pitched a tent. It was an isolated and very beautiful spot and our Mujus enjoyed it as much as we did. At last we had nothing more to fear from hostile villagers, but even here in this loneliness I noticed that our porters did not dare to take a few sweet potatoes. This is not the first time I have had occasion to observe what a strongly developed feeling for private property they have. When they are at war with each other they plunder and pillage, but in peacetime they would not steal a fruit, not even if they could do so with impunity.

But back again to the unfriendly village in which we spent the previous night. Unfortunately we could take only the contents of the dropped sacks with us because we had to cut down our loads to the last ounce to spare our porters. Therefore although we could have used the sacks quite well we had to leave them behind in the village. Hurriedly we packed the rest of our things together and were very glad to shake the dust of this obviously hostile settlement from our feet. But I have an idea that the villagers felt much the same way when they finally saw the backs of us. They were probably every bit as much afraid of us as we were of them. In fact we weren't more than a few hundred yards away from the village when their "house arrest" was raised and men, women, children and pigs poured out of the huts making a tremendous amount of noise. From a distance I saw them pounce with delight on the jute sacks we had had to leave behind and a few pounds of rice we had been unable to carry.

I think they must have thought we were plenty big magicians, because we had more baggage when we left than when we arrived, and we had still left some things behind, things they had never seen in their lives before.

For our part we were glad to get away without trouble and with a whole skin—but I shouldn't like to have to go back the same way again; not for all the tea in China. To go forward is the only thing for us now.

When we reached the pass Gerard took over the porters once more to do the next stage with them. I remained behind and guarded the loads they were unable to take with them. I used the hours of waiting to collect rhododendron flowers and to photograph carnivorous plants. Whilst so engaged I noticed a small black snake making towards me with what looked like aggressive intentions, and so there was nothing else for me to do but kill it, though I didn't care to do so. But after all, the snake might have been poisonous.

After four hours the porters came back at last to fetch the remaining loads. They cast anxious looks in the direction of the hostile village and then made off very quickly.

June 2

Today we found a friendly village to bivouac in, but most of the villagers are sick. They are suffering from yaws, malaria, cascado, and some of them probably from consumption.

Although our porters had nothing more to fear, they have been anxious all the way. They were very unwilling to do a journey twice, particularly alone—they would sooner carry weight till they dropped. Gerard and I were in agreement about it so we strapped on our heavy rucksacks, and we all staggered forward over a hardly distinguishable path. Only when we got quite close to the village in which we are now resting did it take on any clearly recognisable form.

Once again we were met by deathlike stillness, and Gerard and I were already wondering whether we should have to reckon with hostility again, or whether perhaps the villagers hadn't spotted us yet, when we suddenly heard the familiar sound of "*Nabrava! Nabrava!*"—the shout of greetings that promised a friendly reception but at the same time expressed a certain anxiety.

When we came nearer to the villagers we could see why they were scared. The men who slowly and shyly came out of their huts looked more miserable and more poverty-stricken than any we had seen

192

30. Orchid fibres and a bone needle

in the villages we had previously passed through. One glance was enough to see the ravages of yaws.

We found it very easy to come to terms with these villagers, because they were only too glad that we had not come as enemies. For an axe we received a pig and before long at least two hundred-weight of pork meat was braising in the usual cooking hole. Apparently the "bush telegraph" had got to work at once to announce our arrival, because as soon as the food was ready over a hundred hungry mouths turned up, and they certainly weren't all from this village. However, not one of them was sent away from our "banquet" hungry.

As we are probably now in the last mountain Papuan village we can afford to be generous with our presents, which has two advantages: it lightens our loads and ensures us the friendliness of the Papuans. We presented them with tobacco, salt and large quantities of cowrie shells, and in return their women lugged up sweet potatoes. The women are sick too and disfigured by skin blemishes. Not even the younger women were pleasant to look at. Their breasts hung down flabbily and were covered with scabs. Their only item of clothing was a small loincloth of pandanus leaves. They were kept constantly busy bringing up sweet potatoes and looking after a sick man in one of the eight huts. He seemed to be on the point of dying. A little while previously a woman must have died because near our tent there was a still glowing pile of ash, and on a pole hung one clean and one dirty loincloth, and one old and one new net—the only things these women possess in life and certainly all the dead woman had to leave behind.

Tomorrow we propose to try to find a pass over the last mountain chain in order not to have to follow the enormous sweep the Baliem River takes here. Before us now lies the No-Man's Land between the mountain Papuans and the coastal dwellers, who are still unknown to us.

The nearer we come to our objective the more extraordinary it seems to me that no one has ever previously thought of exploring this biggest and best-known river in New Guinea, and being the first to penetrate from the highlands through to the coast. Gerard tells me that the idea has, in fact, been mooted before, but that people have

31. The rapids on the Baliem River are twenty-five miles long

always let themselves be put off by the difficulties and dangers of the undertaking. The District Officers were, of course, tied down to their respective areas.

According to the inhabitants of the valley we passed through yesterday the neighbourhood is called Voleron, but they say that the river here, which has a good, firm bridge below the village, is called I-Ba.

We are curious to know how the inhabitants of this village will behave when we start off. Will they disappear as all the others have done so far, or will they help us with the porterage?

June 3

That last village was undoubtedly the poorest and most primitive I have yet seen anywhere here. The amount of sickness is depressing. It is difficult to understand how such a wretched community can continue to exist and isn't long since extinct. On the other hand, the situation in this particularly barren area wouldn't be all that much better even if the inhabitants could be cured, because the agricultural yield is so small. Their numbers would increase, the infant mortality rate would decline, and the result would be famine. The only proper solution would be to cure these people and provide them with tools and instruct them in modern methods of agriculture. They could then clear more land, increase the tilled area and produce more sweet potatoes, sugar-cane and bananas. Medicaments alone are no use, and at the same time something must urgently be done to see that they can provide themselves with food. It seems to me that their fear at our arrival changes so quickly into joy when they realise we are not enemies because they are in such need—with the presents we give them they can buy themselves food in the neighbouring valleys. We must strike them as messengers of benevolent spirits.

The good impression that we have made on them nevertheless does nothing to ameliorate our porterage problem, and when the time came for us to leave this morning we were faced with the same old problem. These Papuans didn't hide themselves, and they stood around and watched us with interest, and every time we said anything to them they replied "*Hano*," which means more or less "Of course, certainly." But that didn't help us at all and we set off without any supplementary porters, hoping, of course, that a few would run after us offering their services, as sometimes happened. But it didn't this time. To make matters worse, I couldn't find the path, and we wandered around, taking pig tracks or finding ourselves in those blind alleys in which the Papuans attend to the needs of nature. The natives didn't even show us the right way. They just stood there and said "*Hano!*" if addressed, and watched us until by our own efforts we ultimately found the path to the upper village.

The evening before a number of the natives had come down from this upper village to join our feast, and one of them even helped to carry our baggage. But when after about an hour we came to their village of fifteen huts there wasn't a soul to be seen anywhere.

Fortunately we soon found a good path that led up to a ridge and then down a very narrow sunken lane on the other side. This lane was so narrow that our rucksacks rubbed against the side walls, which were about twelve feet high, and covered as though with a roof by the overgrowth. At times no light penetrated through this thick roof at all and now and again we were going forward in complete darkness.

We ran into one difficulty after the other down this lane. Most of the time we were stumbling over tangled roots. Then the way went up again through a mossy oak forest until we reached an altitude of between six and seven thousand feet, where we found our way blocked by a paling from some recent blood feud. We therefore turned back, and searched for new tracks which we ultimately found and followed. Deep down below us were thick veils of mist that cut off our view, and we knew that we should now have to reckon increasingly with it, since the great watershed to the south was now behind us.

Our knowledge of the neighbourhood was based entirely on air photos, and from them we knew that there were no further fields along the Baliem here, and that the river itself curves in a great arc round a high limestone ridge. It was this bend that we now wanted to cut off.

We went down steeply through mossy forest, and to our great surprise we came after about half an hour to a real clearing. We hadn't expected to come across any human beings here and we were astonished to find traces of native tillage. The big clearing was uninhabited, and it was another hour or so before we came to a few wretched huts which presumably housed the natives who had once made it.

For the first time during the whole expedition we took a village by surprise. We were first discovered by a boy of about ten years old as we were already standing amidst the huts. He was so surprised that he stared at us with eyes like saucers and seemed unable to utter a word. Near by were two men chopping wood with stone axes. As soon as they spotted us they dropped their axes and called out the usual "Nabrava!" They were both emaciated. Their backs were bent and they looked sick men. As they wore the traditional penis-sheaths we knew that they still belonged to the mountain Papuans. Happy and relieved that we harboured no evil intentions towards them they showed us the way.

But the path, which up to now had been more or less passable because it connected the Papuans on the other side of the mountain ridge with the impoverished natives here, soon became so difficult that one could hardly call it a path at all. It took us ages before we managed to find a way out of a steep field in which sweet potatoes, taro, sugar-cane and a few banana plants were growing.

From time to time our Mandur, the leader of our Mujus, had to go ahead with his matchet to hack the hardly visible path clear of the worst obstacles. In this way and across very difficult terrain we came to the bed of the river Somneg. At least, that was the name the two old men in the last village had given us. The valley of the Somneg is steep and its stones are slippery, with the result that we still made only slow progress. In addition a variety of natural hindrances forced us to make constant detours. Again and again we were compelled to hack our way through the jungle around vertical drops and steep slopes. The Mandur and Johannes took it in turns to go ahead. Suddenly we found ourselves above a waterfall whose edge hung over so far that the water cataract did not hit the floor of the ravine until about 250 feet away. The Mandur began to hack a new path for us along the slope to the right, and the other Mujus helped him. But after about half an hour of this they returned to say that it was impossible to go any farther in that direction. Although we could not see it, the river took a bend and blocked our way in that direction too. It therefore seemed more sensible to try the other side. One of our Mujus with the splendid Christian name of Kasimirus discovered traces of an old path that led over a spur. We followed this path and after about an hour we reached the bed of the river again. It was much broader here because a tributary flowed out of a side valley and greatly broadened the stream.

By now it was half-past four. We had done a nine-hour march with heavy packs. We had crossed over a pass and now that we had reached the valley again we looked around for a bivouac site. It struck us as too dangerous to pitch camp in the dry part of the river bed, because at any moment a tropical downpour could start, and the rushing waters would then sweep us away helplessly. We therefore cut a clearing in the jungle. It had to be a fair size because of the leeches hanging from the trees. If we had camped under them they would simply have dropped on us.

June 4

Despite our precautions the camp belonged to the leeches more than it did to us. They wriggled their way through every crevice, and I even discovered a few in my mosquito net. It was particularly disgusting to reach out for the torch in the darkness and find them on the handle.

It rained a bit during the night, but not enough to make any very great difference to the volume of water. When we made our way along the river early this morning we could readily wade across it from side to side to take the easier path.

Gerard was rather pessimistic again yesterday, and it is a tendency I have found that many of the Dutch in New Guinea suffer from. They aren't prepared to try anything unless they are pretty certain that it will succeed and they are never happy taking big risks. However, everything went smoothly and according to plan today, and Gerard dismissed his doubts. Actually he's the perfect partner for me. He is every bit as thorough as I am, and he is much more careful, and that's often a very good thing for me. His reliability is beyond all

197

doubt and has contributed greatly to our joint expedition. Whether he's arranging for a plane to drop us rice, or whether he's carefully rationing our short supplies, whatever he does is done well. This morning we were both in very good spirits, forgot the leeches, and didn't bother too much even about the mosquitoes.

It was more difficult to keep up our spirits when it suddenly began to pour. We had to pitch camp in the middle of the jungle, and it was an hour before our last porters finally arrived, anxiously protecting themselves from the rain with fern leaves.

There's no drinking water around, but we collected so much rain on the roof of our tent that our water supply is guaranteed for the time being. That's the plus side of the downpour, but there's a minus side, too—there isn't the slightest hope of getting a fire going in this dripping wet.

After our bloodsucking night we had a bloodsucking day, and it was *our* blood that was sucked. I had such an intense experience of this revolting plague that now, in a half-way dry tent, I don't want to think about it any more, or write a great deal about it. Now and again there were leeches in such vast numbers that they dropped from the branches in clouds on us, or worked their way up the legs of our trousers. When there are so many it is just impossible to defend yourself against them. The only solution is flight. They are so small and so agile thet thay can easily wriggle their way through the lace holes of your boots. Their favourite place is in your ears, but they are also quite fond of a beard, and once they have settled there they are very difficult to remove. It's a painful business too, once they've got the little teeth they have on either side of their suckers fixed into you. You can't get them off then without tearing your own flesh, which immediately begins to bleed freely, and very rapidly becomes inflamed.

On the way through the river bed I went as far ahead of Gerard and the porters as possible in order to find a suitable spot from which to film. My efforts paid off, because this landscape is one of wild and completely untouched natural beauty. Water pours down in glistening cascades over moss-covered rocks, it thunders through narrows, shoots out at the other end with redoubled force and throws great clouds of spray into the air. However, I was fortunate enough again and again to find knee-deep places where I could wade through the water, sometimes on one side of the river, sometimes on the other, I was so deeply immersed in my filming that I didn't notice how quickly the time was passing and that I was on my own still. When I finally realised this I put down my rucksack on the bank and went back for about half an hour. I didn't come across either Gerard or the Mujus, so the only conclusion was that they had left the river and gone up the slope somewhere, having perhaps spotted a better path. I therefore went back to my rucksack and continued my way down stream. I kept shouting in all directions, but I got no reply. I must confess that by this time I was beginning to feel a little uncomfortable. After all, it's a pretty serious matter to lose your companions in the jungle—particularly when they have the food and the equipment. I therefore kept telling myself that whatever I did I mustn't panic. Thank goodness my doubts lasted only about an hour and then suddenly I heard a couple of our Mujus hacking their way down a slope. They had been sent by Gerard to let me know the position of the column and to tell me that during my absence the leader of our Mujus had found something that looked like an overgrown path, and they had naturally taken it. Gerard had fired into the air several times in order to signal to me but the sound of the shots had been lost in the thundering and roaring of the water. Everything was now in order again and we went on contentedly together, but I had to promise Gerard that I wouldn't go on ahead on my own again like that.

For an hour we climbed up this steep path, and gradually we began to doubt whether we really were going the best way. Incidentally to call this wretched track a path was something of a mockery. We had to hack our way forward laboriously, and it was probably years since any natives had used the path either in war or out hunting. Indeed, perhaps it was nothing more than a game track.

At least we consoled ourselves with the thought that it couldn't get any worse; and, in fact, after tremendous efforts we reached a mountain ridge along which there was a real path. After a while it sloped gently downwards and in this way we reached the bottom of the valley again. Arriving at the river we stopped for a short rest. It was raining once more.

When the rain became less heavy we started off again. We had hopes of crossing a broad landslip that lay ahead of us without getting too wet, and in part we succeeded, because the next real downpour started only when we had practically mastered the mud and rubble of the landslip. On the other side there was a pandanus hut offering us shelter from the rain, which was now pouring down with tropical violence.

But we didn't stay very long in the hut either, because despite the pouring rain there was no fresh water to be found either to drink or cook with.

On an average we haven't done much more than perhaps a third of a mile an hour today. Going downhill it was rather more perhaps, but going uphill it was certainly less. Our present bivouac site is only about 2,800 feet or so above sea level, which means that during the past couple of days we have descended something like 3,200 feet. In the next few days we shall have to go down another 2,500 feet or so into the lower valley of the Baliem River, which is called the Catalina there. As we go down farther and farther we should at least have the advantage of finding easier terrain.

June 5

Once again it rained throughout the night. The small bit of blue sky I saw this morning through the foliage of the enormous trees that towered over our camping site is now covered over with thick cloud. The trees are growing so close together that it is a sort of a race between them to get at least their upper branches into the sky and catch a little sunshine. We could see this fight for the sunshine most clearly with the pandanus palms; in their efforts to get up to the light they had formed root triangles almost thirty feet high. But even the oaks and the casuarina trees growing luxuriantly along the river have sent their branches up to improbable heights in this struggle for light. A great number of different kinds of birds from the yellow-white cockatoo to the brilliantly coloured parrot, are all living in their branches. During the night, which is of almost oppressive stillness here, I was woken up by the sudden squawk of one of these birds. It was obviously a sound of alarm, but in the end it fell quiet again and the enormous silence of the night descended once more over our camp.

Owing to the wet it took us particularly long to get going again this morning. It was ten o'clock before we managed to light a fire to cook rice for our Mujus. They did their best to get one going last night, but they didn't succeed, and this morning they were trying for two hours before they finally succeeded. For an hour before that they had been washing the rice. They have probably seen Europeans doing it and now they imagine they are doing something particularly wonderful when they copy this folly.

Our Mujus are all unusually agreeable and helpful chaps. They aren't, in fact, much different from any other of the Papuans I have seen. They're not very big; they have flat noses, thick lips and crinkly hair. But they are not so powerful as the Danis or the Uhundunis. Nevertheless they are good porters and they have earned a good reputation for themselves with a number of expeditions. But I'm afraid their loyalty develops according to need rather than from any inner qualities. The fact is that when they act as porters for an expedition they naturally pass through territory which is unfamiliar to them and inhabited by hostile tribes. If they were to desert the column they would probably be killed by the first local natives they met. They know this perfectly well, of course, and so they much prefer to stay obediently and loyally in the neighbourhood of their Tuan. But if they happen to be in familiar country then they're more difficult to keep together than a herd of swine. Let them out of your sight for a moment or two and they've gone. They like to do as they please, and although they make good porters when they must they don't really like going long distances in one stage. Gerard once asked one of them whether he'd like to be a policeman, and received the answer: "Pay good. Food good. But too much walking." He was obviously thinking of the daily patrols, and the idea didn't appeal to him.

The ideal solution of the porterage problem would be to fly Danis or Uhundunis to where you need them. They are certainly the best companions. Not that they're more intelligent or more stupid, or more faithful or more treacherous than all the other tribes, but they're much stronger and therefore able to stand more. In this matter of physical strength it is important for the leader of an expedition to know just how strong his natives are in order not to overtax them. As they cannot accurately estimate their own strength they just do as they're told without objection. You have to be careful not to overtax their strength, because if you do you will find them dying on you like flies.

We had another quite good day today. We pitched our camp on a terrace about 160 feet above the river. Our altimeter gives our position as just over 2,000 feet above sea level. That was a good performance in a comparatively short time, because we didn't get off until after ten o'clock in the morning and we had to pitch camp by four o'clock. In addition, after we had crossed a bed of limestone sinter on the way, we came across indescribably tangled jungle. Gerard was gloomy again, but fortunately it doesn't last long with him. When at the end of the day he discovers that our progress has been satisfactory he just laughs at himself and very quickly recovers his optimism.

We had to cross two small and one large stream, and just before we got to our present camping site the river disappeared altogether in a deep, narrow limestone gorge with a 250-foot waterfall, which we also had to cross.

Our camp site is once again in the heart of thick jungle. Before we pitched camp we carefully examined the surrounding trees to discover whether they were inwardly rotten, because rotted and decaying trees are a big danger in the neighbourhood of a camp site. There is always the chance that one of them will fall during the night, and in doing so it can bring others down with it, and that could be a catastrophe. On the other hand, this tendency on the part of one falling tree to bring others down with it is very useful for the natives when they are making a clearing, since it saves them a lot of labour.

We don't often see the river now, but we seem to be out of the high mountains since we can hardly see a ridge over the thickly growing tropical forest. We made another discovery though. Our inadequate path led us by a hut made of foliage and covered with pandanus. The leaves are still greenish which means that it can't be more than a few months old. Our supplies are running low and we could do with a human settlement. My mind's eye pictures the joys of a banquet of roast pork. About half an hour after that we came across the first sago palm. Our Mujus were beside themselves with delight to see their beloved sago palm once more, because it is the chief source of nourishment in their part of the world, Tana Mera. To these signs of human agriculture came a few wild banana trees without fruit. Nevertheless they helped to raise the spirits of both porters and Tuans. At any moment now we hope to meet our first coastal Papuans.

June 6

On account of the dreadful dirt and mire our Mujus made a sort of platform of tree trunks for Gerard and me yesterday evening. But our contentment didn't last long. Hardly had we got off to sleep than the supporting beam broke with a crack and we found ourselves lying in the dirt. These are the sort of minor accidents you meet with on your way through the unknown jungle, but they're too unimportant to get excited about.

June 7

It's getting dark already and I haven't much time to write down even the most important items.

Yesterday when we left our terrace site we had something more or less like a path for about a quarter of an hour, but then it disappeared for good. Deep limestone holes in the jungle forced us to hack our way up slopes until we had gone up something like twelve hundred feet and were once again at a height of 2,800 feet above sea level. By this time it was afternoon and we were looking for a way of climbing down again, because towards the end we were going west by north-west, whereas our general direction should be south-east.

Nightfall compelled us to bivouac in the middle of the slope. It wasn't a very agreeable site, and, above all, it swarmed with leeches again. Our Mujus suffered from them very badly because they go bare-footed. However, they have a very quick and effective way of dealing with them: they just take a matchet and scrape them off with the blade.

Our camp site was once again deep in mud and we all felt miserable with the result that hardly a word was said. But at least after casting around a bit we did find some water, and what with this and the rain-water—it was still pouring—we soon had enough to cook rice for everyone.

Early this morning we started off after a night without much sleep, and without water and without breakfast. After going for about an hour we came to a powerful tributary of the Somneg, and in my opinion it carries as much water as the main river. We then rested and had breakfast.

We had to cast around for two hours before we finally managed to clamber down to the river over a vertical limestone face almost two hundred feet high. Before this we had searched up river and down river for somewhere negotiable, but without success and so finally we decided to make ourselves a sort of rope ladder from liana and climb down that, and this we did, but it was midday before we finally got down to the river.

We found a fine terrace about sixty-five feet above the river and there we first cooked our food. When we had eaten, our Mujus began to fell one giant tree after the other in the hope that one of them would fall with its top over the other side of the river and thus form a bridge for us to cross. But they all fell at an angle into the water and the powerful current seized their foliage tops and carried them away downstream. Their plan wasn't successful, but our porters put up quite a performance. They didn't take more than half an hour to fell trees seven feet thick, though they certainly picked out trees that slanted out over the river and began to crack and break before they were half cut through.

When this plan failed the Mujus tried to build bridges from rock to rock over the river. They managed this up to the last thirty-five feet or so, but the current was too strong and the small rounded rocks were too slippery to offer a proper foothold so our Mujus had to give up this plan too. Then they made one more attempt by felling a giant tree, and finally gave it up. The only thing was to hope that by tomorrow the water level would have sunk and that our bridge building would be more successful.

Right next to us, towards the east, is a small, crystal-clear river

204

which has eaten a deep ravine through the chalk rocks. Apparently we must have gone round it on our way over the heights.

Owing to the many detours and the constant going up and down, the actual distance we have covered today is pretty poor, but we're only about thirteen hundred feet up now and that at least is good. Somewhere or other the river must reach the sea, and then we shall finally be at sea level. This means that we shall soon have reached the southern edge of the mountains where the river runs into the plain at a height of something like eight hundred feet. From there we shall then have about 125 miles to the sea.

Our supplies are running short. We have enough rice and tinned stuff to last for just six days. This morning Gerard discovered that in the night our Mujus have stolen a few tins of corned beef and fish and eaten the contents. For the next few days they will therefore get only rice, sugar and salt. The long-term rationing scheme that Gerard had worked out and strictly adhered to was upset by this theft, and against his will he now had to cut down our rations even further.

June 8

We got up at the first crack of dawn this morning. I instructed one of our Mujus to prepare the breakfast, and all the others had to take their axes and go down to the river, where we now made a last attempt to fell a giant tree and get it to fall over the river so that it could serve as a bridge. But once again we were unsuccessful. Like all the other trees yesterday, the final thirty feet remained out of reach as before. Some of our Mujus then went upstream to see if they could find a more favourable spot, but after a while they returned shrugging their shoulders. We already knew that downstream the vertically falling rock-face barred the way in every direction.

We now tried quite a different tack. With endless patience our Mujus built small bridges between the rocks jutting out of the water. They worked away with admirable skill and courage whilst Gerard and I kept our eyes anxiously on the water level, because a tropical downpour could release a bore upstream perhaps twenty feet high to rush down the river and sweep all our porters away helplessly. Fortunately there was no heavy rain and after a few hours' work the first strong pole reached the other side of the river. It was strengthened by a second one, and at midday the first of our Mujus crawled forward on his belly over the still fragile bridge. His success caused the others to set up a howl of delight, and after that everything went rapidly.

Whilst the bridge was being strengthened and consolidated, Gerard and I struck camp. An hour later the crossing took place with all our baggage. Although they had to carry the loads our Mujus balanced their way elegantly across the improvised bridge, whereas Gerard and I, who had nothing to carry, went over on all fours.

There was now an agreeable change in the weather, the clouds parted and the sun shone down brightly and warmly into the gorge as we left it. Unfortunately on the other bank there were almost vertical limestone faces and we had to cast around for a long time. In our search we climbed a mountain ridge and there at last we discovered a clearly visible path before us.

The leader of our Mujus went ahead and hacked the way clear where necessary. Despite occasional hindrances we made quite astonishingly rapid progress. After two hours we found ourselves at a clearing in the heart of the jungle. Our Mujus stopped dead, drew back and fell silent fearfully. A "ghost fence," which seemed to mark the village boundary, held them up and they refused to go on. To encourage them I went ahead and we came to four inhabited huts. But the moment the natives spotted us they rushed into the jungle in panic-stricken fear. We took a closer look at the huts. From the cooking pit and the fire places I concluded that the natives here still belonged to the mountain Papuans. Old stone axes, many bows and still more arrows were propped against the walls. The natives had fled in such panic that they had left even their weapons behind. Their fire was still burning. Because of the mild southern climate the huts were airily built. On the whole the clearing and the settlement made a very primitive impression. I found a few sweet potatoes growing between fallen tree-trunks, and here and there a banana tree.

I tried to persuade Gerard that we should make a halt here and satisfy our hunger with the sweet potatoes, but he was in favour of going on and so were our Mujus.

We didn't stay very long therefore, and went on until we came to a second clearing on which the natives were apparently still engaged. We did not rest even there, but pushed on, and all the time the path was becoming less and less recognisable, and indicated that these few natives lived on their clearing like an island in the jungle sea. On the way our Mujus discovered a nibung palm, whose heart—the not yet developed leaves—they regard as a particular delicacy.

The ground remained limestone which meant that water didn't collect, and we were already beginning to fear that we should have to bivouac without any, but at about five o'clock, that is to say almost at the very last moment, we came to a small stream running through a sinter gully.

In the immediate vicinity of our camping site were a few tremendous sago palms with leaves at least fifty feet long. Our Mujus explained that someone owned these trees and that they must therefore not be touched. To make up for not being able to touch the sago palms they went off to search for the larvae of tropical insects, which they subsequently roasted at our camp fire and ate with great pleasure.

We made quite good progress today, and after the short distances we had covered on the other days, this evening was a contented and satisfactory one. It can't be much farther on to the plain now, and I am enjoying the feeling that at least we shan't have to go back the difficult way we came. The hours when I felt fear on account of hostile and warlike Papuans now seem far off.

Gradually Gerard and I are beginning to rid our baggage of ballast that has become useless. We have already left two sacks with cowrie shells behind by the bridge, though our porters would gladly have taken them along because in their own neighbourhood they would represent quite a considerable value. Because of this I had to stay behind with the sacks at the bridge until Gerard and the porters were out of sight. Had I not taken this simple precaution I am quite certain that one or other of our Mujus would have slipped back surreptitiously and carried off the cowrie shells.

Today we found traces of wild pigs and cassowaries, and now and again we heard the crooning of wild pigeons. We couldn't see them;

the jungle is too thick for that. But at least they are another proof that we are approaching the plain. The tangled jungle roof above us is still so impenetrable that we cannot take our bearings from the sun and have to use the compass.

This expedition is a constant psychological up and down for Gerard. When we've done a good stint and reached our objective for the day his spirits are sky-high, but when we can't find a path and make no progress despite all our efforts he is right down in the dumps. He invents the most incredible oaths when his rifle or his rucksack catch on a jutting rock or in a thorny bush.

Our Mandur is an ideal leader for our porters, and he seems to have a very definite sense of responsibility. He is usually at the head of the column with a matchet in each hand cutting rhythmically to right and left to clear the worst hindrances out of our path. A second Muju goes behind him, also with a matchet in each hand, to put the finishing touches to his Mandur's work.

The two have had a very great deal to do today. After about an hour there was no path to be seen at all and they had to hack out a new one laboriously. And the whole time we were going either up or down, through gorges, past waterfalls, across large and small valleys. Once or twice we tried to climb up the steep slope which dropped down to the river, but that proved impossible so we just continued to hack our way obstinately towards the south-east.

It is raining uninterruptedly. The clouds above us were sometimes so thick that you might have thought that it was evening instead of day. Despite the difficulties we made quite good progress, and when it really was evening and we pitched our camp even Gerard was satisfied with the day's work.

We had been going for almost nine hours, and our heavy rucksacks had got heavier and heavier. But I forgot all our exertions at once when I stood on a ridge near our camping site and saw the great plain shimmering before us in the misty blue of the evening twilight.

Our Mujus felled a huge tree at the upper end of the steep slope. In falling it took another one with it, and that took still another one,

208

32. *The first length of liana to make this bridge was shot across by arrow*
33. *This chief has twenty-five wives* (OVERLEAF)

AAN DRAGERS UITBETAALD AAN LONEN EN PREMIES.

NAAM	BEDRAG LONEN	BEDRAG PREMIES	TOTAAL BEDRAG	HANDTEKENING OF DUIMAFDRUK.
KONAJAP	f 181,=	f 26,=	f 207,=	→
PAULUS JOROMOK	- 130,=	- 15,=	- 145,=	→
BENJAMIN WATAN	- 130,=	- 23,=	- 153,=	
ARNOLD KOENGMOT	- 130,=	- 2,=	- 132,=	
JOHANNES KEWDRIB	- 130,=	- 7,=	- 137,=	
ROBERTUS TAMIN	- 130,=	- 1,=	- 131,=	→
KASIMIRUS TALIJOP	- 130,=	- 7,=	- 137,=	→
LINUS SONJAP	- 130,=	- 1,=	- 131,=	→
KOJAP	- 130,=	- 1,=	- 131,=	→
ESMUNDUS	- 130,=	- 12,=	- 142,=	→
TOTALEN	f 1351,=	f 95,=	f 1446,=	

UIT BETAALD TE
AGATS, 23 JUNI 1962

G. VAN DER WILLEM

and so on until trees were falling like ninepins—an unforgettable sight. We no longer saw the last trees arrive below and heard only the crackling and snapping of their branches and the heavy impact of their trunks. With the trees gone we now had a clear and uninterrupted view out over the plain, and we were all highly elated, including our Mujus. It was quite clear that all we should have to do now would be to go down into the next valley—there would be no other side to climb up. We can move down the slope diagonally and gradually approach the great river bed. Yesterday we were still fifteen hundred feet up, and today we are even about 2,500 feet above sea level.

A week ago today, last Saturday, the wireless broadcast a few details concerning our expedition, but so far we haven't heard either from Agats or Merauke to tell us that the coastal District Officer is already on his way to meet us. However, as it was agreed that he should, I am not very worried about the omission. Of course, should the Indonesians invade in the Agats area that would alter the situation. Before we left, Dr Valk and I reckoned that the expedition would be about three weeks on the way, and that if necessary those who were to meet us would wait a further week for us on top of that. If we hadn't turned up by the end of this extra week they were to sound the alarm. On June 12 exactly three weeks will have passed since we set out. It looks almost as though we shall be at the agreed meeting place right on time. But there's one thing you soon learn on this sort of job, and that is that prophecies are dangerous. There's the weather for one thing, and you can't do anything about that. Then there's the possibility of having to make detours. And finally there's the behaviour of the natives.

June 10

An exciting day lies behind us. First of all there was quite a disappointment over the way, which went for about a third of a mile through a gorge and took us about an hour to master. But worse was to come.

Suddenly and unexpectedly we came to an area pitted with funnel-like craters and covered by thick jungle. Only the sharp

209

points of the limestone rocks, overgrown with thorns, jutted out. Nearby were vertical rock faces and then deep holes again, which were quite dangerous. We tried to get from our altitude of sixteen hundred feet up to over two thousand feet. We worked our way eastwards, that is to say in the direction of the river, but it was hopeless. One deep crater followed the other. From the edge of one the Mujus would hack a way across to the edge of the next—and so it went on until by about four o'clock the landscape became a little more friendly.

As some compensation for these exertions we actually and unexpectedly found drinking water at our camping site. There had been no water at all in that craterous area, and we had already warned our Mujus that there would be no rice today.

All the way I had the smell of fermenting rice in my nostrils, and the few grains that were still dry we now had to take out of the damp jute sacks and put into my two camera cases. In the meantime we have eaten the half-fermented rice.

But when are we going to reach the plain at last? Our Mandur climbed to the top of a tree and looked round very importantly in all directions and came down to inform us that without doubt we should have many days' journey ahead of us. This shocked us a bit because we had reckoned that three or at the utmost four days would see us through. Gerard was quite cast down by the Mandur's depressing prophecy, particularly as the wretched path had been giving us trouble for hours. He reminds me of my father: if he's upset he bawls at everyone and everything, including his rucksack and his rifle. But it doesn't take long for him to calm down and then he's amiable and considerate to everyone. Gerard is one of those people who think things over carefully and analyse them in detail. One look at his lean, haggard features is enough to tell you that. He could easily be a scholar, and he uses up more energy in thought than in physical effort.

Yesterday evening I ate eggs from jungle turkeys for the first time in my life. They were excellent and certainly every bit as good as hen's eggs. Our Mujus found four eggs under a pile of leaves. According to them a turkey hen usually lays eight eggs at a time about the size of goose eggs. But as these birds aren't much bigger than a good-sized hen in Europe laying eggs must be quite a painful business for them. Their cackling is something like that of geese, too, but louder.

Cockatoos play much the same rôle on behalf of the wild animals living in this jungle as do jays in our woods at home. As soon as you get anywhere near them they set up a terrific din and thus warn all the animals around that interlopers are at hand.

All day long the compass was our only guide. We had to rely on it not only for finding our way through the jungle, but also for getting across the crater landscape. As we had constantly to work our way round these craters there was a very considerable danger that we should lose our sense of direction and perhaps find ourselves going round in circles, and this the compass prevented. The sun, which would have given us our direction in the ordinary way, was constantly hidden behind threatening rain clouds.

June 11

As we could get nothing from the broadcasting station at Agats today I had another look at the calendar. I've discovered that today's a bank holiday: it's Whit Monday. It hasn't been much of a holiday for us. On the contrary, it was a dreadful day.

The night itself was bad enough to start with. The fermented rice weighed heavily on my stomach, and as I lay there, unable to drop off to sleep, I heard our porters being sick from time to time—the rice hadn't agreed with them either.

We first descended from our mountain ridge because I was hoping that we would be able to get along faster by the river bed without having to use our compass all the time, but before long we found ourselves in an area of deep chalk craters again, and finally our way was completely blocked by a steep rock face. There was nothing for it so we turned in our tracks and went the whole way back along the way we had come in streaming rain! On the way back the usual night storm surprised us at four o'clock in the afternoon, and the rain came down in torrents. It was too much for our porters and they revolted, and when we tried to pitch our camp in the downpour only the Mandur and another Muju named Paulus lent us a hand. The

211

other eight porters crouched together a little distance away looking miserable and disconsolate. To stir them up a bit Gerard shot once into the air and then a second time over their heads. There was no danger, but the Mujus threw themselves down on their bellies and it was a good half an hour before they came creeping up, one after the other.

Although the situation was serious and needed to be taken seriously I couldn't help seeing the funny side of it. There I stood in the mud and rain in my birthday suit doing my best to wring the water out of my soaking clothes. When the porter carrying my load finally came up I seized him by the throat and threatened him that if he failed to follow us again I'd break every bone in his body. Then I lifted him off his feet and flung him into the mire, telling him he could consider himself lucky to get off so lightly this time.

Whether they realised that they were at fault or were just feeling hungry it's difficult to say in retrospect, but despite the wet they managed to get a fire going and then they asked politely for their rice. On the way they had felled a number of nibung palms and eaten the rudimentary leaves. Added to Gerard's meagre ration of rice it was enough to still the worst pangs of hunger. The hope of the porters that we should be able to kill a wild pig or a cassowary or two was not to be fulfilled, because it was already too dark and the best time to go for them is in the early morning.

Gerard was so exhausted he went off to sleep before the rice was ready, and when it was finally ready he could hardly stay awake long enough to eat it.

June 12

Unfortunately I had a great deal of trouble during the night from the "lice" which infest the jungle turkeys whose eggs I had consumed with such relish the day before. These particularly disagreeable insects are actually a kind of tick. You can hardly see them with the naked eye, but they are capable of working their way under your skin. And in addition to the rain and these loathsome creatures came the ubiquitous leeches, which obviously make a banquet out of me.

Our camp site was over nine hundred feet up, and when I crawled

212

out of our tent in the morning swathes of mist were moving across the site and a fine rain was falling. The valley was very narrow at this point, and once again we were hoping that this was the last gorge before we emerged on to the plain.

We made only slow and laborious progress. Although we were on the march for seven hours yesterday, the actual distance we managed was less than a mile. In the meantime I know from experience that even in relatively favourable terrain where we can hack our way forward towards the south-east without having to make many detours we can't do more than about five hundred paces an hour, or about two hundred yards as the crow flies. But the question of time is now becoming a very important one indeed, because our food supplies are running very low. There is probably no hope at all of falling in with any village here in the mountains, and so for the first time I am beginning to wonder seriously whether we have a reasonable chance of getting out of it alive.

Of course, even a day like that isn't just hard work and exertion. Sometimes we caught a wonderful sight of waterfalls thundering down into three-hundred-foot-deep craters and then disappearing. But the beauties of nature aren't all that entrancing when there's fire under the soles of your feet and you know you've got to press on as quickly as possibly if there's to be any hope of getting out of this No-Man's-Land. In consequence although we noted many beautiful things there was little time or inclination to enjoy them. For some days now I have noticed that delight in these unusual beauties of nature comes chiefly at night just before going to sleep. That was because the mould of the forest floor glowed and flickered in the dusk from the decomposing bacteria it contains.

If you happen to have a geologist like Gerard with you on such occasions you can learn a great many interesting things and enjoy a good many fascinating conversations. But even the expert isn't in a position to say anything definite about the likely state of the terrain to be met with during the next day's stint. Gerard is well up in all possible geological formations, of course, but owing to folds, land-slips and various accretions even he can't prophesy with any certainty what the actual surface will be like. For example, geologically speaking marl and silt should lie above limestone, but, in fact, we usually found that porous limestone was the upper layer, and it made our progress difficult and disagreeable. In addition, being porous, the limestone let the water through, so there was none when we wanted it. Again and again we clambered down lower in the hope of finding silt loam, which would be much easier for us, but we usually found that on account of a fold the limestone was uppermost again, and that's just how it was today.

The day began with a display of friendliness on the part of our porters. Esmundus, the fellow I had pushed into the mud for a lesson only the previous day, actually helped with my packing, for the first time, and without being asked either.

First of all we descended to about nine hundred feet without encountering any particular difficulties, but then as we moved along the gorge we had to climb up to fifteen hundred once more. At this point we stopped for a midday rest and to wait for the stragglers to catch up, because now they were not properly fed our porters were much slower. We were unable to find any nibung palm hearts, and we had to make do as best we could with the concentrated extract Gerard doled out. Our food stocks were steadily diminishing, and therefore I made no objection to his very strict rationing. On our way we have learnt at least one lesson that may come in useful to others in the future: no one can hope to cross this jungle without taking his own food with him. Nature provides too little in the way of fauna and flora for an expedition to live, so to speak, off the land. Settlers could, of course, make a clearing and live here indefinitely, but for that they would have to grow their own food and vegetables, keep domestic animals, and go hunting to supplement their food supply. But to go through this jungle without taking your food along? Not on your life—and that quite literally! The noise of our progress, and in particular the constant blows of our matchets, was quite enough to drive off any bird or animal we might otherwise have been able to shoot to eke out our food supplies. At least the noise had one advantage: the snakes could also hear it, and they too fled before us so that we had no trouble with them at all.

Finally the last of our porters came up, but by the time he arrived it was really time to think about starting off again, but that, of course, would have been senseless. The slowest of our Mujus were the weakest and they needed rest, so we stayed there for another half an hour to give them a breather before we started off again.

Immediately the descent became very steep, and the way went through thick jungle, which meant constant hacking. After making our way for several hours in a south-easterly direction we finally found our river again. We hadn't seen it for five days, but its distant roar had served us as a guide to our general direction.

At this point the river ran swiftly between vertical limestone faces, and we were gradually coming to believe that the mountains had no intention of ever releasing the river and allowing it to flow peacefully out into the plain. Gerard is in none too good a state. He's been complaining of pains all day, and just now he moaned that he'd had to go on his "teeth" for hours. He meant "toes," but when you get to the point of exhaustion you find it begins to affect your speech. It wasn't a suitable moment to laugh either.

Our camp site is perched rather like a bird's nest about a hundred feet above the river. The slope is so steep that it is thanks only to the ingenuity and skill of our porters that we are able to camp in such a spot at all. When despite all our searching we could find nowhere to camp they built a terrace against the steep slope with timber. For this purpose they collected strong branches and poles which they placed horizontally against the slope and supported from below by vertical poles. And that's where we're sitting now, daringly and rather dangerously. Beneath us the river is forcing its way through a bottle-neck. It's not more than perhaps sixty-five feet wide at this point, which means that it must be very deep. It's running swiftly and silently almost as though it were passing through a narrow canal.

The good temper of our Mujus has survived the day. It's still raining it's true, and it has been all the time, but at least we're now by the river again and we haven't got to fight our way round those jungle craters, which often confused our sense of direction, and this makes them more cheerful.

We are something like three hundred feet or so above sea level at the moment, which means that the river is not more than about a couple of hundred feet above the plain here, and that very soon now we should be out of the gorge. From the edge of the mountains to the coast the river is about 125 miles long, and so it can't have more than a gradient of about 220 feet or so still to descend. Now although I know that most things here are different from things anywhere else in the world, one may surely assume that rivers aren't going to flow at less than zero. On the other hand, our altimeter might well be out of order.

In a few minutes we shall be leaving our "eyrie." At last a morning on which the sun is shining once more! A feeble ray or two is even penetrating into our gorge, and we are correspondingly cheerful. It is days since we experienced anything of the sort.

It was a peaceful camping site, peaceful for the ear and peaceful for the spirits. Our mood was serene because we were hopeful that we were very near to our objective now. And it was peaceful to the ear because the river was no longer roaring and thundering, but shooting almost noiselessly through its bottle-neck about a hundred feet below us. We are now confident that we shall be out of the wood in two or three days at the utmost. It is exactly three weeks ago that we set off from Wamena.

The first part of our journey today went upwards steeply for over three hundred feet to the uppermost edge of the gorge, then the path went fairly level, with neither ups nor downs, for another couple of hours, until at midday we could see through the trees ahead that the river turned sharply eastward as our own map indicated. At this bend we expected to find a big tributary flowing into the main river from the west.

Temporarily the terrain became more difficult again and the jungle even thicker, and quite suddenly we found ourselves amongst limestone ridges very difficult to negotiate. But difficult or no, we had to go forward. Then about sixty-five feet or so below I spotted what looked like still water between overhanging limestone walls. Only when I looked more closely could I make out eddies. I just couldn't imagine what water it was. A tributary? Hardly. At this point the river was at least three hundred feet or so away. One thing was clear: we must be at the last loop before the river finally turned eastwards to join the Baliem four or five miles on. The estuary of the Baliem,

216

which is called the Catalina here, is the place where we have arranged to meet, and where the police launch from Agats should be waiting for us.

But for the time being we had to climb upwards laboriously over limestone ridges and make our way in a westerly direction through jungle. At about four o'clock in the afternoon, the leader of our porters, who usually went ahead with Paulus to hack a path free, had had enough and insisted that we should now pitch our camp.

There is no water anywhere here, but some of our Mujus went back and fetched some.

Whilst we were pitching camp Gerard and I discovered that we had passed through a depression, and with this the mystery of the "still" water I had seen swirling in the neighbourhood of the bend was solved. It was the expected tributary, but for part of the way it flowed underground. So once again we have reached our objective for the day, and as a reward the porters have each received half a packet of shag.

It was once again a typical experience for these parts. The day began with great hopes, sunshine, jungle not particularly difficult to penetrate, not a great deal of limestone, and the prospect of reaching the last bend, seeing no more mountains, and having no more gorges ahead. And what actually came about was just the opposite: impenetrable undergrowth, constant hacking, limestone ridges, new mountains and another gorge. I could hear Gerard cursing steadily behind me. But as so often before, the achievement of our daily stint consoled him and made him optimistic once more.

It is difficult to imagine how little the jungle provides here in the way of food. Really hardly anything at all, Nature's biggest gift to us today was a single palm pith, and our hopes of coming across some more turkeys' eggs were disappointed, though our Mujus did find a place that had been completely stripped of foliage. What jungle turkeys do is to collect all the foliage for ten to twenty yards around, make it into a vast pile, and then lay, their eggs in the middle of it. But there were no eggs in this one. Gerard and I gave the heap a wide berth because apart from eggs—if any—such heaps harbour the *kutumaleo*, one of the most treacherous enemies of mankind to be found in the jungle. The name *kutumaleo* comes from the Malay and

217

isn't altogether an accurate description because *kutu* means louse, and these insects are ticks. They can hardly be seen with the naked eye, but they can worm their way under the human epidermis. Once there they make their presence felt by setting up an inflammation which produces an almost intolerable itch. After a short time a hard blister forms, and when it has reached a certain size it bursts and leaves a suppurating wound. As our blood was already infected by all kinds of tropical bacteria we were particularly susceptible to these microscopic parasites. Our blood just no longer had sufficient powers of resistance. And so we had to put up with broken *kutumaleo* blisters turning into suppurating ugly wounds. Strangely enough our Mujus appear to be quite immune to them.

The high-light of the day was when we discovered traces of cassowaries at last. The flesh of these big land-running birds, which use their long hard legs as weapons, would make a very tempting meal. Incidentally those long, hard legs can be dangerous to human beings too. Unfortunately, however, the traces were all we did come across—not a sight of a bird. In all probability the cassowaries had been warned in good time, no doubt frightened off by the noise we made slashing our way through the jungle.

With a rather empty feeling in the pit of my stomach I thought over our food situation. As a matter of fact I have been thinking about it for days now. So long as we press on the noise we make frightens every animal away and spoils our chances of bagging anything for the pot. But if we rest for a day and make no noise there is no guarantee that we shall bag anything. And that would mean that we had wasted a day's food, added nothing to the larder, and lost a day's travelling time. Gerard and I are both in agreement that we can't afford to take such a risk; it's too dangerous. Food or no food, we've just got to press on. You need time to stalk animals or birds and we just haven't got it. Our last store of rice is diminishing in an alarming fashion. Apart from the remains of our rice we have some salt and a small quantity of sugar. It's high time that we arrived at our destination.

We have now pitched our twenty-third camp. This day brought no relief whatever. Limestone ridges, streaming rain, and mountains overgrown with thick jungle. We had to fight our way forward foot by foot.

At midday when the jungle opened up a little we saw the last mountain barrier. It really was the last, and behind it in the half-light lay the enormously broad plain. From now on our way led steadily downward, and at about two o'clock we came to our river again. It flowed past broad and majestic without turbulence or eddy. Our faces were alight with renewed hope now, and the idea immediately occurred to me that from here we could use a raft.

However, we continued our way forward on foot. At first we went for a while along the bank of the river and then suddenly we debouched on to the plain.

The jungle became thinner and we stopped for a short rest. We found a few palm hearts which we ate with great appetite and in the best of spirits. Then we went on for another hour. We wanted to reach the spot where the Somneg flows into the Baliem-Catalina, but we found ourselves up against unexpected difficulties. The Somneg became broader and broader and finally fanned out into four separate arms and compelled us to make detour after detour. The exhaustion of our porters did the rest and so we pitched our twenty-third camp by the outside arm. I am lying there now and writing up this diary.

Shortly after we reached this camping site some of our Mujus went down to the bank. Suddenly they began to shriek blue murder and rush off in a panic. Wondering what could have so alarmed them I went down to the river bank myself, and what I saw gave me a shock too. It was the first crocodile of our expedition, a really big brute. It had crawled up on to the bank and it was now making its way at an astonishing speed back to the water at the very place where our Mujus had been standing. The crocodile had obviously been sleeping quietly on the bank and probably had no disagreeable intentions towards anyone. It let itself sink slowly into the water and then swam off. A little later we entered the river at the same spot to take a bath.

The wash down with antiseptic soap was something we all needed. Gerard and I carefully washed out the *kutumaleo* wounds and the leech bites. Our Mujus were not immune to the attention of leeches and blood ran down their legs just as it did down ours.

Two hours later, when it was already dark, I was still attending to my various wounds and injuries, including those I had suffered during my fall, which had not entirely healed up yet, and bandaging what needed bandaging. Counting all my various wounds and bites brings me to just about a hundred. As we are not going on any farther today the bandages will at last have a chance of doing some good. I have bandaged a good many wounds at various times for myself, for Gerard and the porters, but I might just as well have saved myself the trouble because after a while they always got wet and dirty. In addition they always slipped and in the end they usually came off altogether. A bandage can do any good in this part of the world only if you put it on at night and you then get a little rest.

Gerard has distributed antibiotics and we've all swallowed them in the hope of cleansing our bacteria-poisoned blood and reducing the glandular swellings in the crutch. Personally I'm fairly well off; the intensive medical treatment I had in Wamena seems to have given my body powers of resistance that poor Gerard's doesn't possess. His wounds are causing him a great deal of pain and trouble. He curses frightfully but bears them manfully.

Our porters are feeling pleased. They've managed to catch a tree lizard on the way. These creatures often sit perfectly still on the branches of trees, and thanks to their protective colouring they are almost invisible. But one of our porters spotted this fellow, and before long they will have eaten him.

It was again and again an astonishing experience for me to watch the Mujus at work hacking a path through the jungle. You watch one of these powerfully-built fellows wielding his matchet, and then with a sudden side-swipe he will cut down some small tree or bush which wasn't in the least in the way and need not have been touched. But such unexpected side swipes with the matchet have nothing to do with clearing the path. As the trees or bush falls you will see him snatch something with a movement like lighting. You would have mistaken it for a leaf, but he has recognised it as a lizard, and that's what happened today. Gerard or I would never have spotted it in a month of Sundays, but the natives have eyes as sharp as needles. And when they've seized the lizard they wring its neck with a movement so swift that it probably hardly has time to feel any pain. After that its body is packed in leaves and tucked away in the baggage to be eaten at the next rest.

Whilst the Mujus were busily preparing their lizard for cooking Gerard broke the unpleasant news to me that we had no more tinned food at all, so the two of us will have to live on boiled rice laced with concentrated extract.

Big birds are noisily circling over our camping site. They are mostly "annulary birds," so-called because of the age rings round their beaks. It is interesting that these birds always fly in threes: a pair and a young bird. Gerard and I can't make up our minds whether it's a strong family sense or some protective measure.

Whilst our Mujus were preparing the camp site Gerard and I proposed to have a shot at the birds, and the thought of roast flesh once again made the saliva collect in our mouths. But our Mujus grinned and advised us not to bother, telling us that the flesh of those birds was so tough and hard as to be quite inedible. Pity! But when the natives, who will eat almost anything, say a bird is too tough to enjoy, then you can bet your boots there's nothing in it for a white man.

However, we did discharge a couple of shots—not in the idea of hitting anything, but in the hope that they might be heard as far as the Baliem, where, so we hoped, the police launch from Agats must already be waiting for us. However, there was no answer to our signal. The only noise that broke the silence was the sound of flying foxes which had come out in the fast falling darkness to do what we had been doing during the day—looking for food, though presumably with greater success. At least they, together with the annulary birds, were an indication that we had finally made our way back into a part of the world which had fauna as well as flora. Another day's march and we should probably find animals that could be shot and eaten—with pleasure. And that will be very necessary, because it is quite possible that the police launch will not be able to penetrate upriver as far as the agreed meeting place, in which case it will have to wait for us farther downstream in the plain. The truth is we don't really know whether the launch is there at all, or even whether it will be, because when we made our arrangements with the Dutch they told us that very little was known about the navigability of this part of the river, and what rapids or other hindrances might be met with. The Baliem-Catalina River towards the mountain area is completely unexplored territory—which means that we can still meet with disagreeable surprises. For this reason we also fixed an alternative meeting place should the first prove impossible. This second rendezvous is on the Catalina in an area which has already been explored from the coast side.

There is, of course, another possibility which could completely upset all our plans. The first attempts of the Indonesians to land paratroops on the south coast were a failure, but further attempts, and perhaps a large-scale invasion are regarded as on the cards. If this were to happen the police launch would be unable to keep our rendezvous. However, so far our transistor hasn't given us any such disagreeable news. If such an invasion took place and prevented a meeting we should have a two or three weeks' journey by raft down to the coast, a stretch of about 125 miles. Of course, though rather unwillingly, we have taken this possibility into account, and our baggage contains everything necessary for building ourselves a raft.

I also have a design for a seaworthy catamaran drawn up for me by Colin Putt.

Now that we really are about to enter the enormous south plain of New Guinea I am once again interested in a question that has not yet been satisfactorily answered: did the mountain Papuans of Central New Guinea make their way into the mountains from the north or south of the island? During the next few days I hope to meet natives of this southern plain and be able to make my own comparisons and work out my own theories. What I have read on the point so far, and what the Dutch officials and missionaries say, suggests that the mountain Papuans come from the south, and perhaps even from still farther away; namely, Australia. In any case there are certainly numerous ethnographical indications of a close relationship between the Papuans of New Guinea and the Aborigines of Australia.

The features the mountain Papuans have in common with the tribes in the north of the island are considerably fewer but the similarity in language is considerably greater.

It rained heavily all night, as though someone up there were pouring it down in buckets. It is nine o'clock in the morning now, but it's still raining.

Gerard and I have made a short tour of inspection to see if we can get a more accurate picture of our whereabouts. We have discovered that we have, in fact, already reached the spot first agreed as a meeting place, but there is no sign at all of any police launch, and that is a disappointment.

The veils of falling rain constantly change the appearance of the landscape. Sometimes they are so impenetrable that they hide the islands in the river and make the mountains invisible. At such times one could believe oneself already on the plain. But then the rain diminishes, the mist clears—and the pleasant illusion is over. The mountains and the steep faces are still there. The arm of the river beside which we have pitched our camp has become so swollen by the rainfall of the past few hours that the water is now rushing past not more than four or five feet away from our tent.

We ought already to be on our way, going down river, and looking for some safer spot beyond the confluence of the Somneg and the Catalina, but for the moment we can do nothing but wait until the surface of the water drops a little. In order to get a general picture of our further progress we have once again studied the sketchy maps we have of the area. A number of islands are marked as being in the river, but we can't rely on that. The latest of the maps we have is now over twenty years old, and as everything here really is "in flux" we have to allow that the landscape may well be different today from what it was when the air photographs which formed the basis of our latest map were taken.

The stretch we have in the meantime put behind us was short but difficult. Right from the start we waded, waist deep, through canals and side arms. Sometimes they were so deep that we couldn't ford

223

them, and in such places we just felled a tree in the traditional Muju fashion to serve as a bridge, though the necessity considerably slowed down our progress. In the end we had to capitulate in face of the vast flooded area. To attempt to go forward on foot was just hopeless. Our porters suggested that we should start building a raft right here and now.

In the given situation it was—as much as it went against the grain with me—the only sensible proposal. We cleared a small site which was more or less safe from inundation, and there our porters got to work to build a raft. It was quite obvious that they already had experience, for they did their work skilfully and confidently.

First of all they felled three very large trees of about three feet thick each, which they then stripped of bark. The inside of this bark is very slippery and with it they made a slide along which the trees were manhandled into the water. The trees they chose were about twenty feet long with the ideal specific gravity of 0.5, so that one half of the trunk would lie in the water whilst the other half floated above it. When the three of these stripped trunks were in the river our Mujus pulled them into a quieter tributary where they could get on with their work without being in danger of being carried away by the current. In each of the trunks they hacked three notches. Then they felled three thinner trees and laid their trunks across the others in the notches, lashing them firmly into place with rattan. Fortunately there is a plentiful supply of rattan liana in the jungle here, and you can find it growing up to six hundred feet long wherever you turn.

We now had a framework of three longitudinal and three lateral trunks floating in the water, with the three thinner, uppermost trunks altogether out of the water. The Mujus tied still more trunks to this basic framework, using liana to lash them firm and make a solid platform.

At midday, by which time the raft was by no means completed, the rain stopped as suddenly as it had begun the previous evening. And almost as quickly the water level in the stream began to sink. Our porters had their work cut out to get the raft out of the shallows before it settled on to the bottom and push it into the still strongly flowing current of the main stream. Once there they fastened it with rattan to trees and continued their work on it.

224

37. Native dugouts in the river harbour

It was beginning to get dark when our Mujus stood before us grinning all over their flat-nosed faces—the raft was ready. And they were hungry, so hungry that the amount of rice we had would certainly not have been sufficient to satisfy them. But then, as though sent from heaven, a pigeon flew over our camp site. Gerard seized his rifle, raised it hurriedly and fired. Unfortunately he missed and the pigeon flew on its way. We now tried our luck with the fish, and a number did bite and get caught. They were about a foot long with drooping barbels. Greatly delighted and heartened by this success our Mujus now set out in search of palm hearts of which they ultimately found quite a number, and so they returned to camp in the best of spirits to enjoy a tasty and satisfying evening meal.

Tomorrow we begin what I hope is the last adventure of this expedition—our journey by raft to the coast. Now that we have succeeded in catching perfectly edible fish again I am looking forward to this final stage of our journey without anxiety; at least we ought not to starve. And we shan't have to cut paths through the jungle or climb up and down steep hills, or stumble over chalk ridges. We shall just sit on our raft and rest, and nevertheless we shall go on our way, propelled by a current which never ceases day or night.

I am particularly happy because during the past few days my knee and shoulder injuries have not given me too much trouble. And another thing, on board our raft I shall have time and opportunity to keep my wounds clean and give them a chance of healing up.

June 16

I am lying on my belly writing. Beneath me our raft glides on steadily, gently swaying as it moves. Gerard is sitting next to me. There is a satisfied look on his face too.

But our journey by raft did not start off all that well. It hardly rained at all during the night, and by the morning the surface of the water had sunk still further. When we walked from our camping site to the raft, which was about a hundred yards or so upstream, we discovered that the surface of the water was something like thirteen feet lower than the evening before. Nevertheless the raft was gently

225

38. This "cannibal" wasn't all that savage

bobbing up and down without touching the bottom. Once again we realised what a good thing it was that our porters came from an area of rivers, and were therefore used to them. Just as they demonstrated their skill and experience yesterday in the building of the raft, so they showed it today in the loading of it. And when we got started the steering was also no problem, and they were well able to deal with any difficulty that arose. Using branches, they took depth soundings carefully and expertly. Then they carried the loads on to the raft and piled them up in the centre, afterwards lashing them down with the inevitable rattan. When everything was finally ready they set out their lines hopefully, but this time they were not successful, and our breakfast consisted of palm hearts with a little rice, very little rice in fact, and no fish.

After breakfast we all went "on board"—two Tuans and ten porters. Under our combined weight the raft sank quite considerably until we were actually touching the bottom. But our expert Mujus knew at once how to deal with this contretemps. Several of them leapt off the raft into the water, armed themselves with strong branches, thrust them under the raft and levered it loose. The raft now set off gaily, but before we had gone fifty yards or so my first sigh of relief had turned into a groan. The water in the centre of the river was now so shallow that we had to sail under the trees close to the bank. The water certainly did not flow so fast there, but at least it was deeper. And now on board our raft we unexpectedly found that we had to do all over again what we had done every day for the past three weeks in the jungle: a couple of Mujus stood at the front with their matchets and laboriously cut away the low-hanging branches of the trees at the side of the river to allow us to glide under them. It seemed that even on the water our progress was to be attended with difficulties. Now and again the two would wade into the water ahead of the raft, whilst the others held it back until they had cut a way free. It took us about an hour before we had laboriously hacked through the first barrier of branches.

When we were through we all heaved a sigh of relief, but our satisfaction did not last for long, because now the bottom of the raft began to crunch on the gravel and finally we came to a halt altogether. The raft was stuck. This time everybody had to get off, and it took us

226

a good half an hour before we managed with the help of poles and a great deal of energy to get the raft floating and on its way again.

This time I suppressed my sigh of relief, but I need not have done. Life's like that. Since then we've been making good progress, with no tangled branches to bar our way and no gravel to grind over. We are gliding downstream at about three to four miles an hour, and Gerard and I are admiring the skill and speed with which our Mujus manoeuvre the raft past obstacles jutting out from the water without fouling them.

But all good things come to an end in time, and I had just about got used to our stately tempo and was reckoning out that we were now making more progress in an hour easily than we had previously made in a whole day laboriously, when suddenly our rate of progress increased rapidly. We were now going too fast for comfort, and suddenly ahead of us we saw a huge tree-trunk over the water athwart our course, its great side branches barring our progress and threatening disaster. We were gliding straight towards it at the dizzy rate of ten miles an hour. The situation looked hopeless, but at least our Mujus had not failed to recognise the danger, and apart from shouting wildly they were paddling like mad. Unfortunately their efforts didn't seem to have much effect. It looked as though we were being drawn straight towards that obstacle as though by invisible strings.

You often react very strangely to dangerous situations. When I saw the catastrophe rapidly approaching all I felt was a great urge to film the end of our raft voyage, because it seemed quite obvious that the end was at hand. I therefore stood to one side of the raft and filmed the coming doom. My idea was to stand there right to the last moment, and then, as we crashed, to try to save myself by leaping over the branches, particularly as the trunk was largely above water, which meant that our low-lying craft would shoot beneath it. The trunk would obviously scrape our baggage off the raft and mangle anyone unlucky enough to be in the way. The only thing therefore was to jump at the very last moment in the hope of picking up the raft again on the other side, and I shouted as much to Gerard whilst I was still filming.

But what actually happened was once again entirely unexpected.

227

We were only a few yards from the tree-trunk, and I was already automatically tensing my leg muscles for the leap when there was a sudden terrific crash. I caught a glimpse of three of our Mujus being catapulted into the river and I felt a sudden jarring pain in my legs.

For a moment or two I just didn't understand what had happened, but then I realised that we had ridden up with all the force of the current on to one of the submerged side branches of the great trunk. I had been thrown forward by the impact and barked my shin against our aluminium cooking stove.

But there wasn't much time to think anything out very clearly. We were slowly spinning round now, and then once again the raft fouled something under water and we were shaken up again like dice in a cup as though by some giant hand. A series of less violent bumps followed, and gradually we were able to take stock of what had happened to us and our raft: the first crash had caused it to spin to the left, and this was a bit of luck because on that side there was a channel free enough to allow it to slide through. The second bump, and all the other bumps, increased our momentum to the left towards this blessed passage.

Of course, all this was a matter of seconds only. Immediately behind this wretched tree-trunk the water was flowing smoothly and steadily again, and as we glided on we stared at each other unbelievingly, hardly able to credit our good fortune.

The Mujus who had been flung into the river bobbed up again and swam after us. We were no longer going so rapidly, and they clambered aboard, their expressions as bewildered as ours.

From the first shock to this moment no one had said a word, but now we found our tongues again—particularly when we discovered that we were no longer travelling on a rectangular raft, but on a wooden rhomboid. I started to collect my cameras and film cases, which were lying around higgledy-piggledy on the raft. Thank goodness nothing of any importance had been lost overboard. And the rattan had once again proved how tough and reliable it was—it held our rhomboidal raft together as tightly as ever.

Our way down river continued peacefully now and the weather alternated from sunshine to gusts of rain. But not even the rain could upset our porters. We were now gliding along on the sparkling surface without trouble or difficulty, and that was all that mattered.

We had almost forgotten our clash with the tree-trunk when there was suddenly another violent jolt. I had just spread my things out to dry when once again we were all pitched off our balance. The raft had come to a dead stop. It had caught up in another submerged tree-trunk, and there we sat, our small island held as though in a vice with the water of the otherwise quiet river lapping around us. Several of our Mujus immediately leapt into the river and used their feet to discover the position of the obstacle. When they had satisfied themselves just where it was we all went to the opposite side of the raft in order to tip it up by our weight so that it could be pushed over the obstacle. Three of our Mujus did the pushing, but at first they were unsuccessful. But then they planted themselves with their feet against the obstacle and their shoulders against our raft and heaved in the direction of the current, and that did the trick. We sailed on once more, and this new collision had the advantage that the previous process was reversed—our raft was once again rectangular and no longer rhomboidal.

The second incident made me more cautious, and I refrained from laying my things out in the sun to dry. We were all staring into the water in expectation of the next obstacle now, but though we experienced a few more dangerous moments, no further serious collision occurred.

It was generally quiet around us, and there was hardly a sound apart from the gentle lapping of the water against the boles of our raft. Then suddenly at about midday we heard the steady chug-chug of an internal combustion engine in the distance. After that it wasn't long before we spotted the khaki uniform of a Papuan policeman. He was standing on a sandbank. Immediately afterwards we saw a native dugout with an outboard motor with which a European was fiddling. No doubt this was the Dutch police officer who had come from Agats to meet us. Gerard fired his rifle into the air elatedly, and after a certain amount of manoeuvring—in their excitement our Mujus had almost overlooked the tree-stumps sticking out of the water—we were able to shake hands with our new Dutch friend, District Officer R. C. de Jongh, who congratulated us warmly on our successful passage across the mountains and through the jungle

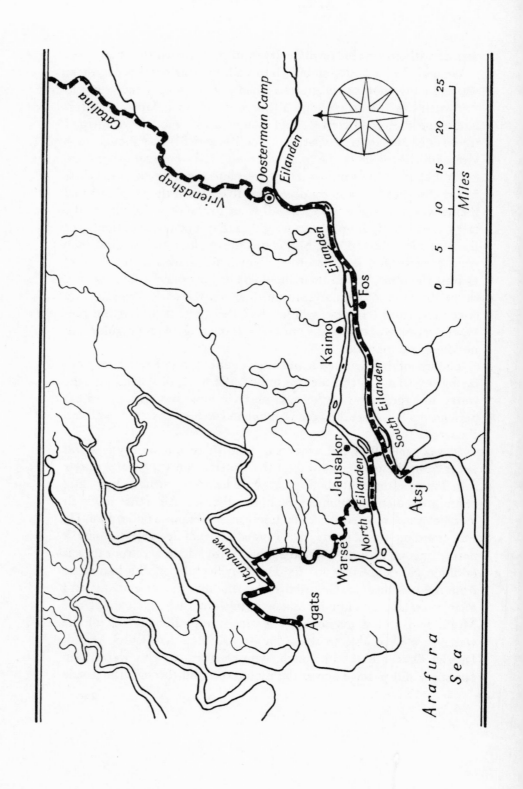

His congratulations were all the more sincere and welcome because he knew the neighbourhood very well and told us that he could well imagine the exertions which now lay behind us.

After weeks of life lived at its most primitive level, after weeks of hardship and privation under Stone-Age conditions, we were now once again in direct contact with Western civilisation. De Jongh was its representative, and nothing in his face indicated that he was in the slightest degree put out by our late arrival at the rendezvous. However, I apologised for us all for having made him wait four days beyond the fixed appointment, but he immediately assured me that it had been no trouble at all and that everything was in apple-pie order. I really needn't have worried, he assured me. It was all part of his duties anyway, and altogether a very useful trip, because no official from Agats had previously penetrated northwards so far inland to visit the natives there.

However, the truth is that accident played some part in our meeting, because on discussing the matter we discovered that there had, after all, been a misunderstanding about the rendezvous. Thinking that we had agreed on the same spot, the Dutch District Officer and I had in reality had different spots in mind. However, all's well that ends well, and there was even a new and pleasant surprise awaiting us. In a quiet backwater of the Catalina, moored against a sandbank, lay a much larger vessel, gently bobbing up and down. It was a Dutch police launch, known as a Mappi boat because such craft are used on the Mappi River to the east near the Digu. The name of this particular Mappi boat is *Saham*, a word in the Mimika dialect meaning kangaroo.

Three journeys with the native dugout were necessary to bring us and our baggage from the raft to the *Saham*, which had an awning and was large enough to accommodate us all in comfort. The prow of the small native craft which cut through the water so elegantly was decorated with traditional carvings.

When the dugout came alongside the launch there was a wonderful bunch of bananas hanging on the rail. My mouth watered, and I think if we hadn't immediately been invited to help ourselves, Gerard and I would have been hard pressed not to have forgotten our good manners. We had hardly stepped on deck when a fat hen

231

scuttled across the boards in front of us, clucking excitedly. My imagination, I am afraid, immediately pictured it plucked, trussed and done to a turn on a dish. I asked if I might buy it and, having received permission, I did so. Apart from the "Captain" there were two Papuan policemen and a helper on board.

At a good speed we now made our way downstream, and said our last farewell to our raft before it gradually faded away behind us. Without difficulty or incident we reached the main camp, which De Jongh had pitched at the place we had agreed upon as the alternative rendezvous. He had gone forward this very day for the first time to the advanced meeting place since previously there had not been sufficient water to float the *Saham*. De Jongh had just left a message behind for us and was about to take the *Saham* back to the main camp when we turned up on our raft. This happy accident spared us another day on the raft, and, above all, another day of famine. On board the *Saham* we did the journey in a little more than an hour.

Now we are in the main camp, which lies about sixteen feet above the river on a fine broad terrace. But De Jongh told us that only the day before the water level had been so high that they had been flooded out and had had to seek safety on board the *Saham*. For us, who had lived for weeks in dirt and wet discomfort, this typical bivouac of a District Officer was more like paradise. The Dutch build such camps with deliberate care and neatness as an example of cleanliness and order to the natives. There are two wash-places and a big tent, and everything is on piles. And even the clay path to the landing stage is sprinkled with sand. But when it rains heavily the landing stage and the path both get flooded and you can step direct into the boat from the camp huts. But if there has been no rain for some time then the surface of the water drops so far that the landing stage is high and dry and you have to clamber down ladders to the water.

We admired the efficiency with which everything is arranged, particularly when we learnt that most of the work is done by the natives themselves. Most of the Papuans here also go around naked though some of them wear coloured vests and shorts presented to them by the Dutch authorities. All these men come from the nearest village along the river. When De Jongh arrived here for the first time

232

a few days ago they all fled, but the next day they cautiously made their way back, half-curious, half-scared. But when de Jongh had presented them with a steel axe and a few articles of clothing they came again the following day without fear. They are even more primitive than the Danis in the last Papuan mountain village were, and I feel certain that they are still cannibals, though as they speak a dialect I don't know I can't talk to them about it. But even if I had been able to talk to them I don't suppose for one moment that they would have told me the truth—they would probably have been too much afraid of the Dutch authorities.

Our evening meal consisted of a marvellous Indonesian dish De Jongh prepared himself, and we finished off, as a sort of crown to a wonderful day, with French brandy. It was now that I finally realised that all our troubles were over: hunger, wet, cold and danger. Impulsively I toasted Gerard and thanked him once again for the splendid comradeship he had given me. The rest of the evening we spent chatting, and—as is usually the case when danger has passed—we suddenly remembered all sorts of comic incidents. We laughed heartily about Gerard's colourful curses, and about our man-sized crash with the raft. The past three weeks of our expedition now unrolled again in our mind's eye. The last fourteen days have been the best for me: my condition steadily improved until at the end of the expedition I felt definitely fitter than at the beginning. Many of my wounds have already healed up, and the after effects of my various falls are beginning to wear off.

This morning De Jongh managed to get in touch with Merauke, and let them know that we had got through safely. I was also able to send a telegram to my family. This was presumably the first radio telegram from the River Catalina to Europe.

June 17

We have reached the confluence of the two big rivers, Vriendschap and Eilanden, and we are going to stay the night in the Oosterman camp established here by the Dutch authorities.

Last night we were delighted for the first time for weeks because it was raining. First of all, we were on board the *Saham* and therefore

233

in the dry, and secondly the downpour added a great deal more water to the river and made it possible for the *Saham* to go at her top speed, about ten knots. I spent the greater part of the morning sitting comfortably in a deck-chair, smoking my pipe and making notes about the course of the rivers we have got to know during the past few days. Our damp and already rather mildewy things are drying out in the warm headwind we are encountering. Just now and again the *Saham* scraped a submerged tree-trunk, but we hardly felt anything. Before long we reached the village of those natives who were with us in the main camp. From a distance I could see to my surprise that some of them were wearing reddish head coverings. These, it turned out, were gifts from the District Officer. Otherwise the Papuans were stark naked as usual.

We stopped for a while at the village, and during the short time we were there I saw neither women nor children—the natives were obviously hiding them from us. A few older villagers were crouched around between the huts. They looked quite wretched and obviously suffered from cascado sickness. I succeeded in bargaining with them for a primitive stone axe and a few arrows in exchange for a couple of knives. This axe, of course, does not come from my Ya-Li-Me in the north. The blade is made of flint stone, which the local Papuans get from the river bed, and the haft is a bamboo root.

At two o'clock in the afternoon we reached the end of the Catalina, and thus the Vriendschap. Four hours later we arrived here at the camp situated at the confluence of the Vriendschap and Eilanden Rivers.

Now that the riverain system is behind us I am going over it again in my mind. The great River Baliem begins in the northern highlands cuts through the mountains in the Baliem Gorge, and changes its name in the plain to the Catalina. The general direction of its flow is southward, even after it joins the bigger River Vriendschap coming from the north-east. The River Vriendschap then joins the still bigger River Eilanden, which flows from the east, and the camp is situated at their confluence. The southerly direction is not maintained for long after this and then the River Eilanden turns westward, growing broader and broader until by the time it pours into the sea it is several miles across. The Pacific Ocean between here and Australia is called the Arafura Sea. It was in this estuary neighbourhood that young Michael Rockefeller was tragically lost last November.

Although we are in dry, rainproof huts here I am not looking forward to the night with much confidence, because hardly had we settled ourselves down comfortably than myriads of tiny, almost invisible, flies called *agas*, overwhelmed us. The irritation of their bites is so intense that it's almost driving me mad and I can hardly write. De Jongh has taken a boat and gone out on to the river in the hope of getting away from them.

Quite the best thing of the day was our evening meal when we ate the greater part of our fat hen roasted. The rest—there isn't a great deal—we shall eat on the boat tomorrow morning.

June 18

The natives we have met since we arrived on the plain are slimmer and rather taller than our inland Danis, but they probably aren't as tough and tenacious. What they do have in common—apart from the distended "sweet-potato belly"—is that there isn't an ounce of fat on their bodies, though they are equally unreasonable and immoderate in their eating. I am quite sure that if they were given unlimited quantities of rice, sweet potatoes and sago they would interrupt eating only to cook more. When they have stuffed themselves so full of food that there isn't room for a morsel more they just vomit and then start eating again. At their roast-pork banquets, at which sometimes as many as a hundred, and even more, pigs are prepared, they do nothing but eat for days on end.

Yesterday we met the first crocodile trapper I have come across here. It's odd to see a Papuan in a native dugout with an outboard motor. The fellow was on his way to his hunters to bring in the crocodile skins. There are strict rules and regulations and very definite ideas concerning private property amongst these crocodile trappers too. For example, no crocodile may be killed unless it is at least ten inches across the shoulders. The hunting districts are also carefully delimited. Later on we met two crocodile trappers who belonged to a different area, and our D.O. immediately sent them back to where they came from.

In this area almost all Papuans carry a bit of Western civilisation with them, though it may only be a piece of stuff, a metal strip, an old felt hat, or a ragged vest. But only their own ornaments go into their hair or through their noses.

Our next objective is the village of Fos. It lies shortly before the place where the River Eilanden separates into a southern and a northern arm. We are to meet a bigger vessel there and go with it to Atsj. I am hoping to add a few ethnographical items to my collection from these villagers. Incidentally, our Mujus are staying on board the *Saham* and they will go with it direct to Agats.

I have been making inquiries from our Dutch companion concerning the famous wood carvings of the coastal province of Asmat, which have attracted great attention on account of their artistry. He tells me that at the moment it would be very difficult to get hold of any carvings done in the typical iron-wood as at the moment the coastal Papuans are celebrating their larval feast, which goes on for several weeks. The natives regard this as the close season for carving hard wood, believing that if they did, the larvae, which they hold in high esteem as a delicacy, would then grow as hard as the wood and be unsuitable for eating. On the other hand, De Jongh thought I might be able to find and purchase one or two carvings in the stores at Agats.

However, for the moment we are still on board, and as we travel down river splendid parrots with red and black heads fly over us from time to time. They cost a lot of money in Europe, because very few of them survive the journey and the change of climate.

It is evening and we have reached Atsj where we are going to stay overnight.

This morning at eleven o'clock we arrived in Fos. The Dutch are building a school there—a tremendous innovation for a village with a few hundred inhabitants. Another building that impressed me was the men's house, a long, representative building in a prominent site in the centre of the village. It has twelve cooking places, and it serves the bachelors of the village and those men whose wives happen to be pregnant. The floor of this men's house is made of bamboo and it is very thin. With my weight I have to tread carefully for fear of breaking through. But this thin bamboo weave has one very big advantage:

236

all the dirt falls through the floor as through a sieve, with the result that the standard of cleanliness here is exceptionally high for Papuans.

I should have liked to make a film of the women here in Fos, but as soon as we landed they all retired to the family houses, and inside those it's dark. However, a boat arrived with two women and I was able to take a few feet of film. They wore a kind of very rudimentary shorts made of bast, but apart from that they were naked. Both the men and women of this village have slim, good figures, quite unlike the stocky little Danis on the other side of the mountains. However they wear the same kind of ornaments in the same way: pieces of bamboo and bone in the strangest shapes worn through their nostrils, and necklaces of coloured tree seeds or dog's teeth.

The larger vessel we were to join was there waiting for us, and after a short while we went off with it in the direction of Atsj. I had been told that because of the full moon and the tide the larval feast would be at its height today, and I am hoping to be able to film the great event. It is celebrated with the same enthusiasm as the roast-pork feasts, in fact the fat larvae, or maggots, are regarded as an even greater delicacy. Long columns of natives set out to collect them from the decaying stumps of sago palms, and later on they eat them to the accompaniment of throbbing drums and ritual dances.

When we arrived I was greeted with the disappointing news that the larval festival is not being celebrated yet because the natives have not so far succeeded in collecting a sufficient number of the requisite maggots. The festival has therefore been postponed until tomorrow and I can't wait that long.

In the last light of day I set out for a walk through the village, which is a large one and has over a thousand inhabitants. It wasn't long before I was surrounded by a horde of noisy, inquisitive boys. I was hoping to be able to film something. On my walk I noticed rows of huts on each side of the road, and I came across several men's houses. They were built here rather higher above the ground than in Fos. I was astonished at the great number of pirogues, as the native boats are called, drawn up along the bank of the river. They are painted in bright colours and ornamented with carvings, which suggests that their builders are art lovers. Close at hand natives were

237

engaged in building still more boats. Most of these men were completely naked. Only very few of them wear shorts, or a kind of loincloth—"contact gifts" from the Dutch authorities.

I strolled around in the village for perhaps an hour and a half, and never did my lively companions leave me even for a moment, or take their eyes off me. Here too the women hid themselves at first, but with the aid of some brightly coloured beads I managed to entice some of them out of their huts.

Time is running short for us now. On Wednesday, June 27, a plane leaves Merauke for Hollandia, and I want to go with it under all circumstances. So far I have done what I wanted to do without bothering my head a great deal about the political and military situation, but now that my expedition is over I must start taking it into account. The nearer we come to the coast the more one becomes aware of a certain uneasiness in the air. Obviously the authorities are reckoning with a new invasion at any moment, and this means that every day is a matter of importance for us now.

The day after tomorrow a government vessel will be waiting for us in Agats. We can't assume that it will wait for us if we're not there in time, and we can't afford to miss it. This vessel will take us from Agats along the coast to Merauke in three days.

This has all been discussed and arranged, but I know from experience how things can go wrong, and therefore I have made arrangements for us to go on even without the government vessel if necessary. My New Zealand mountaineering friend Colin Putt has prepared me a detailed plan—I think I mentioned the matter before—for building a catamaran from two native dugouts, and I have the necessary tools and other material with me in our baggage. Of course this will really be a last resort, but the growing unrest and the repeated invasion scares are clear evidence that this "last resort" might become necessary at any moment. If the Indonesians do invade before we get away it may be impossible for us to use normal means of transport. Should this situation arise then we propose either to sail from the coast of New Guinea across the Arafura Sea to Australia, or along the coast and through the Torres Strait to the Australian part of New Guinea. However, for the time being our route is, as arranged, via Agats and Merauke to Hollandia.

238

Apart from such worrying matters my thoughts are altogether concerned at the moment with supplementing and extending my ethnographical collection. I had already succeeded in securing a number of ornamentally carved spears, paddles with splendidly carved handles, and lovingly woven baskets in bast, when chance brought a rare treasure my way: a modern woodcarving of Christ on the cross—but a Christ with the breasts of a woman. At first this startled and quite shocked me, but it wasn't long before the curiosity was explained. The crucifixes the natives see at the mission stations all show Christ with the usual loincloth, but just such a loincloth, woven of bast, is the one article of clothing Papuan women wear, whilst the men go around stark naked. What could therefore be more logical for their simple minds than to assume that Christ must be a woman since he wore a loincloth?

June 19

Time is getting short. This morning our D.O. received news that the government vessel is already in Agats waiting for us. As it belongs to the Merauke administration the captain can't delay his departure. This means that we've got to get started at once. However De Jongh went off to a neighbouring village to arbitrate in a dispute, and so I had to spend a few more hours in Atsj, but at least my time wasn't wasted. The local Patrol Officer arranged a splendid river regatta for me with native dugouts. Each side sent about twenty-five boats into "battle." These Asmat Papuans stood upright in the boats, and not a stitch of clothing covered their brown muscular bodies as they dug their paddles into the water rhythmically. It was wonderful to see their supple, feline movements as they paddled faster and faster towards each other. And the wild shouts they uttered as they swept into battle were quite hair-raising. One attack followed swiftly on the heels of the other; and when one was ended the Papuans knocked with their feather-decorated paddles against the gunwales of their boats. The scene must have been even more picturesque in former times when in addition they were armed with coloured shields and went into battle as though in a mediaeval joust.

It isn't so very long ago that the Dutch first established a little civilised order here, and before that the natives were not only head-hunters but cannibals. In fact in those areas which have not yet been brought under Dutch administration they still are both. The films I shot in Asmat certainly suggest that "Cannibalism is good for you!" because amongst the older men, who were quite certainly cannibals in their youth, there were some splendidly built and particularly muscular fellows. They showed no signs of senility or physical decay, and thanks to hunting and building and paddling their dugouts they were in excellent physical trim.

When this warlike game was over a number of the natives brought various things in the hope that I would buy, and—perhaps for the last time—I took advantage of their offers. In exchange for knives, beads and watches I obtained two very fine drums, one or two shields, several crocodile knives, and a variety of neck and nose ornaments. I also came into possession of twenty more stone axes, but they were all without hafts, and were made of flint stone found in the river bed.

In the meantime our D.O. has returned from his arbitration efforts, which were, it appears, quite successful. The cause of the trouble was, as so often, rape. The wronged and indignant husband gathered all his friends around him, his clan was up in arms, and all the able-bodied men got into their canoes and paddled off to the clan to which the offender belonged. Although both clans were of the same tribe this did not prevent trouble, but fortunately the D.O. arrived before the brawl had developed very seriously, and one broken arm—let's hope it was that of the sinner—was the only casualty. The D.O. managed to part the two camps, but it is quite likely that when his back is turned the trouble will start up again in accordance with the long-standing rules of this game of vengeance followed by counter-vengeance, and so on *ad infinitum*.

We shall be leaving in a few minutes.

We went back a little way up the southern arm of the River Eilanden in order to reach a canal through which we could get to the northern arm. The journey proceeded uneventfully and by late evening we hope to be in Agats. For hours we manoeuvred through a highly ramified riverain system, nosing our way through canals sometimes so narrow that palms and foliage from both sides scraped

240

against our boat. We have to get to the River Utumbuve, on which Agats lies. By the time it was getting dark we had lost our way in the maze of side arms and tributaries, and finally the channel became so narrow that we had to put back. However, soon after this we did reach the Utumbuve, and, pressing on despite the darkness, we arrived in Agats shortly after nine o'clock. Fortunately these river boats are used to travelling at night and they are all provided with searchlights.

Agats   *June 20*

When we arrived here yesterday evening the tide had just reached turning point and was beginning to flow back to the sea. When I went on deck this morning I could hardly believe my eyes: the surface of the water had fallen by about twenty feet, and the landing stage towered above a waste of mud like a great scaffolding. Yesterday its platform was level with our deck, now it is high above us. Now and again a native dugout passes us silently and it is raining in torrents again. The patrol boat for which we left in such a rush yesterday hasn't arrived yet, and about an hour ago we received a message to say that it will probably be a day or two late. But it only confirms what I already know from experience—patience is the virtue you need most here, and the ability to wait. Different standards apply, and, of course, such boats are naturally very dependent on the tides.

I used the day—amongst other things—to re-bandage all my wounds. The tropical sores are steadily healing up and the glandular swellings are almost gone, but for the past fortnight now I have been greatly irritated by about a hundred tiny bumps about the size of a pinhead. They are all over my body and they itch terribly. An experienced settler gave me the highly theoretical advice to cauterise them with a red hot needle the moment they appear. Poor Gerard is so covered with festering sores that he's being treated at the local first-aid depot here.

In many respects Agats is something of a rest cure. For one thing there aren't many mosquitoes, and we are living in proper rooms with windows and doors. In the evening you close them all, spray the room with insecticide and then you can sleep undisturbed without a mosquito net.

241

As it now seems altogether doubtful when the expected vessel will finally arrive, our friend De Jongh has asked for another. This one will go from Merauke to Pirimapun, which lies between Merauke and Agats, about nine hours' journey to the east from here. This alteration of the original plan suits me very well, because the inhabitants of Pirimapun are said to have the least contact with civilisation of any of the coastal natives. I am therefore looking forward to making their acquaintance. Once again: it's an ill wind . . .

I have a feeling that the often contradictory reports about the arrival, delay or position of vessels put out by the wireless are due to the general state of political and military tension. As the broadcasts are monitored by the enemy, the Dutch will generally avoid giving anything away, and perhaps they deliberately give misleading information.

June 21

This morning I visited the near-by native village of Suru. The weather was very changeable: at one moment it was pouring with rain, and at the next the sun was burning down. It was low tide and the tributary of the Utumbuve which is straddled by the village of Suru is carrying very little water at the moment. The bare mud flats and the native dugouts drawn up on the mud made a rather sad and depressing spectacle. But I found that the men's house in Suru was in a beautiful position at the confluence of this side arm with the Utumbuve proper. Right along the whole front of the building was a ladder and the men were crouched on it whiling away their time by doing nothing at all, but done up in their festive headdresses and their broad nose rings. Sounds of woe were coming out of one of the huts and when I inquired the reason I was told that the family had just lost its breadwinner.

In the family houses here too I was offered quite a lot of things, but it is already clear enough that they are no longer articles made for use, but knick-knacks for selling to tourists. The difference was particularly striking, because only just a little while previously I had seen the excellent and authentic items in the possession of the D.O. But the natives manage to get rid of this inferior stuff, too, because

242

sailors and tourists are frequent visitors, and they are always out to buy souvenirs. Lampengs are the recognised currency here. Lampengs are flat wads of tobacco which can be bought in the shop of the one Chinese trader here at 1.50 florins a time.

In the afternoon the sunshine got the better of the rain for a while, and my camera case and rucksack, which are still damp from the last days of our expedition, are beginning to dry out.

I am looking forward to Pirimapun and I hope that we may be able to interrupt our journey there for a while. The settlement lies on Cook's Bay at the estuary of Cook's river. This is the spot where the great Captain Cook attempted to land a couple of hundred years or so ago, but was compelled to beat a retreat by the hostility of the cannibals. In February 1779 he met his death in somewhat similar circumstances on the beach at Hawaii.

June 22

Different news! Having made up my mind that I was going to get a chance of meeting the natives of Pirimapun the D.O. now informs me that he had received a wireless message to the effect that the vessel originally intended to pick us up will arrive after all. It is expected during the course of the day and we shall probably leave tomorrow at about midday.

Yesterday evening I visited the Catholic missionaries here and was at last able to find out something reliable about the tragic death of young Michael Rockefeller. For the past six months, that is to say since I have been in New Guinea, I have been hearing different and often not very credible rumours, beginning with a wrist-watch alleged to have been found in a cannibal village, and ending with a bone knife alleged to have been made quite recently from a human thigh-bone. Now I learned that none of all this is true. The only things that were found were two red tins which he had tied round his waist as a sort of safety belt and which were ultimately washed ashore.

Michael Rockefeller came here to collect examples of native art along the coast. He lost his life whilst sailing in a catamaran of the type we were proposing to use if need be to make the crossing over the Arafura Sea to Australia. He was on his way from Agats to Atsj. He did not choose to go by the river route, the way we had just taken in the other direction, but preferred to go by sea along the coast, an area in which he was particularly interested. He built the catamaran himself together with his companion René Wassink, using two native dugouts attached by boards and with a protective roofing of corrugated iron. To make themselves independent of wind and current they had provided their catamaran with an outboard motor. The two of them left Agats in their catamaran in the morning and visited Yepem and Per, two villages on the coast, before midday. They bought various items that interested them and in the afternoon they set sail fully loaded. In addition to the steel axes they had with them for bartering they now had a load of ethnographic items they had purchased, and the catamaran was rather deep in the water and not so manageable. Late in the afternoon they reached the estuary of the northern arm of the River Eilanden, from where they intended to go on to the southern arm, on whose banks Atsj is situated a little way upriver. But Michael Rockefeller never got there. In the broad estuary the catamaran was caught where the river water surging out meets the waves of the Arafura Sea, which were just at that time being whipped up by a strong wind. A wave swamped the catamaran, the outboard motor died on them, and they drifted helplessly and waterlogged out to sea. This was at about four o'clock in the afternoon The two natives who were with Rockefeller and Wassink now leapt into the sea to swim to the shore, which was perhaps three-quarters of a mile away, and which they both reached safely. It was night before they could give the alarm in their village and in the meantime Rockefeller and his companion had been carried far out to sea by the estuary current of the River Eilanden. Rockefeller's hope of getting the catamaran to shore was obviously ill-founded and a terrible night began for the two young men.

They were driven farther and farther out to sea, the waves grew stronger and finally the catamaran capsised. They succeeded in clinging to the wreck and in this way they survived. By daylight each had come to a different conclusion as to what was best to be done in their plight. Wassink felt that their only hope was to stay with the wreck and trust that a plane would spot them and a boat pick them

244

up. His view, on which he acted, proved correct, and he was ultimately saved. However, Rockefeller decided to attempt to swim ashore as the two natives had done the day before—except that the shore had then been perhaps three-quarters of a mile away and was now between nine and ten miles distant. His decision was not prompted by panic, but came logically from the temperament and character of a young man who found it intolerable just to wait for something to turn up, and preferred instead to be doing something. Incidentally, the attempt to swim ashore was not altogether hopeless; the tide was now flowing inland and he had a good chance of mastering even that long distance. Against Wassink's urgent dissuasion Rockefeller determined to chance it, so he tied two empty canisters to his waist, pushed off, and started his long swim. It was the courageous, but nevertheless unfortunate decision of a young man who found it impossible to remain passive in such a situation and just had to act. Looking back on it, one can see that he really hadn't much of a chance. Even if his strength had held out could he have escaped the sharks, and, further inshore, the crocodiles of the River Eilanden? These considerations suggest that Michael Rockefeller probably didn't think about the matter for long before putting his decision into action.

Even in the extremely unlikely event that by great good fortune he did manage to reach the shore, the situation would still have been extremely unfavourable: an uninhabited, marshy jungle in which there were no tracks and no huts—nothing but crocodiles, leeches and poisonous snakes.

No doubt rumours will continue to circulate concerning Michael Rockefeller and his fate, but the above account is the sad and unpalatable truth.

June 23

The constant chopping and changing about the arrival of this vessel that's supposed to be coming to pick us up is beginning to get on my nerves, and I am having to check myself in order not to get irritable. It's Saturday today, and on Wednesday, that is to say in four days' time, my plane leaves Merauke for Hollandia. The latest news is that the vessel will arrive here tonight. Let's hope the message is accurate, and not just put out to deceive the Indonesians.

I went to the village of Suri again and found a wood-carver there who is already working only for the tourist trade. It appears that his artistically carved hafts for the stone axes are a particularly profitable and fast-selling line. They're quite handsome to look at, but you really couldn't do any serious axe work with them. However, I bought one or two from him in order to supplement my collection of authentic stone axes with this modern imitation.

On my return to Agats I met the local doctor, who happened to have been in the neighbourhood of Atsj where he fixed up the arm broken in the trouble the D.O. settled successfully last Tuesday. I have frequently had cause to notice that the Dutch go to a good deal of trouble to help the natives, and always with the knowledge that they are not likely to be successful. For example, as this doctor told me, he is quite convinced that as soon as his back was turned his patient broke off the plaster used to set his arm, and will in consequence go around for the rest of his life with a crippled arm.

I got my hair cut today. The last time I had it cut was six months ago. As there was no other barber available I let a Papuan do it. By European standards he's no artist at the game, but all the same the result isn't too bad, and at least I feel that I have taken another important step towards civilisation. I didn't let him shave off my beard. I'm going to keep that until I get to Hollandia, where I shall have proper equipment to tackle the job.

It is now late afternoon, and what we have hardly been daring to hope any longer has come about at last—our boat has finally arrived, and tomorrow morning early the last part of my journey begins. It will take nine hours to get to Pirimapun, but because of the state of the tide it will be evening before we can enter Cook's Bay.

As our porters will be going by a different boat we paid them off today. They received a total of 1,500 florins, inclusive of bonuses for special industry. In addition each man received a watch, and I shared the old clothes amongst them. They will get a subsistence allowance and a tobacco ration for their journey to Tana Mera, where they live.

After the pay parade we parted company with them. They had

246

been our loyal companions for six weeks, and we had endured a good deal of hardship and fatigue together. It is against their nature to show any feelings at all, but I have the impression that they are quite satisfied.

June 24

It is Sunday and this circumstance has again delayed our departure. The D.O. had to intervene firmly. The Captain of the *Korff* insisted that Sunday was a day of rest, and he didn't want to put out at all. In the end it was agreed that the boat should start at eight o'clock, but by the time the argument was over and the sago for the crew of eight stowed away it was almost nine. Just before we finally departed a couple of our Muju porters turned up to see us off. In view of their reserve in all matters involving feeling this is a quite extraordinary demonstration of attachment and regard.

For about half an hour our way went down the Utumbuve, which grew steadily broader and broader until finally we reached the estuary and put out to sea. The captain hove to at an isolated marker buoy, got his bearings, and off we went on a south-easterly course into the notorious Arafura Sea. It certainly lived up to its bad name, and the vessel pitched and tossed violently. But I just managed to avoid being seasick with all the dreary discomfort it involves.

There are four bunks on board: two for Gerard and myself, one for the Captain, and a fourth for the other passenger, an American missionary. He made good use of his bunk and spent the whole voyage in it, sweating and looking very pale and sickly.

Unexpectedly soon—at about four o'clock in the afternoon—we arrived off Pirimapun and were able to put in at once. We had a very special pleasure in store for the young District Officer there, who spoke excellent English. It was a package of letters, already three months old. In his delight he opened it at once.

As Pirimapun is particularly subject to tidal changes the native huts are all on stilts up to twenty feet or so high. Once again, as so often here, we saw nothing but men—the native women had hidden themselves. Lying around abandoned and neglected on the shore were native ancestral and mortuary poles whose carvings indicated a high degree of artistic talent. I could have bought some of them for a song, and they were good enough to have delighted the ethnographic museums in Europe, but I had to content myself with admiring them, because the transport costs would have been more than I could afford as a private person.

Pirimapun has an "airfield," though in reality it is no more than a bumpy strip overgrown with grass. Shortly before dusk we spotted a plane flying so high that we could hardly make it out at all. As it made no attempt to come in to land we wondered what it was. The late-night news on the wireless resolved the mystery: it was in all probabilty a Dutch transport plane carrying reinforcements into the area around Merauke, where they are expecting an Indonesian invasion. Another item of news made me prick my ears: a plane of the Melanesian Air Service was reported to have crashed at the take-off in Mulia, and amongst the three passengers was one of my companions on the Carstensz expedition, Bert Huizenga. I heaved a sigh of relief when I heard that everyone had escaped without any very serious injuries.

It was a year ago that P. D. Gaisseau shot those films at Pirimapun which have since made his name. They were made before he started on that outstanding expedition which made him the first man to cross the island.

I am now back in my bunk again, and the *Korff* is throbbing her way on through the Arafura Sea. Thank goodness my *kutumaleo* bites have almost healed up. The last thorns are suppurating out, and I can lie down without pain. My knee is all that really troubles me now. It creaks and complains at every movement, and the doctor in Agats found it difficult to believe that I could have travelled over three hundred miles on foot with a knee like that.

The news item we have all been fearing has come at last: Indonesian parachutists are reported to have landed in the neighbourhood of Merauke. The Dutch claim that the airfield is firmly in their hands, but what will the situation be when we arrive there the day after tomorrow? Shall we even be able to land? And if we manage to land shall we be able to take off again? Today is Sunday, and my plane is to leave for Hollandia on Wednesday. I have already determined that in an emergency I will do my best to get to the

Australian part of the island by boat, or, if necessary, even on foot. I certainly don't intend to wait until the situation has cleared itself up. Who knows how long that will take?

During the night the sea became very rough and disturbed. We pitched and tossed so heavily that I couldn't sleep. I went on deck and found a wonderful night sky—one half of it impenetrably black and threatening, and the other a brilliant galaxy of stars dominated by the Southern Cross.

Once again a day lies behind us and it has got dark again. We passed through the Marianna Strait, discovered by the Lieutenant Korff after whom our little ship is named. He also discovered Frederik Hendrik Island. Hour after hour the strait became narrower and narrower before we finally reached the open sea again, where we are now lying at anchor. Owing to the numerous coral reefs the Captain will be able to continue our voyage only in daylight. This means that we shall arrive in Merauke tomorrow afternoon. I'm wondering what the military situation will be by that time.

The Captain emerged from his bunk at four o'clock this morning, and half an hour later we started up again. A rather sallow half-moon gave us enough light, and after about half an hour we were far out to sea. A day now began which I would prefer to forget as soon as possible. The Arafura Sea is notorious even for its normal seas, but on this particular day it showed itself from its very worst side. The American missionary had company: both Gerard and I found it impossible to keep on our feet, and we lay in our bunks gritting our teeth against the waves of sea sickness that attacked us. This wretchedness lasted almost thirteen hours, but it ended at last with our arrival in Merauke. During this whole time we did not have a bite to eat or exchange a single word.

Just as we arrived in Merauke harbour one of the big New Guinea coastal vessels, the *Kasimbak*, was sounding her siren as a sign that she was about to leave for Port Moresby. If I had only known that! How much time and money I should have saved: the enormous detour *via* Hollandia and the expensive air fare! But now, after great difficulties, our air bookings have just been confirmed by wireless, and so, willy-nilly, we shall have to fly. Our baggage can follow us the week after by ship.

I find it difficult to get used to—we are staying at a real hotel here, even if it is crammed full. Journalists from all over the world have turned up in Merauke to be on the spot to report whatever political and military happenings take place. The Dutch authorities have seconded a major who knows this part of the world intimately to be their guide and mentor—and keep them out of trouble. First of all it would be dangerous to allow them to do just as they liked, and secondly the Dutch Government is not too keen on publicity in connection with the war it now has on its hands with the Indonesians.

In Merauke itself you see no sign of warlike developments. The general atmosphere is relaxed and totally unmilitary, although Indonesian parachutists are reported to have landed not twelve miles away.

Tomorrow morning we must be on the airfield at six a.m. to take the plane to Hollandia. I shall have a lot of farewell visits to pay there, and the packing will take up the rest of my time. On the following Friday I shall take a TAA plane via Lae and Port Moresby to Sydney.

Hollandia   *June 27*

On January 11, almost six months ago, I left here for my expedition into the highlands of New Guinea and right across the island. The stages of the expedition come back to my mind: Wamena; Ilaga; the then unclimbed peak of the Carstensz mountain; Ya-Li-Me the "source of the stone axes"; Baliem Gorge; Agats; and the last days of our voyage to Merauke. And once again I recall the friends who were with me on those various stages: Bert Huizenga and Philip Temple, Russel Kippax and Gerard van der Wegen. We went through hard, wonderful and unforgettable weeks together. What more can I say about my partners in conclusion than that I would gladly start off again with each one of them on some new expedition? And now I

250

have returned to the starting point, which has become the finishing point.

This morning at four o'clock we were woken up in our hotel in Merauke. I hadn't really slept a great deal because the pitching and tossing of the boat was still in my limbs. Two hours later we started. Once more I saw part of the plain, and later on part of the mountains under our plane, and after a three-hour flight we touched down in Sentani, the airfield twenty-five miles outside Hollandia.

It was more than just a return; it was almost a return home. But the day after tomorrow there will be a new parting. And this time there will perhaps be no *Wiedersehen*.

Epilogue

THE experience of a great expedition is always a double one: first of all the gathering of impressions, observations, knowledge and material; and then at home again the re-living of the experience in your mind, the arrangement and appraisement of the spoils. I am engaged on this now. And, particularly when I re-read my diary, I recall many an idea I had on the way but didn't enter into it because there wasn't enough time, or the cave in which we were resting was too wet, or I was too taken up with the immediate experience of the moment.

But that's not all. Some of the things we experienced, the things that occupied us, worried us or gladdened us, already begin to look different in retrospect. For example, when Phil Temple and I were so terribly thirsty that we decided that once we got back we would always start the day with a glass of wonderfully cool beer. When we actually got back and could have done it we didn't dream of doing it. Or with Gerard van der Wegen on the final days of our journey through Baliem Gorge when our rations were cut down steadily further and further: listening to the hunger noises in my belly I kept thinking of baked potatoes in their jackets. It was an obsessive vision, and it filled me with longing. At that time I could have sworn that I would be satisfied with baked potatoes in their jackets for the rest of my life—and the height of luxury would have been an egg on top on Sundays.

And now? The oath that might have been sworn under dire stress is already forgotten, and luxury in the matter of eating has already become something more than an egg on top of a potato baked in its jacket. The fact is that man has an extraordinary capacity for forgetting disagreeable things.

But, of course, it works the other way round too. My desires and my longings have changed conversely with the circumstances. In Europe and surrounded at every step by the achievements of civilisation the moment always came sooner or later when I began to long for the simple life—the attraction of life probably lies in the contrasts it is in a position to offer. Before I started off on my expedition to New Guinea I was feeling this very longing, and I felt that I could live for years right next to the heart of nature with nothing but primitive satisfaction for my desires. But it didn't take very long to cure me of this: not quite six months amongst the primitive people of the Stone Age was enough to confirm my belief in the value of a comfortable bed, central heating, air conditioning, and everything that goes with them. The fact is that we all belong to the surroundings we are brought up in.

And the others, those whose lives are so very different from ours, they too have their surroundings, their way of life, which we must respect. I therefore don't feel any very great indignation if you care to call the Papuans, amongst whom I have just been living, "savages," provided you don't use the term in any pejorative sense, because a so-called savage is a human being too, and with a little tact and insight I got on very well with them. They don't look at life in the way we do. But does that necessarily mean that their way is wrong? For example, I took steel axes to them, one of the achievements of our civilisation. But the result was not always as overwhelming as one might have thought from our point of view, believing firmly as we do in the superiority of our civilisation. The Papuans certainly admired the sharpness of the steel axe and the high polish of its blade, and they were always quite proud to possess one. But my argument that with a steel axe you could do the same amount of work in half the time as compared with a stone axe—in other words, what is certainly for us the biggest advantage of the steel axe over the stone axe—made no impression on the Papuans at all. They are just not open to such an argument. Why should the thing be done any quicker? To what purpose and to whose advantage? I remember once telling my Tibetan friends that a jet plane would fly a certain distance much quicker than a piston-engined plane, and all I got for this, as it seemed to me, important item of information was blank and embarrassed silence. Finally one of the Tibetans asked uncertainly: "But why?" And I must confess that there was no satisfactory answer I could give him.

We are well on the way to forgetting that there's any other way of life but our own, and this always has a strange effect on me. This last expedition of mine "into the Stone Age" reminded me forcibly of it. Here are people who are living in exactly the same way that our forefathers lived twenty thousand or thirty thousand years ago—and we hardly know anything about the way they live. Here is an untouched island in an engulfing sea of civilisation, the biggest Natural History Museum in the world, and there is so very much to inquire into and so much to explore, and yet I am quite certain that before long we shall know more about the moon than about this part of the world where primitive human beings live. I shall certainly never forget them, and I hope that this book will serve to let a great many other people know of their existence and their way of life.

My expedition to the Papuans involved more hardship than any of my other expeditions—its various phases and the privations involved have been noted down in this diary. I have never returned from an expedition so physically battered, and I have never before been so near death so often as I was in New Guinea. I still can't go in for sport because of my cracked knee-cap, the last ticks of the jungle turkeys are still suppurating under my skin, and whole areas of my body are still numb because nerve tracks have been severed as a result of my various falls. But it wasn't slippery paths, steep rock faces, perilous bridges, hunger, thirst or vermin that were my chief enemies, but water—water in excessive quantities that is. My experiences with outsize waterfalls and torrential streams—not forgetting the Arafura Sea!—have taught me that there is probably no force on earth to exceed the elemental power of moving water. Indeed I couldn't have had it brought home to me more clearly than when I stumbled into that waterfall on my way to the "Source of the Stone Axes"—Ya-Li-Me.

And even when all danger seemed over I still had one more escape from death—and by a hair's breadth! I had booked my return flight in Hollandia *via* Australia and India, but before the plane left I was approached by the American magazine *Life* with the request that I should meet one of its representatives at some convenient point on my

255

way back. I proposed Sydney, Bangkok or Calcutta, and if none of these places was suitable then Frankfurt on my return. The *Life* people decided on Bangkok, and so I broke my journey there. The plane I would have been in but for this arrangement went on without me and two hours later it crashed in the neighbourhood of Bombay, and all the ninety-four people on board, including the pilot who had flown me out of New Guinea, were killed. But for *Life* I should be dead now.

Well, it really is all over and I'm safe home again now, but there is just one obligation arising out of my expedition which I have the greatest pleasure in fulfilling: namely, to thank all those who contributed in any way to the success of my journey into the Stone Age. If in this connection the only names I mention are those of Messrs Bot of The Hague, den Haan of Hollandia, and Dr Valk of the Geological Institute in Hollandia, this is because I was in particularly close touch with these gentlemen during the preparations for my expedition. It is just impossible to mention the names of all the people who helped in one way or other to make my wonderful experience in New Guinea amongst the Papuans and way back in the Stone Age such a success. My thanks go out to them all.